THE ENTREPRENEURS

THE ENTREPRENEURS
An American Adventure

Robert Sobel and
David B. Sicilia

Illustrations compiled by
Martin W. Sandler

Houghton Mifflin Company

Boston

1986

To our parents and
to the memory of
Uncle "Cookie" Jules Sicilia,
entrepreneur

Library of Congress Cataloging-in-Publication Data
Sobel, Robert, date.
    The entrepreneurs : an American adventure.

    Bibliography: p.
    Includes index.
    1. United States — Industries — History.
2. Technological innovations — United States — History.
3. Inventions — United States — History.   4. Entrepreneur —
History.   I. Sicilia, David B.   II. Title.
HC103.S683   1986   338'.04'0973   86-10650
ISBN 0-395-42020-2

Printed in the United States of America

J 10 9 8 7 6 5 4 3 2 1

Book design by Larry Webster

Acknowledgments

Davis Dyer and Alan M. Kantrow of The Winthrop Group, Inc., and the *Harvard Business Review* made invaluable contributions to the structure and content of this book. Along with these scholars, David G. Allen, Elizabeth Altman, Daniel Dupre, Margaret B. W. Graham, George D. Smith, and Nan Stone eased our task by offering the fruits of their research for the companion television series, "The Entrepreneurs: An American Adventure," sponsored by Wang Laboratories.

The manuscript was edited with intelligence and sensitivity by Nan Stone and Janet Silver. Our thanks also to Martin W. Sandler, Carol Weiss, Alfred D. Chandler, Jr., Susan R. McWade, and Daniel Dupre, who commented on earlier drafts.

Our editor, Larry Kessenich, and our agent, Barney Karpfinger, contributed in many important ways to the realization of this project.

The volume's engaging and informative illustrations were selected by Martin W. Sandler and Carol Weiss, who wish to express their gratitude to Lorene Mayo and Vanessa Broussard of the Smithsonian Institution, to the staff of the Prints and Photographs Division of the Library of Congress, to Ann Hobart, and to Melissa Deptula for their much-needed assistance in the selection process. The book was designed by Larry Webster, whose care and skill will be obvious to all who turn these pages.

We also wish to thank Janet Silver for her important contribution in writing the captions that accompany the illustrations.

Finally, several entrepreneurs — the directors of The Winthrop Group and Martin Sandler Productions and the executives at Wang Laboratories, especially Jane Carpenter — deserve special mention for their imagination, willingness to take risks, and unrelenting support of this book.

Contents

Foreword

THIS BOOK IS A LIVELY, well-conceived story of American entrepreneurship. No study reveals so well the rich diversity of American entrepreneurs and their creative ventures. As the authors emphasize, entrepreneurship is a difficult concept to define. They do, however, follow the dictum of Joseph Schumpeter that the entrepreneur is an innovator, who reshapes patterns of production and distribution by developing new products and processes, by opening new markets and sources of supply, and by devising new forms of organization.

As to defining entrepreneurial qualities, they are quite properly less precise because they question whether there is such a person as a typical or quintessential entrepreneur. They do consider Juan Trippe, who at the age of twenty-eight became president of Pan American Airways and made it the first American overseas airline, a good example. "While there is no quintessential entrepreneur," they write, "Trippe possessed a surprising number of the qualities that often characterize the breed." He was "an opportunist" who "was never reluctant to exploit personal and family ties." He was "a visionary, not only one of the first to see the commercial possibilities of air flight but also the originator of an international and then a global strategy." His "restlessness" caused him "to personally scout the globe for prime landing spots and key routes." His shrewdness made him fully aware of the need to secure government mail contracts for the success of his strategy. Like many of the breed, he was much more an empire builder than an organization builder. Even before his retirement in 1968, the global empire he had created was faltering badly.

The personality, goals, and methods of many — probably most — of the entrepreneurs described here differed from those of Trippe. Indeed, the purpose of the sketches in Part I is to show the extraordinary variety not only in the entrepreneurs themselves but also in the nature of their enterprises. The activities of Thomas Edison, King Gillette (safety razors), Adolph Zukor (film), Charles Darrow (games), John Johnson (magazines), Mary Kay Ash (cosmetics), and Fred Smith (Federal Express) were as different as were their personalities, education, training, and business experience.

Diversity remains the theme of the chapters that follow. In each of these, the entrepreneurs described are grouped together around a few very broad themes. For Part II, "The Land and Its People," the theme is the creation of new processes to facilitate the most efficient use of the nation's resources. Part III, "Expanding America," focuses on the creation of new and more efficient forms of transportation. Pioneers in the processes of production is the focus of Part IV, "Made in America," and Part V, "Giving 'Em What They Want," does much the same for marketing and distribution. Finally, "Instant America" reviews the activities of some of the best-known entrepreneurs in communication.

The book is, then, essentially a series of biographical sketches. The authors find unity of a general sort in exploring the fascinating diversity of their subjects rather than attempting to analyze the similarities and differences in entrepreneurial performance, training, or personality. Although they say little about the interactions of one set of innovations upon another or about the essential preconditions necessary for many of the innovations described, they note that the creation of one set of entrepreneurial enterprises became the base for another and quite different set of innovations.

The authors are more interested in empire builders than organization builders, that is, in the creation of entrepreneurial ventures rather than their continuing history. Still, a few entrepreneurs discussed did both. J. Edgar Thomson of the Pennsylvania Railroad and Theodore Vail of AT&T are examples. We also learn of the work of Alfred Sloan, the organization builder who made William C. Durant's General Motors a viable and profitable enterprise, and of the Resors, who reshaped the J. Walter Thompson advertising agency. However, though it is mentioned, little is said, except for the case of Sloan, about the modern challenge of "intrapreneurship" that is carried on within the large enterprise. Such entrepreneurship permits followers — smaller companies in an industry — to overtake powerful leaders. The recent invasion by the Japanese of American markets provides a striking example. Such achievement is based on the ability to reshape in small but complex and sophisticated ways the existing processes of production and distribution.

But such analyses are not the purpose of this book; nor should they be. The book's purpose, as the title announces, is to celebrate an American adventure — to tell the story of creative innovators who established new products and processes that brought them fame and often fortune. Indeed, the story told is that of one American dream: start your own business and make millions. These stories are good reading. They are also excellent history, accurately describing the dynamic personalities whose achievements were central to the transformation of the American economy from a rural agrarian and commercial one to an urban industrial and technologically advanced one. These entrepreneurs and their achievements have been central to continuing economic growth and productivity in the United States from its beginnings to the present day.

Alfred D. Chandler, Jr.
Harvard Business School

MILLIONAIRES OF THE UNITED STATES.

I

The Entrepreneurs

ENTREPRENEUR. Americans have fallen in love with this French noun, which the dictionary tells us means "one who manages, and assumes the risks of, a business or enterprise." In 1985 Lee Iacocca's autobiography topped the best-seller lists, and guides to starting your own business, self-help books for careers in management, and descriptive accounts of successful companies are now crowding out volumes about dieting and cats on bookstore shelves. Scores of seminars are now being conducted at business schools in an attempt to uncover clues as how best to isolate and distill entrepreneurship and infuse it into modern corporations. We're even hearing a new word — "intrapreneurship" — used to describe how individualistic risk-takers can transform large corporations grown arthritic and moribund.

An irony of this current fascination is that the entrepreneur has occupied center stage in the American economy from the very beginning. The first European settlements in North America were entrepreneurial ventures (and failures at that). Before Virginia and Massachusetts Bay were colonies, they were companies in which investors risked their incomes, and in some cases their lives, in hopes of realizing a better life later on. From colonial times onward, entrepreneurs have sought opportunities, planned strategies, invented new products and services, taken risks, and found better ways to create industries and fortunes. Indeed, the American soil proved fertile ground for developing new businesses based on minerals from aluminum to zinc, on manufactured goods from corn flakes to computers, and on services from small shops to financial supermarkets.

Most Americans think of our leading citizens as being politicians, social leaders, entertainers; entrepreneurs are the unsung heroes of our past. These men and women saw challenges and opportunities where others saw nothing at all. Some were responsive, recognizing the opportunities arising out of changing circumstances; others actively created opportunities. In either case, they seized on ideas and worked tirelessly to overcome obstacles, sacrificing savings and sometimes their personal lives in the quest for new products and services. They took risks — though they often found creative ways to make the risks acceptable — and shaped how we live, from the way in which we earn our income to the ways we're likely to spend it.

According to the first great theorist of entrepreneurship, Joseph Schumpeter, entrepreneurs perform an important function, "creative destruction": they rethink conventional assumptions and discard those that may once have been useful but no longer apply. "The function of entrepreneurs," wrote Schumpeter in 1942, "is to reform or revolutionize the pattern of production by exploiting an invention or, more generally, an untried technological possibility for producing a new commodity or producing an old one in a new way, by opening up a new source of supply of materials or a new outlet for products, by reorganizing an industry or so on."

In short, Schumpeter understood that the entrepreneurial strategist combined in a new way factors that were available to others. In retrospect, of course, the new combinations created by the likes of King Gillette and Mary Kay Ash seem fairly simple, if not self-evident. But they require a special kind of imagination that few, it seems, possess. Seen in this way, not everyone who founds a new business or develops a new product is an entrepreneur. The Chinese laundry of the late nineteenth century, the tailor shop run by an East European Jew in the 1920s, and the Korean-managed fruit store of today sometimes have been the seedbeds of an entrepreneurial vision, but usually they made the grade through hard work and long hours, not the creation of any new product or service.

What of the entrepreneurs themselves? Can we identify other qualities of the typical entrepreneur? Is Thomas Edison, John Johnson, or Fred Smith the quintessential entrepreneur? A few students of this subject are now attempting to develop such a profile. One study has concluded that entrepreneurs tend to be shorter than average height. Another study singles out birth order as a key variable: innovators tend to be the oldest or youngest child in their families. But generalizations of this sort, however fascinating, will probably remain of limited usefulness, for there will always be exceptions.

Besides the uncommon imagination of which Schumpeter spoke and wrote, entrepreneurs display other common characteristics. Their willingness to take risks suggests a higher tolerance for uncertainty and ambiguity than most people have. And entrepreneurs are disciplined and focused on the task at hand, almost to the point of obsession.

In America, where entrepreneurship is as old as the nation itself, businesses have never been slow to proclaim their presence. Following the famous 1889 noontime land run in Guthrie, Oklahoma, these settlers made sure the shop signs were ready even before the store owners arrived.

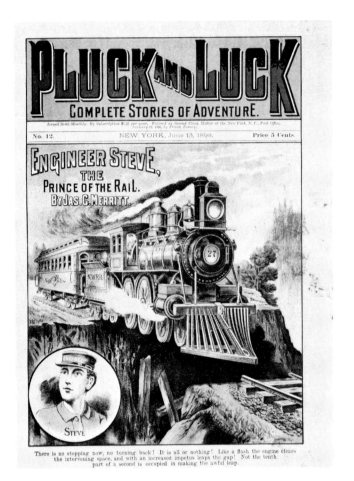

There is no stopping now, no turning back! It is all or nothing! Like a flash the engine clears the intervening space, and with an increased impetus leaps the gap! Not the tenth part of a second is occupied in making the awful leap.

"Stop beating that horse, you brute!" cried Fred, darting up to the cartman and grasping the rung as it was raised high above his head.

Money, of course, matters too. Yet while the vast majority of entrepreneurs are profit-seekers (a few, like Robert Moses of New York, have had a tremendous impact within nonprofit settings), it would be a mistake to assume that money is the only, or even primary, motivator for all. Rather it is the contest, or what social scientist David McClelland more tactfully has called the "need for achievement." Entrepreneurs often have little time to spend the money they earn, since for them twenty-hour workdays aren't unusual. Most thrive on challenges, even when supposedly on vacation or relaxing.

This drive for success often has its costs. Entrepreneurs notoriously suffer serious personal problems; many are brash, self-centered, difficult to live with, narcissistic, impatient with structured organizations, and blind to the effects of their actions on others. Much of this, no doubt, is because potential or actual failure is their constant companion.

Sometimes society has suffered in a similar way, such as at the hands of the more ruthless and legendary "robber barons" of the late nineteenth century. It has only been in recent years, however, that business historians have begun to examine seriously the contributions made by industrial magnates to the growth of the American economy and the advancement of modern managerial methods.

A more balanced view is now possible, one that acknowledges the fact that, because they were all deeply concerned with important economic chal-

Beginning in the 1860s, enormously popular magazines for boys created a new American hero — the entrepreneur. Combining talent, ambition, and plain old good luck, these resourceful self-made men achieved fame and fortune by seizing every opportunity at hand.

lenges — and willingly accepted risks to meet them — entrepreneurs played a key role in the economic growth of the United States. Schumpeter recognized the value of such reshuffling of the factors of production. Capital would have little value unless employed in productive projects. Labor would achieve little unless entrepreneurs dreamed up ways to organize it.

At each historical juncture, entrepreneurs both affected and were affected by the relentless march of social and economic change. Consider King Gillette, who changed a part of the daily routines of millions of American men by developing the safety razor. Yet Gillette's innovation could not have been successful if the social climate for its acceptance had not been ripe and the technology needed to mass produce it had not been available.

Indeed, the ability to make the seemingly ordinary into the extraordinary within a given context is a perennial achievement of the entrepreneur. Frederic Tudor made a fortune harvesting a commonplace substance — ice — while Fred Smith entered a very old business — shipping the mail — in a most contemporary way. In this way, entrepreneurs have been especially adept at understanding the constantly unfolding nature of opportunity, while the passage of time has insured that no one has succeeded — or failed — in quite the same manner.

Still, entrepreneurs often appear in particular roles in different eras. Inventors, visionaries, traders, investors, organizers, and opportunists are a few of the entrepreneurial types that appear throughout the history of American business.

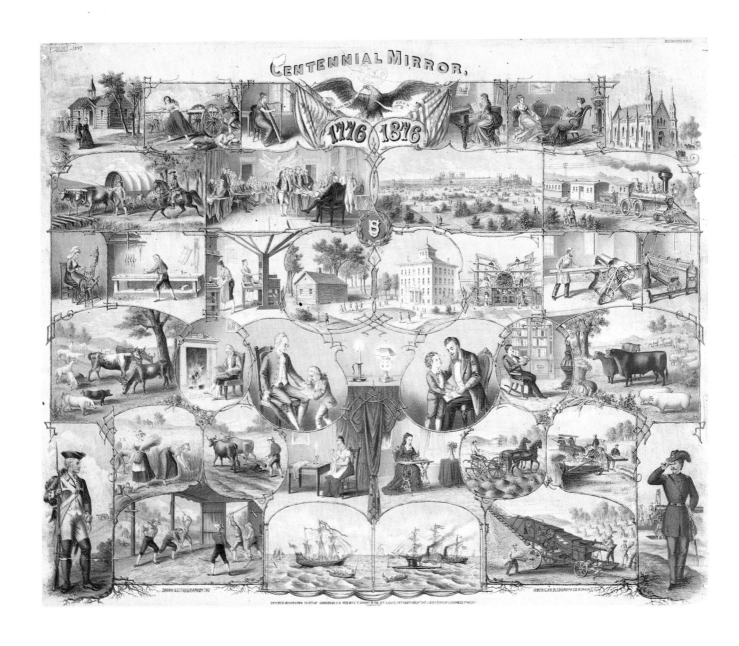

The Centennial Exposition in Philadelphia was a history-making salute to progress. At America's 100th birthday celebration, the triumphs of America's entrepreneurs and inventors were proudly displayed alongside tributes to the nation's citizens, customs, and culture.

These recurring roles give credence to Mark Twain's dictum that while history does not repeat itself, it rhymes.

Seen historically and collectively, therefore, American entrepreneurship emerges as an important, instructive, and richly textured phenomenon. By examining entrepreneurs in many guises and historical settings, and by focusing on the challenges they faced and the achievements they realized, we can begin to see a composite image of these brash, unconventional, original people, who are incapable of standing still for long and who have played such an important role in the rise of the American economy.

Thomas Edison: The Inventor As Entrepreneur

IN THE SUMMER of 1876, the United States marked its one hundredth birthday with a history-making salute to its progress: the Centennial Exposition in Philadelphia. In a massive tribute to the triumphs of American men and machines, the Centennial Awards Committee bestowed more than twelve thousand awards on inventors and entrepreneurs. The recipients form a pantheon of ingenious American tinkerers: Cyrus McCormick, builder of the automatic reaper; Samuel Colt, inventor of the repeating revolver; George Pullman, manufacturer of the famous sleeping car; George Westinghouse, designer of the first air brakes for trains; Norton P. and Charles R. Otis, sons of the creator of the modern safety elevator; and Alexander Graham Bell, pioneer of the telephone.

That same year an inventor who would tower above the rest, Thomas Alva Edison, built America's first independent research and development laboratory at Menlo Park, New Jersey. During his astonishingly productive life, Edison would become the source of more than a thousand patented inventions and the father of a dozen major industries. Edison was twenty-nine years old in 1876 and for the next half century would tirelessly conduct experiments in the new science of electricity.

His fame spread quickly. By 1890 he was already known as the Wizard of Menlo Park. In that year a pulp novelist, Garrett Serviss, even went so far as to publish a book, *Edison's Conquest of Mars*, in which the hero foils the plans of the invading Martians by inventing an "electric balloon" that takes an expedition to the red planet and destroys its evil leaders with disintegrator rays. Such was the stuff of legends. By the turn of the century, Edison was perhaps the most well-known individual in the United States, an American whose reputation abroad was rivaled only by that practical genius of an earlier age, Benjamin Franklin.

Separating Edison the man from the heroic myths around him is an important task, not least because Edison's true personality and contributions to technological progress are more instructive than the figure who emerges in popular lore. Edison occupies a place as our greatest inventor partly because of what he accomplished, partly because of how he worked, and partly because of the way he presented himself. All of these factors, as we will see, came together in his most famous product, the incandescent lighting system. The story of that innovation shows not only Edison's systematic and determined approach to invention but also the limitations of that approach.

Thomas Alva Edison, known as "Alva" or "Al," was born in Milan, Ohio, in 1847. His father, Samuel, was an easygoing optimist who liked whiskey, women (in his late sixties he took up with a pretty teenager in Port Huron and fathered three illegitimate children, whom Alva refused to acknowledge), and his independence. He had fled to the States from Canada after taking part in the unsuccessful Mackenzie rebellion. In contrast to her husband, Nancy Edison was a pious, strait-laced woman who had lost two children already and would lose another the year of Alva's birth. Pouring her ambitions for herself and her family into her youngest child (who grew up much as an only child since his surviving brother and sister were some seventeen and eighteen years older), she was demanding, strict, and stern, eager to imbue him with the morals and culture his father so conspicuously lacked.

Edison never accepted his mother's strict religiosity, a fact that later was to cause considerable consternation in a nation that revered him. But Nancy Edison did oversee a goodly portion of her son's education, chiefly because his chronic ear infections, the source of his lifelong hearing impairment, often kept him home and left him a restive, difficult student when he could attend school. Moreover, much of his education came from books, selected by himself or by his parents, such as *Parker's Natural and Experimental Philosophy*, a grammar school science text that he devoured on his own.

This austere portrait of Thomas Edison with the first phonograph betrays little of the prolific inventor's personal investment in his latest creation. Partially deaf since childhood, Edison had long been intrigued by the technology of sound.

At his laboratory in Menlo Park, New Jersey, established in 1876, Edison was able to indulge his wide-ranging scientific curiosity. His method of operation combined systematic adventurousness with irrepressible tinkering and a willingness to explore all experimental avenues.

When Edison left school at twelve — a customary step for boys from families like his — his father got him a job hawking newspapers and sundries on the train that ran between Port Huron and Detroit, then a booming industrial city known for its pharmaceutical and chemical companies as well as its disorderly streets and wharves. Edison worked on the train for three years, and the job fit him like a glove. The five-hour layover in Detroit gave him plenty of time to explore the city, and his undemanding duties onboard left him free to mingle with the passengers and satisfy his curiosity. Intrigued by chemistry, Edison collected supplies and conducted experiments in the baggage car until his habitual absent-mindedness led him to forget a bottle of phosphorus, which nearly set the train on fire.

Since his pay was small, Edison soon got into the habit of keeping an eye open for the main chance. His best-known coup occurred in 1862, when the first reports from the battle of Shiloh were trickling into an anxious country. Arranging to buy 1,000 copies of the *Detroit Free Press* on credit, he got the Trunk Line's telegrapher to wire a report of the battle to every station along the way. The crowds clamoring for more news grew larger at every stop, and by the time the train neared the end of the line Edison had raised the price of his papers from a nickel to 25 cents.

Faced with the need to choose a trade, Edison opted for one that meshed

with his restlessness and his scientific curiosity: he became a telegrapher. Although not particularly deft, and sometimes hampered by his poor hearing, he was a good worker but not at all a reliable one. In his first job his inattention caused a train crash, and his career thereafter was marked by multiple moves and short-lived engagements. (In 1865 alone, for instance, he held jobs in Cincinnati, Memphis, and Louisville.)

Telegraphy had attractions other than its rough-and-tumble lifestyle, however: it was on the cutting edge of electrical technology. Edison had already begun to experiment with devices for encoding and sending messages by the time he moved to Boston in 1867. Many of his early patents would be related to telegraphy, but his first patented invention, filed on October 13, 1868, was for an electrical vote recorder.

Scorned by politicians who preferred more leisurely and less tamper-proof ways of keeping score, the machine proved unsalable. This reinforced Edison's conviction that, while he was concerned with a wide variety of scientific problems, he would pursue only those that would lead to a usable product or service and that met a clear need defined by the marketplace and not his own imagination — which is to say he was an entrepreneur in a scientist's smock.

Later on, however, Edison strove to portray himself as a scientific pioneer, blazing paths in the wilderness, unconcerned with pedestrian, commercial interests. "The inventor [meaning himself] tries to meet the demand of a crazy civilization," he wrote in 1914. "Every new thing is resisted, and it takes years for the inventor to get people to listen to him and years more before it can be introduced, and when it is introduced our beautiful laws and court procedure are used by predatory commercialism to ruin the inventor." In reality, Edison was a shrewd businessman, ever prepared to call upon his attorneys to sue anyone who had the temerity to infringe on his patents.

Despite the vote recorder debacle, Edison was encouraged by his experiments in telegraphy and announced in a trade journal in January 1869 that he "would hereafter devote his full time to bringing out his inventions." He secured financial backing for a variety of projects, but all seemed to be languishing; penniless, he moved to New York in 1869.

The vote recorder was followed by an eminently practical invention. Noting the crude stock ticker used at the exchange and brokerage houses, Edison came up with an improved device, which he sold for $40,000. Then followed a carbon telephone transmitter and a nonmagnetic telephone sounder, purchased by Western Union for $100,000 each, and a telephone receiver, sold to the English Bell Company for £30,000.

With these funds and other earnings, Edison established a laboratory at Menlo Park, New Jersey, in 1876, assembled a staff, and created one of the first and certainly the most famous independent research facility in the nation. By 1878 it consisted of a lab, a carpentry shop, and a carbon shed, and as funds became available other buildings, such as a machine shop and library, were quickly added.

Both the equipment and the personnel at Menlo Park were first-rate. Edison had a keen eye for talent and no qualms at all about sharing his work — in private, at least — with men such as Charles Batchelor, John Kreusi, and Francis Upton, who had skills and knowledge he lacked. Public recognition was another matter, however, since Edison rarely acknowledged the part that others played in his successes — a failing that earned him the enmity of some, within the lab and outside it, who felt their contributions had been overlooked. For the most part, though, Edison inspired his workers with his own goals and enthusiasm, and they willingly drove themselves on his behalf. Work sessions, punctuated by midnight feasts and songfests on the organ that was kept in the lab, could last all night. Edison himself often catnapped on a lab table or in the cupboard under the stairs rather than go home to his first wife, Mary Stillwell, who anguished over her husband's neglect for most of their marriage from 1871 to her death in 1884.

The most famous and far-reaching invention to emanate from Menlo Park, of course, was modern electric lighting, a marked improvement over gas lighting in homes and arc lighting for street and commercial illumination. From the first, Edison envisaged creating an entire system, and from his laboratories came dynamos, generators, distribution mains and feeder wires, meters and controls, as well as the famous light bulb.

Edison went about organizing the project in a businesslike and cautious fashion, for he was challenging strong, entrenched interests with technologies and programs that would be quite costly. He understood that he had to fight the gas companies with a superior, less expensive product and service. Nothing else would do, for gas was reliable, relatively inexpensive, and deemed quite safe. He also knew that 90 percent of the gas companies' revenues derived from homes and offices, and for that reason ruled out from the beginning an improved version of arc lighting because its intensity and the hissing noise it made

A rare look inside Edison's Menlo Park laboratory, taken in 1880. The independent research and development facility, which brought together the best equipment and the finest scientific minds in the country, was the first think tank in America. Edison is seated left center, wearing a cap.

would continue to render it unsuitable for interior illumination. The technology might be complex and massive, but the delivery system itself, the light bulb, had to be nonthreatening. To the public, electricity was a novel, mysterious, and potentially frightening new kind of force, conveyed silently, invisibly, and with great power through thin wires. Gas was more familiar; accordingly, Edison described his "lamps" in terms of "candlepower," set them at the same intensity as gas light, and planned to charge his customers for "burners" on bills modeled after those sent out by the gas companies.

To assuage property owners' fears regarding safety, Edison worked out an arrangement with the Board of Fire Underwriters, whereby installers were assured rates would not rise if their wiring was checked before it was hooked up. At the same time, he sent out teams of canvassers to collect information on gas usage and costs, compiling statistics on the number of jets in use, the number of jets per building, and the fees the householders paid. Armed with this information, he could calculate both the technological specifications his generating stations would have to meet and cost restrictions required to compete successfully against gaslight.

It was an expensive proposition; by the fall of 1879, when he perfected the first incandescent light, Edison was spending money at the rate of about $800 a week. In order to raise necessary funds, he was obliged to sell off a portion of his interest in his company. The Edison Electric Light Company was organized in 1878 "to own, manufacture, operate, and license the use of various apparatus used in producing light, heat, and power by electricity." A group of investors purchased one-sixth of the company for $50,000. These included representatives of the Vanderbilt interests, Western Union, and J. P. Morgan & Company, the last acting as the new company's banker. Thus Edison developed excellent ties to Wall Street bankers and never had trouble raising funds. Egisto Fabbri, a Morgan partner, was one of his early shareholders, and J. P. Morgan himself monitored the work carefully. He invited Edison to his office, and when the inventor was too busy to get into the city, Morgan traveled to Menlo Park for demonstrations and discussions about financing and investing.

In Edison's scheme the distribution of electricity would be handled in a novel way. As incandescent lighting was first used in homes, mills, and office buildings, it was powered by "isolated plants," which were small on-site generators. Edison set up a company to manufacture these units in 1881. J. P. Morgan put the first one in his New York residence; the following year, Boston installed them to power the nation's first electrically lighted post office and theater.

But Edison's vision was that electricity would be produced in giant central stations, just as gas was produced from coal in gas houses. It would then be conveyed through underground conduits to nearby customers, who would pay a fee to receive service from the network. Edison's emphasis on underground rather than overhead wiring was unusual and again reflected sound economic and marketing reasoning. Although far more expensive than overhead, underground wiring was much more reliable. Later this proved to be a critical competitive advantage, because the Edison system did not become the target of public or regulatory restrictions in the 1890s, when the proliferation of telephone, telegraph, and electrical wires darkened the skies over many cities.

Together with some of his backers at Electric Light, Edison organized Edison Electric Illuminating Company of New York in 1880 and applied to the city of New York for the right to electrify some of its street lighting. There was intense opposition from the natural gas interests, and John D. Rockefeller,

A dazzling display of the most far-reaching invention to come out of Menlo Park: modern electric lighting. At Luna Park on Coney Island in New York, the new technology literally drove back the forces of darkness.

knowing successful electric illumination would cripple the kerosene business, watched with a baleful eye. But Edison was as astute a lobbyist as he was an inventor-entrepreneur. He wooed the city fathers assiduously, with demonstrations of his invention at Menlo Park and lavish dinners at Delmonico's, and won the franchise. Edison sketched his plans for the press, indicating that the conversion from gas to electricity could be accomplished with a minimum of disruption and choosing his words so as to soothe the fears of any who might be disturbed by the idea of a radical new technology in the home.

> I think that the engines will be powerful enough to furnish light to all houses within a circle of half a mile. We could lay the wires right through the gas pipes, and bring them into the houses. All that will be necessary will be to remove the gas burners and substitute electric burners. The light can be regulated by a screw the same as gas. You may have a bright light or not, as you wish. You can turn it down or up, just as you please, and can shut it off at any time. No match is needed to light it. You turn the cock, the electric connection is made, the platinum burner catches a proper de-

gree of heat, and there is your light. There is neither blaze nor flame. There is no singing or flickering. I don't pretend that it will give a much better light than gas, but it will be whiter and steadier than any known light. . . .

Edison's Pearl Street station went into operation on September 4, 1882, signaling the start of the electric utility industry in America. Costing $600,000, it contained six dynamos, the largest capable of churning out 125 horsepower, quite impressive at the time. Initially, electricity was sent to 58 locations in addition to the Morgan offices. By December, there were 203 customers, and a year later, 513. All of these were located near the Pearl Street station, since there were voltage losses in direct current transmission, which meant only customers within a mile or so of the Pearl Street station could receive service. The electricity generated was 110 volt direct current, quite low powered for safety's sake; anyone coming into contact with a live wire would suffer nothing more than a relatively small shock.

Despite Edison's careful calculations and his unceasing efforts to increase efficiency and reduce manufacturing costs, the station earned no money until 1885, when a 4 percent dividend was finally declared, possibly to work up investors' enthusiasm for an uptown station. The project, however, was part of a much grander plan, which Edison and several associates carried out with vigor during the 1880s and 1890s.

The idea was fairly simple, yet inspired. The rights to Edison's electrical patents (of which there were about 250), would be exchanged for stock in various Edison "illuminating companies" set up throughout the world and financed by local investors, with an occasional helping hand from Morgan and other backers. These companies would also be obligated to buy dynamos, lamps, underground tubing, and other apparatus from the various Edison affiliates that manufactured them. In this way, Edison would bring the "great emancipator" to the world and make a fortune in the process.

Industry leaders such as Samuel Insull, Theodore Vail, and Edward H. Johnson instigated these companies and succeeded in setting up dozens during the first few years. Still, capital requirements were relatively high, and local investors, especially in larger cities, proved reluctant to invest. Boston became the second large American city to have an Edison illuminating company, but not until February 20, 1886 (four days before Edison married Mina Miller), by which time 36 other companies had been founded in smaller communities, many throughout rural Pennsylvania and Massachusetts.

Still, Edison's system was doing well against incandescent competitors. The central station idea, along with underground networks, gave Edison the edge in a now highly competitive and rapidly changing industry. On another technical issue, however, his calculations would prove to be as wrong as these had been inspired. And this time, to his detriment instead of his advantage, Edison was equally dogged in sticking with the technology.

The problem was that Edison's systems operated on direct current (DC), in which electricity flows in one direction, from source to user. Because DC's maximum voltage was relatively low (about 250 volts), it could be used economically only in small areas with high consumer demand. Consequently, as demand for electricity continued to rise, other inventors began to experiment with alternating current (AC) distribution systems that could furnish power cheaply to less densely populated areas. In an AC system, current is transmitted at high voltages, which are then lowered to safe levels before being brought indoors. By 1887 George Westinghouse had patented such a system and begun to put it into operation.

At first Edison simply dismissed the whole idea of alternating current. Then he challenged the system on economic and technical grounds, citing its inefficiency and unreliability in annual reports, at sales meetings, and in publications directed to "expert" readers. These charges had no effect on sales, however, so Edison shifted his tactics — and audience — by concentrating on the issue of public safety. He also supported a series of experiments conducted and publicized by an independent electrical engineer, Harold Brown, designed to prove that AC was more dangerous than DC. (Brown claimed, for instance, that it took 1,420 volts DC to kill a dog and only 160 volts AC.) Finally, Edison backed a campaign to get the New York state legislature to adopt the electric chair for capital punishment. After this legislation was passed, Brown was asked to buy the necessary AC equipment — a purchase he was happy to make, anonymously, from Westinghouse, whose AC became fixed in the public mind as a synonym for death.

Despite Edison's efforts, AC equipment continued to gain ground, and by the turn of the century even the Edison companies were producing AC systems — albeit without Edison himself — since their economic advantages and safety were self-evident.

In spite of this and other failures, Edison richly deserves his popular acclaim. Called "the most useful American" by his contemporaries, he transformed their lives and ours with his inventions: in addition to incandescent lighting, he was instrumental in the discovery of the phonograph, motion pictures, electric traction motors and storage batteries, improvements to the telephones, and the "Edison effect," the phenomenon that led to the vacuum tube and thus to radio and TV. He also added to American industrial capacity with such inventions as multiple telegraph transmission, cement manufacturing, and the mimeo machine. At the time of his death, he was trying to formulate rubber from giant hybrid sunflowers, lest the country be helpless in wartime if supplies from the Far East were cut off. On average he had produced a patentable device every two weeks of his adult life.

King Gillette: The Social Reformer As Entrepreneur

SOME ENTREPRENEURS yearn to bring their products, services, or ideas to what they perceive to be a nation eager to enjoy and profit from them. Others see a gap in the market they hope to fill. Many are compelled by a vision of providing the means to create a better society. King Camp Gillette, who in the late nineteenth century worked as a traveling salesman for hardware companies, belonged to this last group; but to realize his ambition he first had to do something else — become wealthy. And to do this, he invented the safety razor.

Born in Chicago to a businessman father who tinkered with inventions and a mother who wrote *The White House Cookbook*, Gillette was forced to leave school at the age of sixteen when the Great Fire of 1871 destroyed the family business. It was then he became a salesman, first for companies based in Chicago and New York, and then for one in Kansas City.

This was a turbulent period in American history. Labor strife was growing, there were problems on the farms, and in the cities businessmen spoke with fear of a coming wave of socialism. Gillette must have pondered such matters while traveling by rail through the Midwest, where he witnessed industrial growth and urban misery, rich farmland and poor farmers. Out of these observations came his first book, *The Human Drift*, published in 1894 when he was thirty-nine years old. Gillette wrote that most of the nation's economic problems derived from wasteful competition. More important, the system fostered a social climate in which selfishness and greed prevailed. From this came crime, civil corruption, excesses of wealth and poverty, and moral decay. To correct the situation, Gillette advocated the creation of a "World Corporation," which would take charge of all production and for which everyone would work. It would be democratically controlled and seek equality and justice, the elimination of poverty, and, most important, the substitution of cooperation for competition.

These were hardly novel thoughts. In America, Jack London, Ignatius Donnelly, and Edward Bellamy, among others, were saying similar things, along with scores of European socialists. Two years after *The Human Drift* appeared, the Democrats would nominate as their presidential candidate William Jennings Bryan, who was supported by many intellectuals who thought like Gillette.

The time was right for such ideas; but this was the wrong book. *The Human Drift* was barely noticed, an oversight Gillette attributed to his inability to publicize its views. To rectify the situation he would need money, which is where his inventions came in.

Among the companies Gillette represented was one owned by William Painter, a manufacturer of a new kind of disposable bottle stopper. Painter was doing quite well with his product, since America, with all its problems, was on its way to becoming a "disposable society." Other products that could be discarded rather than recycled were also coming to market. Tin cans and cardboard collars were becoming common, and new items appeared regularly. Herman

King Gillette invented the safety razor to support his activity as a social reformer. In the process, he single-handedly altered the daily and time-honored routines of millions of American men.

Hollerith had invented a tabulator that used coded information cards, and he figured his profits would come from the sale of millions of nonreuseable cards, not the rental of machines. In other words, an entrepreneurial opportunity was in the air.

Painter spoke to Gillette about how a fortune might be reaped through the invention of "something that would be used and then thrown away" so that the customer would come back for more. The thought fell on fertile ground; Gillette had already worked on inventions, and he later recalled that "some of them had merit and made money for others." From Painter's concepts he lighted on the idea of the safety razor.

It was really quite simple, though the execution presented problems. In this period men shaved either with a straight razor or not at all, which helped explain the popularity of beards when Gillette was growing up. The presentation of a straight razor to a boy or young man was an important rite of passage. His father would carefully instruct him in its use, showing him how to hone it on a strop or, more commonly, a stone. Along with the razor would come a shaving mug in which the initiate was to create his lather, which would be

Intricate design problems were involved in developing the safety razor and the disposable blade. Gillette's success was due in part to the availability of the technology needed to mass-produce them.

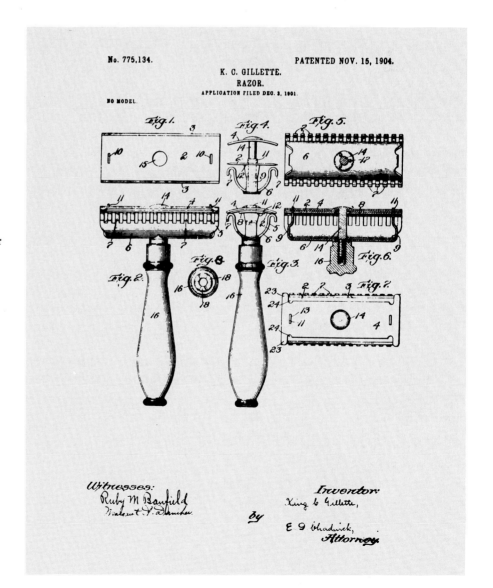

carefully applied as hot as possible before touching razor to face. Close at hand would be a styptic pencil to stanch the flow of blood from cuts, of which there would be quite a few until the novice got the hang of it.

All of this called for no little skill — and time: a really good shave, from beginning to end with a dab of witch hazel, could occupy the better part of half an hour. For this reason, some men opted to forgo the morning shave, preferring instead to frequent a barbershop, which also served as a male club. There a customer could relax as the barber pulled his mug from a shelf on which all the regulars had theirs, and after swapping stories and jokes, perhaps engage in a few songs; this was the heyday of barbershop quartets.

The trouble was that all of this took time, and as the pace of life quickened, that presented problems. For reasons of safety, convenience, and economy, then, a faster method was needed. Moreover, in the aftermath of the Franco-Prussian War of 1870–71, in which the close-cropped German defeated the hirsute Frenchman, short hair became popular, and beards were shorn. For reasons of style, too, there was a need for a simpler way to shave.

It is not known precisely when Gillette started experimenting with ways to create a new razor, but it was shortly before the turn of the century. The idea was obvious enough: a sharpened steel blade would be clamped between plates held together by a screw device that also served as a handle. Enough of the blade would protrude to present a proper edge to the face, but not so much as to nick a less than careful shaver. Gillette carved a model from a block of wood and, with the help of machinist William Nickerson, worked on several prototypes to show to prospective investors.

The invention did not occupy all of Gillette's time. He continued working as a salesman to support his wife and young son and wrote another social reform polemic, *The Ballot Box*, in 1897. Meanwhile, the processes of invention continued. Gillette had to work at fine degrees of tolerance. This meant perfecting the means of producing quantities of special steel, which then had to be drawn and honed to the proper degree of sharpness and cut to fit the razor. All of this required money, certainly more than he was earning. But he did manage to convince friends to invest $5,000 to form the Gillette Safety Razor Company in 1901. He was unable to resolve technical difficulties, and work progressed slowly. Gillette was close to bankruptcy when another group, who had no trouble perceiving the commercial possibilities of safety razors, came up with $60,000 more.

The first sales were made in 1903, when 51 razors were marketed, along with 168 blades. For a while Gillette feared blade sales would decline, as owners attempted to sharpen them on their stones. But the practice was soon abandoned: Gillette priced the blades so low that parsimony became unnecessary. Razor sales came to 90,000 in 1904, when a startling 12.4 million blades were sold. Now Gillette poured capital into advertising, and his razors swept the nation. Barbershop shaves didn't disappear, and many men clung to their straight razors, refusing to accept or even try Gillette's new contraption. But many did, encouraged by the low prices Gillette could charge, secure in the knowledge that even had he given the razors away, profits from the blade sales would more than compensate.

The turning point for Gillette came with World War I, an event that affected many established products. Soldiers and sailors switched from cigars to cigarettes and from pocket watches to wrist watches. The convenience of safety razors (there was no room for a strop or stone in a kit bag, or time to shave with

So safe and simple, a child could use it! When it first appeared in 1903, the safety razor was greeted with overwhelming enthusiasm by a nation eager for convenient, time-saving devices.

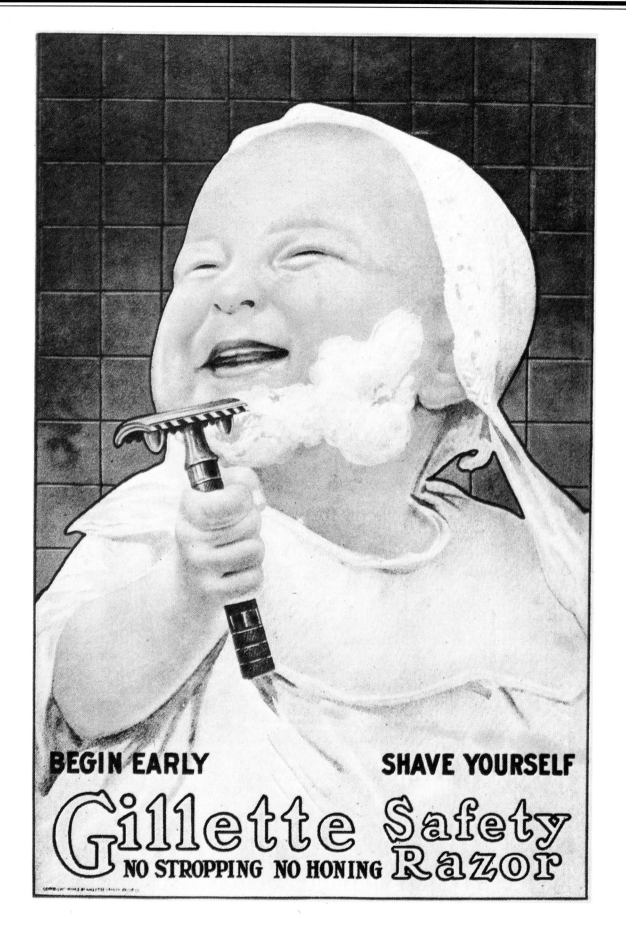

a straight razor) won the doughboys over, and they continued to use them after the war. In the 1920s Gillette ran many promotions, selling his razors in bulk to merchants who gave them away — once again boosting blade sales. Gillette plowed funds back into the business and established factories throughout the world.

Not all the money went into the company. In 1907 Gillette hired a professional writer, Melvin L. Severy, to write *Gillette's Social Redemption,* and in 1910 he came out with another of his own books, *The World Corporation.* In an attempt to publicize himself, Gillette had his portrait placed on every blade wrapper, but this did him little good. He even offered former president Theodore Roosevelt $1 million to serve as head of the World Corporation he planned to establish in the Arizona Territory. Teddy declined. Gillette went on to visualize an engineers' utopia and wrote of how air conditioning could revolutionize the economies of the southern states. But he did nothing about it. Instead he continued on with the safety razor and his social projections.

Gillette died in 1931, in the midst of the Great Depression, when his company had assets of slightly less than $60 million. Years earlier he had written that government had to provide work to the unemployed in hard times, something President Franklin Roosevelt would soon do. For most of his adult life, Gillette strove to bring to fruition his vision of a better world, and failed. What he accomplished was to revolutionize they way men shaved. His impact on the daily life of half the population was greater than that of most entrepreneurs of his time.

Adolph Zukor: The Serendipitous Showman

Adolph Zukor was among the first to recognize that the audience for vaudeville shows like *Parisian Widows* could be successfully transferred to the budding technology of motion pictures.

THOMAS EDISON often categorized his many inventions in two groups: the industrial, which involved power and included dynamos, electric lights, and batteries; and "play things," invented as a result of his personal interests. Partially deaf since childhood, he was naturally drawn to the technology of sound, out of which came the phonograph. And there were motion pictures, embodied in his Kinetoscope, which the inventor described as "an instrument which does for the eye what the phonograph does for the ear" — which is to say it was an adjunct to the phonograph, enabling users to see as well as hear others.

There is no indication that Edison truly appreciated the potential of film, even though he was one of its early practitioners. He invented cameras and projectors, which were sold to film makers and exhibitors who owned theaters and who, in the early years of the industry, looked upon motion pictures as an expensive rival to live entertainment, such as "the legitimate theater" and, more important, vaudeville. While King Gillette charged low prices for his safety razors knowing the real profits came from the continued sale of disposable blades, Edison made motion pictures only to encourage sales of his machines: when he and other patent holders came together to form the Motion Pictures Patents Corporation, it appeared the greatest profits would come from making cameras and equipment, with distribution and exhibition of movies wholly dependent upon the manufacturers for their very existence.

Had Edison thought otherwise, he certainly would have concentrated on film production and perhaps exhibition as well. And had the show business

Zukor's fantastic success as a movie mogul stemmed in part from his uncanny knack for judging the public's tastes. Being filmed here is his 1918 movie *Stella Maris*, with "America's Sweetheart," Mary Pickford.

tycoons of the period appreciated the potential of film, they too would have entered the field. Charles Frohman, David Belasco, Sam Harris, and the Schubert Brothers were giants of the legitimate theater, and B. S. Keith, E. F. Albee, F. F. Procter, and Percy Williams ran large-scale vaudeville enterprises. All had the talent and experience for such tasks, but none possessed the vision and imagination to realize just what film could become. As a result, the field was left to a group of newcomers, individuals who had little or no experience in show business and in fact were beyond the pale of American big business. Almost to a person, these were immigrant Jews from East Europe, who came to the industry through exhibition and then moved into production so as to have wares to attract customers. In 1926 one of the most important of these men, Adolph Zukor, spoke of the economics of the infant industry:

> The main business of the Edison Company . . . was to make these machines. Naturally they all concentrated on the mechanical end of the business. That was very necessary and very important for this reason: In those days you had to buy a projection machine for $75 or $95. People with money or with a substantial business would never think of opening a little store show, but as long as it didn't take more than $300 or $400 to open up a theatre a good many small investors took a chance, and that helped develop the business. . . . The great number of these store shows created a market for the moving picture producers and gave them an opportunity to develop.

Zukor was typical of the immigrants who pioneered the motion picture industry in the years before World War I and became its leaders in the decade that followed. He outlived them all, surviving to see motion pictures go through radical changes that made film arguably the most important medium of the twentieth century until the advent of television.

Born in Hungary in 1873, Zukor arrived in New York sixteen years later with $25 sewn in the lining of his coat. He found employment as a $2-a-week sweeper in a fur shop, where he soon became an apprentice. After learning the trade, he moved to Chicago and a better-paid position, soon forming a partnership with another furrier, Morris Kohn, and later married Kohn's brother-in-law's daughter. The two rose quickly in the fur business, opening shops in both Chicago and New York, and Zukor earned additional income from a fur clasp he invented.

In 1903 the partners agreed that Kohn should remain in Chicago while Zukor returned to New York to take charge of affairs there. Seeking an apartment, Zukor contacted Marcus Loew, a Manhattan-based furrier he met in Chicago, and moved across the street from him. They were about the same age, both had growing families, and the Zukors and the Loews became close friends. Later on, when they were two of the most important film tycoons, Zukor's daughter married Lowe's son.

Like many middle-class Americans of the time, Loew and Zukor enjoyed the theater. The families also went to the nickelodeons that were springing up all over the city. Recognizing the promise of film, Zukor wanted to invest in the business, and after some conversation with Kohn the partners decided to do so. They started out in a small way, lending $3,000 to a friend, Max Goldstein, to open a peep show arcade. Zukor monitored the investment, which he found much more interesting than the fur business.

So did Loew, and he started to think about taking the plunge. Later that year he and Zukor organized Loew Enterprises, which operated a chain of penny arcades. The storefront operations were profitable and multiplied rapidly,

Zukor's Famous Players Film Company brought to the screen well-known artists from the stage, increasing the prestige of the movies and ushering in the studio star system.

as did Zukor's other theatrical interests. In 1904 he opened the Crystal Palace on Fourteenth Street. It was probably the city's most lavish motion picture theater of the time. By then, he and Kohn had come to an agreement: Kohn would take care of the fur business, leaving Zukor free to concentrate on motion picture exhibition.

There soon would be plenty of competition from Jesse Lasky, William Fox, Carl Laemmle, Louis B. Mayer, Harry Cohn, the Warner brothers, and Samuel Goldfish (who formed a partnership with the Felwyn brothers, Goldwyn Pictures, and liked the name so much he took it for his own). Some were in the clothing trade or related businesses; Goldfish and Mayer had been junk dealers before becoming involved in film, while Cohn was a streetcar conductor. None had any training in the arts, though, like Zukor and Loew, most were avid theatergoers. They were businessmen who, as it turned out, possessed an uncanny ability to organize their operations and distinguish the kinds of films all Americans would want to see. All would achieve success, but Zukor was the first. For decades he was their leader and film's most towering figure, and in several ways the individual most influential in molding the industry. Deciding to expand from his New York base, Zukor joined with William A. Brady in operating Hale's Tours, which operated theaters resembling railroad coaches to exhibit the popular movie *The Great Train Robbery.* Other films followed, produced under licenses granted by the Motion Picture Patent Company and its successor firm, General Film Company.

General Film was besieged by exhibitors who hoped to integrate backward: instead of renting films from distributors, they would produce them for exhibition in their theaters, and perhaps others as well. It was a logical move but

presented some difficulties, not the least being the matter of judging the market. Without a keen knowledge of popular taste, a film would fail, the investment wiped out. Zukor, who in 1912 organized Engadine Incorporated as a film distributor, had his own method of judging the appeal of films he purchased. "I would go to a theater, take the first row or sit in a box, and then study the audience to see what effect the film had on them. So I was pretty certain in my mind after the experience I had had in watching audiences that I could use a subject and not go far wrong." Later on he would talk of an "itch in the seat of my pants," meaning that if watching a film caused him to squirm in his seat, Zukor would not buy it.

Such was the thinking of the time, but surely there was more to it than that. Zukor and others had a combination of innate intelligence and good taste, as well as an uncanny empathy with the American middle class. In 1927, when asked if sex was the foundation upon which the industry was based, Zukor growled:

> Did *The Birth of a Nation* depend upon sex? Did *The Covered Wagon,* or *The Big Parade,* or *The Ten Commandments?* or any other of the films which we managers advertised as epoch-making. The story's the foundation of the whole structure. If it's a good story that depends on sex, well and good. If it's a good story that doesn't depend upon sex, just as good. Everyone, of course, likes a pretty attractive woman. It's part, and a very pleasant part, of a scheme of life which we're trying in our imperfect way to put onto the screen. Those directors who make their films drip with sex confess their own shallowness and inexpertness. They're unable to tell a really first-class story, so they try to save themselves by sensationalism. It's like the political orator who hasn't anything more to say and knows he's stuck, and so he goes on: "Behold the starry banner, the proud symbol of our freedom."

With General Film's permission, Engadine purchased the American rights to *Queen Elizabeth,* starring Sarah Bernhardt. The film was a huge success and encouraged Zukor to organize the Famous Players Film Company, which under license produced such hits as *The Prisoner of Zenda, The Count of Monte Cristo,* and *Tess of the D'Urbervilles.* True to the name of his new company, Zukor brought to films such popular artists as John Barrymore, Elsie Janis, Douglas Fairbanks, Lily Langtry, and H. B. Warner, making Famous Players the major link between the legitimate theater and the movies.

By now Zukor had come to realize that it would be possible to create a company that would control all aspects of film, from production to distribution to exhibition, if necessary in defiance of General Films. His first step came in 1916. Joining with Jesse L. Lasky, he took over Paramount Pictures, a leading distributor, and formed Famous Players–Lasky. With this in hand, he moved to unite production and exhibition. This would require far more capital than he or any other industry figure could martial. Zukor now went to Wall Street for financing, the first of the important film figures to do so. He later recalled the experience:

> I approached several different bankers and tried to sell them the idea of big profits in the motion picture business. They were very glad and wished me good luck and hoped I would succeed, but they did not see their way clear to participate in this lucrative business until one day I met Mr. Otto Kahn, of Kuhn Loeb & Co. I thought that on account of his connection with the Metropolitan Opera House and his interest in theaters and artists I could refer to the possibilities of the picture business and perhaps he would be interested. I talked to him a bit and he told me he was much interested.

Americans flocked to Paramount theaters all over the country to see Paramount stars in Paramount movies. Seven thousand people saw *The Phantom of the Opera* on this Saturday in Atlanta in 1925, just six days after the movie opened.

RIALTO THEATRE
WOODBURY, N. J.
THURSDAY - FRIDAY - SATURDAY FEBRUARY 4-5-6

She speaks and sings CHINESE!

譚蔡沙利

Shirley TEMPLE in STOWAWAY

After some discussion, Kahn invited Zukor to meet Jacob Schiff, the head of Kuhn, Loeb, who was the only person on Wall Street mentioned in the same breath as J. P. Morgan. The former furrier spoke of the glowing future of movies. "It was romantic. It had a future. After a few days' negotiation they gave me $10 million."

With financing in hand, Zukor moved to control production. Within two years he had almost two-thirds of the major artists under contract, raiding other studios and depleting their ranks in the process. Together with Lewis Selznick, Zukor formed Select Pictures, acquiring such Selznick stars as Norma Talmadge, Nazimova, and Clara Kimball Young. By 1917 Zukor was turning out or otherwise involved in some 200 films a year, making him by far the dominant force in the production end of the business.

The next move was into exhibition. With the backing of Kuhn, Loeb, Zukor purchased theaters on a wholesale basis, first taking in 135 in the southern states in 1919 and adding 50 in New England the following year; by 1921 Famous Players–Lasky owned more than 300 theaters and was the dominant force in this part of the industry as well. Others followed, so that at mid-decade Zukor was the colossus in the nation's fastest growing business.

All of this activity stirred antitrust suspicions at the Justice Department, which led Zukor to restructure his holdings. Before the government could act, he spun off his theaters and merged them with the Balaban and Katz Chicago-based operation to form Paramount-Publix, which was two-thirds owned by Famous Players–Lasky. This new giant had more than 500 theaters and soon a new name as well — Paramount Famous Lasky in 1927, and three years later, Paramount Publix.

Zukor was at the zenith of his power in 1928 when Warner Brothers introduced talking pictures. He quickly adjusted to the new technology, borrowing heavily to wire his studios and theaters for sound. In addition, he entered the rapidly growing radio business by purchasing a 49 percent interest in the Columbia Broadcasting System. There was talk at the time of broadcasting motion pictures in such a way as to have them receive on radiolike sets, thus eliminating the need for theaters — an early concept of television. Zukor was interested and prepared to put money into such a project; in 1939 he was the first motion picture tycoon to establish a television subsidiary.

The Great Depression intervened, and television had to await the post–World War II period to be proven commercially. Paid theater attendance declined, going from $732 million in 1930 to $482 million three years later. All the major companies lost money, Paramount Publix included, and all had to be recapitalized. Kuhn, Loeb already controlled the company's finance committee and now another Wall Street bank, Lehman Brothers, took command. Paramount Publix was refinanced and reorganized as Paramount Pictures Incorporated in 1935. Zukor was still chairman, but the bankers now held sway.

Zukor would live another four decades — he died in 1976 at the age of 103 — but although he received honors and applause, his reign was over.

The star system that Zukor initiated became the hallmark of American movies. It reached its apotheosis in the 1930s and 1940s with the fabulous popularity of Hollywood luminaries such as Shirley Temple.

During the height of the Great Depression, one out of every four American workers could find himself standing in line for unemployment benefits. The nation was hungry not only for food but for dreams and diversions, a need filled by the game of Monopoly.

Charles B. Darrow: Playing At the American Dream

THE WINTER OF 1933 was arguably the bleakest in American history. The reality of the Great Depression chilled the nation to the marrow. One out of every four American workers was unemployed. Every day, homeless men and women who had frozen overnight in doorways were taken to the morgues of American cities, and soup kitchens were familiar sights; malnutrition and starvation were a threat even on the farm. Young boys were catching rides on freight trains, aimlessly wandering the country in search of — anything. "I don't want to steal," wrote a desperate father, "but I won't let my wife and boy cry for something to eat. . . . How long is this going to keep up? I can't stand it any longer. . . . Oh, if God would only open a way."

To say that business was poor would be a vast understatement. The gross national product, which had peaked in 1929 at $103.1 billion, was down to $55.6 billion in 1933. More than four thousand banks suspended operations that year, causing losses to depositors of $540 million. American corporations had posted a net loss of $3.5 billion the previous year — an enormous amount for the time — and the outlook wasn't promising.

The great real estate boom of the 1920s had collapsed. There were more than a quarter-million foreclosures in 1933, still an all-time record. The value of new construction had been $10.8 billion in 1929; four years later it came to $2.9 billion. This was no time to enter the labor force, and the outlook for new businesses had never been worse.

Americans had few diversions. There was radio, of course, which had the important virtue of being free. Even though one could go to the movies for ten cents at matinees, it was a price beyond the means of many; attendance dropped 40 percent below the 1931 level, and several film companies, Adolph Zukor's Paramount included, were in receivership or being reorganized, with others to follow. Likewise, the miniature golf craze had faded, as it, too, was an expense most Americans could not afford.

Throughout the country millions struggled to survive and, when they could, looked for ways to forget their problems for a while. Song sheets with lyrics of popular tunes that sold for a nickel were big that year. Friends would gather at one another's homes and spend the night singing songs, sipping coffee, and just talking. Or they would play parlor games, charades being a great favorite. Perhaps in order to overcome the overwhelming feeling of powerlessness, they might engage in a strange pastime that was fairly popular, simply called "The Game." Several couples would sit around in a circle, in the middle of which was a button. A problem was posed: "By pressing the button you become a millionaire but at the same time kill a million Chinese. Would you press it?" The question would be heatedly debated, while everyone looked at each other, wondering if and when someone would lunge for the button. Harmless, perhaps, and at times even stimulating. Such games gave one the illusion of command at no cost.

Charles B. Darrow plays real estate wheeler and dealer at the Monopoly board.

Monopoly has become an American classic — proof of Darrow's insight into the American dream.

Whether Charles Darrow of Germantown, Pennsylvania, engaged in such pastimes is unknown. A heating equipment salesman, he had lost his last regular job in 1930. He lived with his wife and child in a shabby house, and in the winter of 1933 another infant was on the way. Like more than forty million Americans, Darrow was poor, taking whatever work he could find. The previous summer he had rung doorbells, trying to get a dime for mowing lawns, and that winter he shoveled snow. Occasionally he repaired small appliances, and in the evening he listened to the radio and tried to think up a gadget everyone would need, that would make him rich. Darrow came up with several ideas. There were a simplified bridge scoring pad that didn't work out and a combination ball and bat that got nowhere. In his fantasies Darrow played his own version of The Game, wheeling and dealing, perhaps in real estate, an area of speculation that had made fortunes for Americans from John Jacob Astor and A. T. Stewart onward. He probably recalled a vacation he and his wife had taken at Atlantic City, New Jersey, at a happy time prior to the Great Crash.

The result of Darrow's private game was a board game known as "Monopoly." It was complicated, having a set of rules that required some study before play could commence and that were subject to interpretations which could lead to arguments. As with many other games, players rolled dice and moved their pieces around the board; but there the similarities ended. There was no objective the players had to reach; rather, they went round and round, landing on "properties" Darrow named after streets in Atlantic City, buying and selling them, erecting houses and hotels, trading, mortgaging, trying to work deals, and going on until one after another player went bankrupt, leaving a single winner. A game of Monopoly could last through the night and into the next day. Often players left exhausted, with no winner. Perhaps without realizing it, Darrow had created a game that would sharply alter the nature of the industry.

Unable to finance production, promotion, and distribution, Darrow took Monopoly to Parker Brothers, one of the nation's oldest and best-known game manufacturers, then suffering from sales declines due to the Depression. The company had been organized by George S. Parker and his brother Charles in 1883 to turn out a game George devised, known as "Banking." It was a success, and Parker Brothers then originated or purchased other board games, becoming a leader in what was a new industry. George Parker was expert at designing games that fit in with the times. For example, during the Spanish-American War, Parker Brothers came out with "Hold the Fort," "War in Cuba," and "The Battle of Manila." Given this tradition, one might have expected Parker Brothers to have been enthusiastic about a game that engaged players in innocent imaginary financial dealings during the Depression, but such was not the case. The company's executives gave Monopoly a trial and came up with a critique cataloguing 52 flaws, leading to the conclusion that the game was far too complicated to have mass appeal. In the end, they rejected it, leaving Darrow to seek other manufacturers or try to produce and market it on his own.

Taking the latter route, Darrow borrowed the funds and with the help of a friend who was a printer managed to turn out some sets, which he peddled from store to store. Few were placed in 1934, but those who did buy Monopoly spoke enthusiastically about it to others, and by word of mouth the game achieved popularity. Typically one family would buy it, invite two others for a game, and the next week these became customers for additional sets. By the end of the year, Monopoly was the rage of the Philadelphia area. Wanamaker's ordered 5,000 sets on consignment from Darrow — his biggest and most important sale.

Wanamaker's placement engaged the attention of Parker Brothers, whose management now reconsidered its earlier judgment, and in 1935 Parker purchased rights to the game. It was an act of near desperation. The company was on the ropes financially, its major product, Mahjongg, the only clear success in its line. Parker Brothers now threw all of its limited resources behind Monopoly and was shocked by the success. By mid-February 1935, the company was producing 20,000 sets a week and still couldn't fill all the orders. By Christmas orders were coming in at such volume they couldn't even be processed. Sales that year reached the unheard-of level of 800,000 sets, and even more might have been sold had they been shipped. Parker now sought help from a clerical firm, whose representatives surveyed the situation and turned down the job of filling the orders, saying it wasn't possible.

Even so, Parker Brothers couldn't believe its good fortune, still half convinced the fad (for that is what it seemed) would die down. And sales did level off in late 1936, leading George Parker to send down instructions to "cease absolutely to make any more boards or utensil boxes. . . . We will stop making Monopoly against the possibility of a very early slump." But sales revived soon after and continued strong. Later on, Robert Barton, Parker's son-in-law, said, "It was a godsend. It rescued the business, which had come within an inch of disaster." He reasoned that Monopoly's success was due to the fact that it was the right product for the times. "Monopoly was definitely part of the Depression era. It let people fantasize that they could win in the real estate market."

But it was more than that. The Depression ended with the coming of World War II, after which America entered a prolonged period of relative affluence — and continued to play Monopoly. More than 90 million sets have been sold worldwide, with no indication of a permanent slowdown.

Charles Darrow never invented another game. He retired to raise cattle and orchids on a Pennsylvania farm and died a millionaire in 1967.

A JOHNSON PUBLICATION

EBONY

FOUR DECADES
OF BLACK PROGRESS
40th *Anniversary*

**1945-1985: THE YEARS
THAT CHANGED AMERICA**

NOVEMBER 1985 $3

John H. Johnson: Apostle of the Black Middle Class

Aᴜ sᴋ ᴛʜᴇ ᴀᴠᴇʀᴀɢᴇ educated American — of any color, sex, or religion — to name the most prominent blacks in American history, and he or she probably will start off with Martin Luther King, Jesse Owens, Jackie Robinson, Booker T. Washington, George Washington Carver, Frederick Douglass, and go on to include Jesse Jackson, Malcolm X, Muhammad Ali, O. J. Simpson, Ella Fitzgerald, and other political, religious, athletic, and show business figures.

There will be no businessmen or businesswomen on that list, no entrepreneurs, no financiers. The reason for this is simple: most of the big businesses everyone recognizes have been the province of whites. The many small businesses that until recently were the backbone of the economy for blacks as well as whites were hardly known. Until well into the post–World War II period, there were no blacks in the top echelon of the steel, auto, food-processing, machine tool, pharmaceutical, or aviation industries — not even at the middle management level. One would have had to go into the ranks of foremen on the

Four decades of *Ebony* covers pay tribute to prominent American blacks in the second half of the twentieth century.

With *Ebony* reaching more than 1.5 million people every month, John Johnson is by far the most powerful black businessman in America.

factory floor to find the few blacks who were able to rise to that status. Before the war there were virtually no significant black enterprises aside from beauty parlors, restaurants, barbershops, groceries, funeral parlors, and the like. The most a black entrepreneur could hope for was a small, local enterprise, dealing with individuals of his or her own color.

Yet the aspirations of black businessmen two or three generations ago weren't much different from those of their white counterparts, which is to say they dreamed of wealth, security, and recognition. They knew little of the kind of success stories that thrilled white America; the black entrepreneur had no image of an Andrew Carnegie, Thomas A. Edison, or John D. Rockefeller to give him inspiration and hope. Truman K. Givson, L. D. Milton, Harry Pace, C. C. Spaulding, and John Merrick, leaders of the black insurance industry, were known to only a handful, although their companies were the largest to be organized and led by blacks.

Ebony magazine, founded and published by John H. Johnson, ended that anonymity. Every year *Ebony* publishes lists of the largest black-owned and -operated companies, and virtually every issue contains at least one article on the subject. As much as *Fortune* and *Barron's*, *Ebony* is a celebration of American business; if *Forbes* is, as publisher Malcolm Forbes boasts, "The Capitalist Tool," *Ebony* is the quintessential *black* capitalist organ and Johnson one of the more important twentieth-century entrepreneurs. Along with Fred Smith, Mary Kay Ash, King Gillette, and other entrepreneurs we'll meet here, he perceived a need, created a product to fill it, sold it to the public, and reaped the rewards.

Johnson was born in Arkansas City, Arkansas, in 1918, the only son of a sawmill worker, who was killed while John was still a child. His mother married another mill hand, and the family lived a life of rural poverty common in that period. "I can't say I had a happy childhood," Johnson recalled. "I had no contact with the world outside, and when you have nothing to compare with, you aren't aware you should be unhappy." He attended a segregated school, where he was a good student. In 1933 the family moved to Chicago, inspired by the dazzling vision projected by the World's Fair in the city that year. It was hardly a propitious time: this was the bottom of the Great Depression, and for a year and a half the family lived on relief. Then, along with many others, the Johnsons were saved by the New Deal. John's stepfather found employment with the Works Progress Administration, and John, now seventeen, went into the National Youth Administration.

Though still quite poor, Johnson was coming into contact with a far wider world than the one he had known in Arkansas, and his character annealed in the process. "The other kids used to laugh at me as they used to make fun of my homemade clothes," he later recalled. "I decided I would show them, and I did."

How to do so was a problem. For blacks, there wasn't much hope for a career in white America in that period, and whatever existed of black business had been all but crushed by the bad times. In 1929 there had been 59 black-owned banks; by 1933 the number had dwindled to 11. In the same period, the number of insurance companies had gone from 110 to 30. While the usual outlets for local business remained, Johnson's ambitions lay elsewhere. He had no contacts or expertise, and even if he had, there would be no place to capitalize on them. But along with most ambitious blacks of the time, he had middle-class aspirations, fed and nurtured by contacts with the majority culture.

Johnson attended segregated DuSable High School, where he was an honor student, leader of the debating team, and, most important, manager of the school newspaper and business editor of the yearbook. Both jobs combined business with journalism. He enjoyed the work and decided to enter that field even though there was no chance for a position at a white publishing firm or newspaper. At the same time, he read Dale Carnegie's *How to Win Friends and Influence People,* from which he derived an important lesson: "Don't get mad. Get smart."

While Johnson might have broken into journalism at a black newspaper such as the Chicago *Defender,* a better opportunity appeared when he interviewed Harry Pace, then president of Supreme Liberty Life Insurance, a leading black company, for a school program. Impressed with the young man, Pace offered him a starting position at his firm and helped Johnson obtain a scholarship for part-time study at the University of Chicago. Two years later, Johnson became Pace's assistant. Among his duties was helping to publish the company newsletter, which contained material of general interest to black Chicagoans. While completing his studies at Northwestern, Johnson was already considering the possibility of a general interest magazine, offered to the general black community and containing the kinds of stories printed in the newsletter.

Supreme Liberty Life was not only a leading company but also the focus of black political and social life in Chicago, and Johnson was becoming part of the city's "black establishment." For a brief time, he considered a political career but in the end opted to enter publishing, catering to others who, like him, had aspirations for a better life, had been embittered by failures to enter mainstream society, and were obliged to seek opportunity within the black community. He

A JOHNSON PUBLICATION ⑥

EBONY

DIAHANN CARROLL TELLS ALL:
Autobiography Details Stormy, Nine-Year Love Affair With
Sidney Poitier

Eligible
Bachelors
1986

Big Weddings
Are Back

On The Road
With B. B. King

JUNE 1986 $2

decided to create a magazine patterned after the *Reader's Digest,* to be called the *Negro Digest.* Pace permitted him to use Supreme Liberty Life's mailing list, and in 1942 Johnson borrowed $500 by using his mother's furniture as collateral to organize Johnson Publishing Company.

Johnson made an initial mailing of 20,000 solicitations for subscriptions at $2 a year and received 3,000 responses. Getting the magazine on the newsstands was more difficult. Johnson's friends would ask for it and, when told the *Negro Digest* wasn't stocked, asked the dealers to get hold of it for them. This prompted orders, copies were purchased, and reorders placed. The ploy worked in Chicago, after which Johnson moved on to Detroit, New York, Philadelphia, and other cities with large black populations. Within a year the *Negro Digest* had a circulation of more than 50,000 and artificial sales stimulation was no longer necessary.

The *Negro Digest* was hardly a roaring success by mainstream standards, but with a circulation that rose to 150,000 it soon became an important voice for striving blacks, as well as for those who were critical of America's failure to enable them to rise in the general population. Similarities to the *Reader's Digest* were manifest, but with a difference: where the larger magazine featured articles on "My Most Unforgettable Character," Johnson had "My Most Humiliating Jim Crow Experience" and pieces by a white author entitled "If I Were a Negro." This was a time when a black was, in the words of novelist Ralph Ellison, the "Invisible Man." Most whites knew little of black America except through caricatures they encountered at the movies and on the radio, and even blacks themselves portrayed their own race as comic stereotypes. Whites would roar at the antics of Amos 'n Andy's "Andy Brown," a good-natured but thoroughly inept businessman, without ever wondering what impact this image had upon black America.

The success of the *Negro Digest* confirmed Johnson's view that there was a large, literate black middle class, hungry for stimulating articles on their common experience and news of developments within their community. The market for publications such as his not only existed but was far larger than anyone thought. If a magazine for blacks based on the idea of the *Reader's Digest* could be so successful, what about one like *Life?* Out of this insight came *Ebony,* a glossy picture magazine devoted to articles on black middle-class life, featuring success stories and other news of interest to the striving community.

The first issue came out in November 1945, and within days the initial press run of 25,000 was sold out. That the market existed was obvious, but Johnson's new *Ebony* could not exist long without advertising. At first this came in the form of small ads from black-owned enterprises, especially cosmetics firms, but there weren't enough of these to support the enterprise. So Johnson aggressively sought ads from large corporations, trying with no little difficulty to convince them there was a large market for their goods and services that had to be approached differently from that of white America, and that, indeed, if this effort were not made, blacks might turn to new products offered by competitors who made the effort.

Within a year, large firms led by Zenith and Liggett & Myers began to place their ads in *Ebony.* These were of a kind rarely seen by white America: middle- and upper-class blacks smoking Chesterfields and gathered around expensive radio receivers in refined surroundings. The ads worked; before long *Ebony* became the vehicle through which big business reached affluent black audiences.

Other magazines followed. *Tan* (1950) was originally modeled after *True Confessions* but quickly expanded into other subjects, and *Jet* (1951) was a pocket-size picture magazine. Then Johnson started publishing books dealing with the black experience. He became involved in the cosmetics industry through Fashion Fair, using his subscription lists and advertising to get a toehold and then expanding it to the point where the company has become one of the most profitable in the industry. Johnson gained control of Supreme Life Insurance as well, and his company took on the appearance of a conglomerate.

In recent years, Johnson has moved into radio, television programming and broadcasting, and cable television. Johnson Publishing grosses more than $140 million a year, and Johnson is listed by *Forbes* as one of the fifty wealthiest Americans. He is by far the most powerful black American businessman, consulted by every president since John F. Kennedy. With a circulation of close to 2 million, *Ebony* remains the focus of his business activities. It has evolved into a significant organ of opinion and analysis of racial matters, while retaining its concern for progress within the black community. All together Johnson's magazines reach over 60 percent of the adult black population. "You can't sell successfully to the black consumer market without me," says Johnson.

With the coming of heightened black awareness in the 1960s, Johnson became somewhat controversial. Some activists singled out *Ebony* as an "Uncle Tom" publication that pressured blacks to emulate white materialism. Critics observed the plethora of cosmetics ads urging readers to straighten hair and bleach their skin, and pointed to pictures of models with distinctly Caucasian facial features. Roy Innis, one of the new black leaders, was representative of this criticism, writing in 1967:

> We can cry "Black Power" until doomsday, but until black children stop saying, "You are blacker than me and so is your mamma"; until black men stop using black as a curse word; until *Ebony* stops asking such asinine questions as: "Are negro women getting prettier?" and stops carrying bleaching cream advertisements; until black people stop saying such things as "she's dark but pretty"; in short until black people accept values meaningful to themselves, there can be no effective organizing for the development of Black Power.

By then, however, *Ebony* had moved quite a distance, with Johnson running strong articles on the civil rights movement and ads altered to make them more acceptable to Innis and others who felt as he did. Indeed, the changing attitudes of middle-class black America can be better traced in the pages of *Ebony* than anywhere else. This was the key to Johnson's continuing success. "About ten percent of the negro people are those who are able to enjoy many of these advantages we are speaking about" he explained. "Not all the people we glamorize believe this is all their world either. We are like the movies — just as they tend to embellish and adorn the normal, I think we do the same. This is not to misstate the truth but simply to express the search for something that will capture the imagination." Black psychologist Kenneth Clark agrees: "It is impossible to measure the morale-lifting value of such a magazine."

"I believe in miracles. I believe my success is a miracle," Johnson once told a reporter. But surely there was more to it than that, for the "miracle" derived from perception, analysis, action, and adjustments to new opportunities. When talking about his new ventures, Johnson observed, "I don't commit too much to anything. I can't afford to. I always feel a little insecure. In fact, I think there is no such thing as security. There is no such thing as permanent success."

The ebullient Mary Kay Ash poses with the symbol of her remarkable incentive program — the pink Cadillac awarded for high sales. Behind the glitz and glitter is a very savvy strategist.

Mary Kay Ash: The Pink Cadillac Approach

MARY KAY ASH created a third-of-a-billion-dollar cosmetics empire, Mary Kay Cosmetics, by putting together several relatively simple components: beauty preparations, a part-time female sales force, an incentive program, hoopla, and tinsel.

Like the ideas behind many enterprises, the Mary Kay notion seems simple enough, so much so that one wonders why others didn't try it sooner. In fact many did; Mary Kay Cosmetics appeared at a time when Fuller Brush, Tupperware, and Avon had well-established industry niches. What she had was an uncanny knack for motivating her sales force. The company's incentive program offers its "Very Important Performers" special forms of compensation, such as the cream-colored Oldsmobiles given to those who manage to sell $3,000 in products a month for three consecutive months. Prizes like these run upward to the penultimate award, one of the company's famed pink Cadillacs, presented with all the glitter and ritual of a Miss America coronation.

The top prize is a diamond-studded gold bumblebee. Why this? As Mary Kay (as she disarmingly likes to be known) often explains, "A bee shouldn't be able to fly; its body is too heavy for its wings. But the bumblebee doesn't know this and it flies very well." This is of a piece with her best-known greeting: "How are *you*?" she asks all who come across her path. And whatever the answer, Mary Kay will reply, "You're great! Fake it till you make it!" She is ebullient and forever optimistic. When asked her favorite book, she replies *The Power of Positive Thinking*, which has taught her that "If you think you can, you can. And if you think you can't, you can't."

Like most female entrepreneurs of her generation, Mary Kay made her mark in an industry in which women were traditionally cubbyholed. (These included fashion, upscale retailing, and, especially, cosmetics.) Mary Kay was preceded by Elizabeth Arden, Helena Rubenstein, and Georgette Klinger, all of whom were every bit as tough and imaginative as their male counterparts but consigned to the cosmetics ghetto by the folkways of their time. When Mary Kay occasionally falls back into the stereotype, it is usually purposeful, like those pink (not black) Cadillacs. When asked how old she is (she is over seventy), Mary Kay will bat her eyes in a coquettish fashion and answer, "A woman who will tell her age will tell anything." The press has referred to her as "petite" and "as sweet as a magnolia blossom." She says the initials in her financial statements stand for "People and Love," not "Profit and Loss." Appearing at the many Mary Kay conventions, she sweeps in on the arm of some much younger swain, to the strains of "Queen of Hearts."

The Pollyanna rhetoric and Rebecca of Sunnybrook Farm appearance seem to have been carefully orchestrated to achieve the desired effect. In fact, Mary Kay Ash is as shrewd, hard-headed, calculating, and adventuresome as any of the entrepreneurs included here.

She has had as difficult a life as any. Born Mary Kay Wagner in Hot Wells, Texas, during the World War I era, by age seven she was caring for her tubercular father while her mother worked in a diner. A good student despite the need to work part-time during the Depression, Mary Kay was married at seventeen to a local radio crooner named Ben Rogers, who bore a resemblance to Elvis Presley and sang with a group called The Hawaiian Strummers. Rogers deserted her after eight years of marriage, leaving her with three children under the age of eight. "I was the sole support of those kids," she recalled, "and that was in the days before day care."

Having to work while raising the children, Mary Kay found employment selling Stanley Home Products part-time door-to-door. There wasn't much money in peddling notions and the like, but some saleswomen did well enough to win the "Queen of Sales" award, which brought recognition and a prize, usually an alligator purse. Wanting to improve herself, Mary Kay borrowed $12 and went to the annual convention in Dallas, where she met that year's queen and asked how it was done, vowing to follow her lead and win the award the following year. This she did, but the prize was an underwater flashlight used to lure fish — not particularly useful or ornamental.

Mary Kay remembered this decades later, when dishing out those Cadillacs and diamond-encrusted gold bumblebees. She also learned to scorn phrases like "He has a family to support" when applied exclusively to men, as it was by Stanley's executives, to hold back ambitious and enterprising women. (Her organization is staffed almost exclusively by women.) But she continued on at Stanley, holding gatherings to sell the company's products and making a fair living at it.

One night Mary Kay attended a Stanley Home party in a poor section of Dallas and noticed that all of the women there, from the young to the old, had smooth, flawless, unlined faces. "It turned out the hostess was a cosmetologist and that she was using her guests as guinea pigs for a skin care product she was working on." The hostess's father was a tanner, and the formula derived from a solution used to cure hides. After the party she gave out samples, and Mary Kay took some home in a shoe box, tried it, found it worked as well on her, and became a regular customer.

Soon after, Mary Kay left Stanley to take a better-paid position at World Gift Company, a Dallas-based home accessories firm, which she helped expand into other parts of the country. Once again she found her path to the executive

Products in the Mary Kay line are limited so that every consultant can become an expert in each item.

suite blocked due to her sex, so in 1963 she resigned. Remarried and comparatively well-off, Mary Kay now considered herself retired and a housewife. But after six weeks she was bored and decided to return to the business world.

As she tells it, Mary Kay drew up two lists: the first, what was wrong with companies dominated by males; the second, how to correct those abuses by being more sensitive to the needs of women, especially working mothers. From these lists emerged the outline of a "dream company" which, in practice, was one in which everyone would be treated equally, promotions would be made on the basis of merit, and products would be not only superior to others on the market but fervently believed in by the sales force.

She already had her first product. The cosmetologist who had developed the skin cream died in 1961, and, more to assure herself of a continued supply than anything else, Mary Kay purchased the formula from her heirs. It was to become the nucleus for her beauty preparations company, Mary Kay Cosmetics.

Lacking experience and financial knowledge, Mary Kay put up $5,000 of her own money as the initial capital, intending to open a store from which the beauty cream would be sold. Plans were halted when her husband died a month prior to the planned opening. Since he was to provide financial and managerial expertise, Mary Kay thought to abandon the idea, a course recommended by her attorney and her accountant, both of whom had been dubious about the venture from the start. But her children and their friends urged her on, and the 500-square-foot store located in a large Dallas office complex opened on Friday, September 13, 1963. The entire inventory was a single shelf of creams.

Mary Kay's twenty-year-old son Richard took charge of the store, while she set out to recruit a door-to-door sales force, which from the first she knew would be central to the company. The structure and rules derived more from her experiences than any theories. For example, Mary Kay decided there would be no sales quotas or restricting rules. Her "consultants," as they were called, could set their own hours so that they had adequate time to care for their families. Mary Kay recognized, as she put it, that "where women are concerned, they cannot function if they have problems at home." This insight was crucial, for Mary Kay's sales force would be composed for the most part of married women or divorced mothers seeking to earn extra funds for their families. In time some salespeople were full-time career women, but at first these were the minority. The company's motto, "God first, family second, career third," indicated the founder's priorities.

Those priorities have not changed over the years. At one point during her career with Stanley, Mary Kay had to relocate to another city because her husband had been transferred. Moving meant giving up the sales organization she had developed in Dallas and the more than $1,000 per month it generated. When she organized her own company, she was determined that saleswomen shouldn't have to lose what they had built up to save their marriages. She developed an "adoptee" program under which saleswomen recruit others and become their supervisors. The adoptee remains with the woman who recruited her regardless of where she lives and trained. In other words, no one has assigned territories, only personal networks.

Mary Kay's consultants do not earn a great deal, less than $2,000 for the year for the typical nine-hour work week. But the consultants have found they can work fewer hours for greater total returns than they might with rival operations. Consultants pay 50 percent of retail for their supplies, which they purchase for cash from the company, and those who bring in new recruits receive a 4 percent bonus on their purchases. To increase motivation, the bonus is 8 percent for those who bring in five or more new consultants and 12 percent for consultants who place wholesale orders of $600 or more a month.

After six months, consultants can start to qualify for directorships — and also for those extra bonuses, the pink Cadillacs and the like. To qualify, consultants must have at least fifteen recruits and pledge to bring in fifteen more as well as meet other quotas. The program is constantly being altered to expand the sales force and the company's scope.

Mary Kay Cosmetics outpaced its better-established rivals by motivating its sales force more effectively and also giving greater thought to its product line. At a time when the offerings of the familiar Avon ladies and others were proliferating, Mary Kay's was limited to the amount a consultant could carry at any one time. (Avon typically has some 650 products in its line, as opposed to 45 in Mary Kay's.) As a result, consultants can take all of their wares to beauty shows and be expert in a few basic products rather than merely conversant in many. Moreover, the company's inventory needs, and hence its prices, are much lower than those of most rivals. Finally, Mary Kay has always stressed skin care, which accounts for nearly half of all sales.

Mary Kay Ash's successes are due largely to her entrepreneurial ability to perceive opportunities in a field many thought to be crowded with entrenched, large-scale operations. Behind that image of a flighty and beruffled and highly feminine matriarch, lavishing praise and love over her consultants, is a hard-driven individual constantly innovating and seeking new methods to develop her company.

Mary Kay has built a loyal sales force with her people-oriented approach to business and sensitivity to the needs of working women.

Fred Smith and Federal Express

THE PERIOD OF THE 1950s through the 1960s was the seed time for scores of fresh high technology corporations, which were transforming American industry. Most of the dramatic entrepreneurial stories were to be found in the development of the new technologies themselves. But there were also several entrepreneurs of exceptional insight who perceived just how widely technological change would ripple through society, affecting the very patterns of our lives.

In the 1960s, the American economy was increasingly becoming based more upon services and lightweight high technology products than bulk manufacturing. The period when semiskilled workers turned out manufactured goods in large factories not far from sources of raw materials, which were brought in by canal, rail, and truck, was slowly fading. Now, highly trained scientists and technicians were developing services and products based upon electronic devices rather than tons of steel. From 1972 to 1982, electronic components production grew by an average of 9.9 percent per annum; in the same period, steel production declined by 4.3 percent per annum. In such statistics we can see the dawning of a new era of industrialization.

One consequence of the shift to electronics was a dispersal of manufacturing facilities. No longer dependent on proximity to raw materials, companies manufacturing lightweight, valuable products could locate facilities in places that would attract sought-after technicians, scientists, and managers. Did they want to reside in an area where cultural pursuits, higher education, recreation, and ambience suited their tastes? Very well, the plant would be located on the outskirts of San Francisco, Boston, or New York. Did a key scientist enjoy skin-diving? The plant would be established in the Bahamas.

But dispersal of people and products introduced a new problem: transmittal of information and goods. While much could be sent electronically, there remained the need for deliveries on paper, discs, tapes, and the like. Suppose a small installation in the exurbs of San Francisco wanted to send a small package to its counterpart in the Boston suburbs and be assured by 3:00 P.M. that it would arrive before noon the following day. Or a supplier in Des Moines needed confirmation that a small electronic part would be delivered as promised to a valued customer in Jackson, Mississippi, within twenty-four hours. Automobile manufacturers such as General Motors and Ford, and other industries that relied upon bulk shipments, to centralized factories, kept fairly large inventories, knowing that a snowstorm or strike might hold up rail or truck deliveries for days, perhaps weeks. Not so high tech operations and others relying chiefly upon information: for them speed and reliability were of the essence, and they were prepared to pay premium prices for both. This meant shipment by air rather than land or water.

It hardly took genius to see what was happening, but it did take entrepreneurial imagination to make the next step.

Fred Smith is often heralded as one of the greatest entrepreneurial successes of recent times. While the distinction is difficult to dispute, something akin to folklore has grown up around Smith's career. He is viewed as a man who was willing to take almost astonishing risks in the relentless pursuit of his vision. The fact that Smith went up against the monolithic United States Postal Service and that he once used casino winnings to meet a critical payroll are favorite examples of his daredevilry.

But given Smith's experience and expertise, as well as the changing context of transportation and communication in America, his actions seem less precipitous, less absolutely tempting of fate. This is not to detract from Smith's achievements; on the contrary, it is to praise them for their vision and intentionality. The Federal Express story should stand as a reminder that many of the best entrepreneurs excelled at judging, controlling, or minimizing risks rather than simply taking them.

Smith was an opportunist in the best sense of the term, which is to say he succeeded by recognizing opportunities where most others did not. The glamor of Federal's sprightly colored jets laden with time-precious cargo as they scurry across the continent should not disguise the fact that Smith is in the transportation business, one of the oldest and most changeable industries in history. Just as Henry Wells of Wells Fargo fame took advantage of new transportation opportunities in the mid-nineteenth century when he initiated his overland express system, and Henry Ford manufactured cheap cars for a burgeoning population eager to turn suburban, Smith had an eye for the opportunities wrought by new technologies, shifting populations, and the evolving nature of demand.

There is no path hacked through the business wilderness that would-be entrepreneurs can travel, but more than most, Smith followed one that in retrospect appeared well marked. His family had close connections to the transportation industry. One grandfather had been a riverboat captain, while his father founded Dixie Greyhound Bus Lines and, with his brother, opened a highly successful chain of restaurants, Toddle House, which specialized in Southern

The advent of the airplane gave a new twist to a very old business — delivering the mail. In 1929, the U.S. government operated the only air mail service in the country.

cuisine. When Smith's father, also named Frederick, died in 1948, the restaurants were sold in 1961 for $22 million, part of which provided his son with his first stake.

Young Fred had done well enough in school, but he was equally if not more interested in extracurricular activities. He started a record company (which still exists) at the age of fifteen, and learned to fly soon after. In 1962 he entered Yale University, where he majored in economics and political science. Still pretty much a run-of-the-mill student, he appeared more interested in social life and worked as a campus disk jockey. In addition, he enrolled in the Marine Corps Reserve Officer's Training Program. Smith's interest in flying grew, prompting him to revive the Yale Flying Club and dedicate his most original academic effort to the topic.

This was a term paper he wrote as a junior. An analysis of existing freight service, it suggested there might be a market for a company that moved "high-priority, time-sensitive" goods, such as medicines and electronic components. Smith had learned that few packages were sent directly to their destination by existing carriers such as the post office, Railway Express, and Flying Tiger. Instead, packages were "hippety-hopping around the country from city to city and from airline to airline before reaching their destination," which wasted not only money but time, the very reason they were sent by airmail or special delivery. Furthermore, "there was not control over the packages by the originating air carrier if the packages had to be carried by additional airlines before reaching their ultimate destination."

Smith's professor was unimpressed. Perhaps there was something to the argument, he conceded, but federal regulation would preclude such a service. Even if the regulatory problems could be overcome, competition from the major, well-entrenched and well-financed airlines would make success highly doubtful. The grade for the paper: "C."

It mattered little; Smith had no intention of continuing his education or utilizing his academic background. Upon graduation in 1966, he was commissioned by the Marine Corps as a lieutenant and served two tours of duty in Vietnam. Leaving the service in 1969, he launched his business career, to be based upon his love of flying.

He started out by purchasing controlling interest in Arkansas Aviation Sales, a Little Rock–based operation engaged in providing maintenance service for turbo-prop and corporate jet airplanes, which had sales of $1 million, chronic losses, and apparently little future. Smith realized all of this and from the first meant to change things. Arkansas Aviation became a clearing-house for the purchase and sales of used jets, and success in this line enabled Smith to increase revenues to $9 million and turn a profit of $250,000 within two years.

During this period Smith mulled over the idea of a company that could deliver small packages overnight. Was there really a market for such a service? There were some companies in the field: Emery Air Freight and Flying Tiger, to name two of the biggest, had started soon after World War II and by 1969 each had revenues of $100 million. But Smith felt he could offer better and more reliable service than these and couldn't understand why someone hadn't moved to capitalize on the situation. And was it true, as his professor had claimed, that federal laws and regulations would bar such an entity?

Smith commissioned two consulting firms to make studies of the situation. From these reports he learned there was a high degree of dissatisfaction with existing freight services: customers reported their deliveries were erratic,

The audacious Fred Smith entered the delivery business in 1971. His feisty Federal Express Company has outdone its competitors with a fleet of sprightly colored jumbo jets that guarantee fast and reliable service.

often late, and in general, unreliable. In other words, there was a market for a company that could pick up small packages in one part of the country and deliver them efficiently and without hitches to another in a short period of time. Indeed, customers were willing to pay premium rates for assured deliveries.

In addition, while over 60 percent of all traffic was between the largest twenty-five markets, 80 percent of small, urgent shipments originated or terminated outside them. More often than not, shippers or receivers at smaller places had to wait for available scheduled carriers to pick up or deliver packages at a distant location. At a time when manufacturing and research facilities were located outside central cities and had an urgent need for rapid deliveries, such services were vitally needed.

Might Smith, or anyone else, provide such assurances? One of the reports noted that 9 out of 10 domestic commercial liners were on the ground between 10:00 P.M. and 8:00 A.M. This meant the air lanes were uncluttered during late night and early morning hours, so that takeoffs and landings would be relatively smooth. The prospects were exciting. Attempting to create a company capable of providing overnight delivery would be not only challenging but, given Smith's interests in flying, fun as well.

Armed with these findings, Smith set about raising money to start just such a company. And now he learned one of the reasons others hadn't gotten there ahead of him. The capital requirements were high, as was potential investors' skepticism about the concept. In a bold gamble, Smith committed all of his capital, more than $8 million of his family's funds. This stake must have impressed private investors, who added another $40 million. Several interested banks contributed a similar amount, bringing the total to $90 million, the largest single venture-capital start-up in American business history.

The company, which Smith called Federal Express, was incorporated on June 1, 1971, with offices at the old Little Rock facility and the slogan "Welcome Transients" over the hangar. One of the first orders of business was to purchase planes. Smith selected a twin-engine executive jet, the Dassault Falcon, largely because it was small enough to slip underneath the Civil Aeronautics Board's certification requirements for nationwide freight services. By ordering 33 at once, Federal received a discount of nearly 25 percent.

Meanwhile, drawing from the experience of older rivals, Smith decided to follow the lead of United Parcel Service and limit package size to 75 pounds and to restrict parcel dimensions so as to ease loading and unloading. In addition, Federal adopted the familiar "hub and spoke" system of routing used by others: packages would be sent to the hub airport, sorted, and then sent out to the ultimate location, with the company responsible for it throughout by offering door-to-door service. For a while Smith considered using Little Rock as the hub but decided instead on Memphis, which offered better terms and had more ample facilities.

All the while special studies flowed into Smith's office and entreaties to potential customers went out. At one point Federal was devoting 10 percent of its net worth to information generating and dissemination activities. "We're a freight service with 550-mile per hour delivery trucks," he proclaimed. "This company is nothing short of being the logistics arm of a whole new society that is building up in our economy — a society that isn't built around automobile and steel production, but that is built up instead around service industries and high technology endeavors in electronics and optics and medical science. It is the movement of these support items that Federal Express is all about."

Initially, Federal would offer three services: guaranteed overnight delivery, a reduced rate for second day delivery, and a "Courier Pak" in which "the company would transport anything that could fit into a manila foolscap envelope for a flat-fee of $5."

Large sums went to developing a distinctive image. Trucks and planes were brightly painted in orange, purple, and white, and there were full-page advertisements in major dailies and 30-second television commercials, stressing both the company's commitment to deliver packages "absolutely, positively overnight" and the inadequate service provided by competitors. All of this was needed not only to draw customers but establish the proper image with potential investors, for Federal was constantly in need of additional financing. "We purchased the credibility we needed to entice capital sources," explained Smith in justifying his huge promotional expenses.

Operations began on April 17, 1973, with service to twenty-two cities. As expected, there were deficits at first, and Smith scrambled to obtain additional funds and soothe the frayed nerves of increasingly skittish investors. A year later Federal fell into technical default; Smith sold his private plane to help pay bills. On another occasion he used $27,000 won at a Las Vegas blackjack table to meet a payroll. Stories of employee sacrifice and ingenuity during those early years are legion. Couriers would leave their wrist watches for security against gasoline purchases and would hide the Falcons when sheriffs came to repossess them. As one employee recalled:

Believe it or not, these packages will reach their destination "absolutely, positively overnight." Federal Express has had huge success with its system of routing every package through its central facility in Memphis.

You've seen that poster, "The Marines are looking for a few good men," where the troops are dressed in combat fatigues. That's Federal Express. This company should have died five or six times in its first three or four years, but Fred refused to give up. Boy, was he tenacious. With sheer bull and courage, he pulled off a miracle. That's the only way to express what he did.

But it was more than that. While Federal was having a difficult time raising new funds to finance its expansion, Smith was helped by unforeseen developments. Federal came into being at a time when airline traffic was expanding rapidly. Total industry revenues, which came to $7.2 billion in 1970 and $11.2 billion in 1972, rose to $19.9 billion by 1977. Finding themselves in the unusual position of being short on carriers, the major delivery services concentrated on their prime markets and dropped service to many smaller cities. As a result, they were unable to service their small-freight customers as well as they had earlier, opening the way for Federal Express to fill the gap. In addition, there was a long United Parcel Service strike in 1974, followed by the collapse of rival REA Express, which provided Federal with new opportunities.

The red ink continued to flow through 1975, but as the year wore on it became increasingly evident that the situation was turning around. For 1976 Federal had revenues of $109 million — and net income of $8.1 million.

Now everything seemed to work to Federal's advantage. Concurrent with the expansion of its services came the beginnings of deregulation. Under terms of legislation passed in 1977, Federal was permitted to operate larger aircraft, and Smith promptly purchased used Boeing 727–100s from the airlines, greatly expanding capacity. That year Federal reported revenues of $160 million and earnings of $20 million, sufficiently impressive for Smith to plan for the first public stock offering. This came in April, 1978: 1,075,000 shares at $3 per share.

By 1980, when Federal's earnings were just under $60 million on revenues of $590 million, the stock was up to $24. Smith and his backers had reaped a fortune; by then his career was being dissected in the business schools as a prime example of entrepreneurship in our time.

Still, Smith's own view of the matter should be considered by those who would oversimplify his risk-taking tendencies. "I think it's unfortunate that to some degree the word 'entrepreneur' has taken on the connotation of a gambler," he said. "I don't see it that way at all. Many times action is not the most risky path. The most risky path is inaction."

II

The Land and Its People

AMERICA has always been richly endowed with resources. But it took entrepreneurs to see the business opportunities in those resources. Without their vision and efforts, Americans could not have extracted metals and fossil fuels, fed urban populations, processed primary products for industry, or organized labor efficiently and productively enough to transform their land from a rural, agrarian society into a great urban, industrial nation.

It was one thing to fashion a gunstock from wood, but another to build a large-scale lumber-processing enterprise such as Frederick Weyerhaeuser's. Tending the family livestock differed from shipping carloads of dressed beef, as did Gustavus Swift, just as Francis Cabot Lowell's efforts to regularize work patterns in factories differed from the household manufacture of goods. The idea is perhaps best illustrated by Frederic Tudor, who made a business out of selling one of the most common substances available: ice.

In natural resources industries, entrepreneurs at first succeeded by finding better ways to extract, process, and ship raw materials. As industrialization firmly took hold, however, it was accompanied by great economic specialization; the critical entrepreneurial challenge became determining where to pursue opportunities in the chain from raw materials to final consumer. Meeting this challenge was Swift's crowning achievement in meat packing, shipping, and storage. It accounts for John D. Rockefeller's focus on oil refining and explains Frank Perdue's strategy of raising chickens and selling them wholesale only.

Francis Cabot Lowell was among the first to look at people as resources to be organized in factory settings for the sake of efficiency and control. The idea of viewing humans as a resource akin to natural resources is disconcerting only if the aim is exploitation. But without the efforts of Lowell and other entrepreneurs who found better ways to organize and regularize industrial work, America could not have made use of one of its richest resources — its people.

Unfortunately, the utilization of our natural and human resources has too often meant exploitation, especially in our early history. During the first two and a half centuries after Colonial settlement, even the most imaginative and expansionary developers could hardly imagine a time of natural resource scarcity, when forests would be honed bare, arable land fully occupied, whole species of wild animals endangered, and many oil reserves depleted. Such was the case by the late nineteenth century, however, when America's first great conservation movement signaled the beginning of a battle to restore the balance between the use and abuse of resources that continues today.

The parallels with American work patterns are striking. The first immigrants enjoyed a standard of living well above the Old World's, yet many were formally bound in indentured servitude for years, struggled in immigrant work teams, or bore the burden of slavery. The first factories melded men and machines, with the latter more often than not setting the terms of work. But this too began to change in the nineteenth century, as workers banded together to gain strength and a growing number of employers recognized that unrestrained exploitation was simply bad business.

Not all of those who excelled in resource businesses contributed to this darker side of business history. Swift helped feed burgeoning city populations, while Rockefeller, his dubious reputation notwithstanding, cut the price of producing oil for illumination and transportation to a fraction of its original cost. The Weyerhaeuser lumber-processing enterprise has spanned the full extent of

At the turn of the century, the beautiful Yosemite Valley was typical of the American West, which offered a seemingly limitless wealth of natural resources and entrepreneurial opportunity. Who could have imagined that such abundance would soon be depleted by overuse?

Below: Farmers were the most plentiful of America's businessmen before the twentieth century — and also among the most crucial to the economy. The Centennial celebration in Philadelphia honored the people who served as the backbone of the nation's industrial revolution.

Right: The dangerous plains west of the Mississippi were the last American frontier to be settled. Those who dared respond to enticing promotions like this one were rewarded with land that proved to be the most fertile in the world, earning the name of "America's breadbasket."

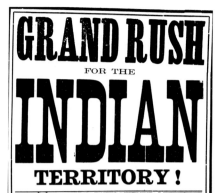

changed attitudes, from the earliest days when its founder, Frederick Weyerhaeuser, aggressively exploited dense forest tracts in the upper Mississippi Valley region, to the present time, when the company owns and carefully manages
5.7 million acres of renewable forest lands.

Agricultural products are still the largest export from the United States,
and food, lumber, and petroleum processing among our biggest industries. In
the beginning, too, land and lumber, fish, furs, tobacco, and indigo were strong
entrepreneurial magnets drawing settlers to the New World. North America
was relatively pristine then. The Indian tribes inhabiting the continent planted
corn and tobacco, but for the most part their economies were based on food
gathering, hunting, and fishing. Rather than till the soil and cut down the forests, they "harvested" animals; and even though their populations were relatively small, they felt crowded. "We have a great deal of ground to live upon,"
an Indian chief told C. F. Volney, an English visitor to America in the early nineteenth century. "A deer will serve us but a couple of days, and a single deer must
have a great deal of ground to put him in good condition. If we kill two or three
hundred a year, 'tis the same as to eat all the wood and grass they live on, and
that is a great deal." Volney concluded that "a thousand acres a head, in a fruit-
ful country, is scanty allowance for Indian population."

But in fact the land was not used to full advantage, something the chief
understood. He was impressed with the way transplanted Europeans farmed
and extracted wealth from what, for him, was little land. Yet he and other Indians would not consider this kind of life for themselves. Volney remarked that
"in all tribes there still exists a generation of old warriors who cannot forbear,
when they see their countrymen using the hoe, from exclaiming against the
degradation of ancient manners and asserting that the savages owe their decline
to these innovations."

Alexis de Tocqueville, that perceptive French observer, noted the differences between the Indians and the whites, implying that while the former adjusted to nature, the latter used and altered it to suit their needs. It was implicit
in their respective cultures. "In order to succeed in civilizing a people it is first
necessary to settle them permanently, which cannot be done without inducing
them to cultivate the soil. . . . Men who have once abandoned themselves to
the restless and adventurous life of the hunter feel an insurmountable disgust
for the constant and regular labor that tillage requires."

The Colonies, and later the United States, until the end of the nineteenth
century, had plentiful land for settlers and the ability to obtain capital (often at
high rates) from Europe, but they also had a chronic shortage of labor. Therefore
it made sense to pursue enterprises requiring relatively little labor but much
land — and individuals able to marshal capital were always in demand.

These realities fostered practices that shocked European visitors and
would trouble today's Americans. By present standards, the early farmers were
wasteful of land, planting crops without a thought to exhaustion or erosion,
setting fire to stands of timber in order to clear the way for planting. But why
not, when there was virgin territory just over the horizon? A farmer moving to
a new locale might burn down his log cabin, not out of spite, but to recover the
handful of nails that went into its creation, since these were by far the most
valuable part of the structure.

In this way, farmers, the most plentiful of America's businessmen before
the twentieth century, were making economic decisions. As transportation and
communication networks improved, and then were revolutionized by the rail-

With the invention of the combine, these California farmers in 1907 could work enormous tracts of land in less time and with fewer men than they had ever dreamed possible. Many farmers began to think in big-business terms, anticipating today's corporate agribusiness.

In the early twentieth century, magnificent forests like this one in Washington State provided Frederick Weyerhaeuser with a superabundant resource for his rapidly expanding lumber business.

The proud loggers who earned a living toppling mighty redwoods in Washington State in the early 1900s probably gave little thought to the destruction their efforts eventually wrought.

road and telegraph, farmers found themselves producing less for their immediate needs and local trade and more for far-flung markets. In the 1850s, for example, wheat from the Great Plains flowed eastward to cities teeming with factory workers, and farmers were impelled to make careful calculations about such things as soil content, future prices and loan rates, and the purchase of expensive equipment like reapers and mowers.

All of this often had dire consequences for the farmers themselves, who could be squeezed between fixed debts and wildly fluctuating prices. Nevertheless, their productivity continued to increase dramatically, and this spurred economic growth. In Colonial times, virtually everyone tilled the land to some degree, and until the second half of the 1800s farming was the full-time occupation of most Americans. Today American farmers comprise only 4 percent of the population, although they feed not only the United States but much of the world. In the process of raising productivity to current levels, millions of farm workers were released from the land to work in industry, and food prices fell for all. Without these events, industrialization would have been impossible.

More than making farming a business, a few farmers became quite entrepreneurial. One of the most striking examples was Oliver Dalrymple, a wheat farmer who in 1875 contracted with the Northern Pacific Railroad to create "bonanza farms" on its land in the Red River Valley of Minnesota and North Dakota. Dalrymple's methods, which were soon imitated by others in the region, produced impressive yields per acre on huge spreads: by 1880 there were 82 farms of more than 1,000 acres in the Red River Valley, and some many times that size. For several reasons, these bonanza farms were short-lived; but they were the precursors to the vast corporate farms that now dominate American agriculture.

For centuries, however, the small farm was a reasonably accessible opportunity for Americans seeking a decent living in the countryside. Land was more than plentiful, by European standards; often the only thing that stood between the homesteader and his first crop was a draft animal or two, some seed and basic supplies, a good degree of hard work, and lots of trees.

Indeed, wood was also superabundant; forests were to early America what oil is to Saudi Arabia today. In the sixteenth century, American forests covered an estimated 822 million acres, with stands of timber of 5.2 trillion square feet. It has been said that a squirrel could cross from the Atlantic to the Mississippi without touching the ground, so dense were the forests. James Fenimore Cooper speculated that "a bird's-eye view of the whole region east of the Mississippi must then have offered one vast expanse of woods."

Frederick Weyerhaeuser and the Wooden Empire

AMERICAN SETTLERS used wood in a myriad of ways in their everyday lives, and many made their livelihood from harvesting and milling timber. But only a rare few succeeded in the business on a grand scale, and none better than Frederick Weyerhaeuser.

The eastern forests would become the basis for four important colonial industries: lumber products, naval stores, potash, and shipbuilding. This last was one of the first important lumber-consuming industries in the New England colonies. The tallest pine and oak were exported for masts; local lumbering and shipbuilding commenced by 1630, with most cargo packed in barrels fashioned from wood from the same trees. A century before the American Revolution, Massachusetts alone had more than 700 ships, some as large as 250 tons, constructed mainly at Boston, Charleston, and Salem.

By the 1640s New England lumber and lumber products were being exported to Europe, and they provided the West Indies with much of its needs. Entire forests were being leveled for domestic uses. There were fewer than a dozen sawmills in New England prior to 1650; by 1675 there were approximately fifty, many large enough to turn out several hundred thousand board feet a year.

Much of the original New England forests had been leveled by the end of the eighteenth century, and as the population moved westward, so did the industry. The pattern was repeated a few decades later in the eastern part of the Mississippi Valley, which was lumbered out between 1800 and 1840. The upper Minnesota and Wisconsin region became one of the next areas to be harvested for timber.

Until the 1840s sawmill operation and timber gathering was a regional industry, generally conducted on a small scale like farming. The primary reason for this was lack of capital. The situation started to change as American industrialization accelerated and transportation improved. Lumber prices, relatively stable for half a century, advanced smartly after the 1837 panic and depression and continued upward. By 1860 lumbering had become the second largest industry (behind textiles), but most outfits were still quite small. Some twenty thousand establishments were in business, typically employing four workers along with the proprietor, with an average investment of $4,000. For the most part, these were little more than sawmills, owned and operated by a family who owned no land other than that upon which the mill stood. Operators would purchase trees from local farmers and others, who transported them to the mill (usually by water) for carving into boards and other shapes. The market, too, was local.

During the Civil War, both North and South demanded large amounts of lumber. Prices shot up again, rising more than 50 percent in five years. Moreover, they remained high in the early 1870s, prompting new businesses to open and older ones to expand. Generally considered an age of steel, this was also an age of wood. From 1859 to 1899 annual domestic lumber production rose from 8 billion to 35.1 billion board feet.

That an industry of such magnitude would produce major enterprises seemed inevitable. While many did appear, none reached the status or achieved the power of that fashioned by Frederick Weyerhaeuser. Not only did Weyerhaeuser think in bigger terms than others, but he mapped out a strategy and engaged in more systematic planning than the rest. Weyerhaeuser was an organization builder of the first rank. Though a ruthless competitor when necessary, he engineered effective partnerships and other associations to meet mutual needs. Unlike his hundreds of rivals, Weyerhaeuser anticipated the need to control timberlands and not just mills. This permitted him to insure the flow of raw materials and soon to set the terms under which others received them as well. Finally, Weyerhaeuser was a far-sighted industrial pioneer, who late in life embarked on one of the most audacious business gambles in American history.

Frederick Weyerhaeuser developed a huge and powerful lumbering empire at the turn of the century by controlling every aspect of the industry.

When Weyerhaeuser began to purchase vast tracts of land in the Pacific Northwest, barren landscapes like this one were becoming more common. Weyerhaeuser would help undo the ill effects of such ruthless exploitation.

Weyerhaeuser arrived in the United States with his mother and sister in 1848 at the age of fourteen, part of the large migration accompanying the failure of the German liberal revolution of that year. They headed west, lured by the inexpensive land of the Mississippi Valley. After working four years in a Pennsylvania lumberyard as a day laborer, Weyerhaeuser moved to Rock Island, Illinois, where he did odd jobs for the crews constructing the Rock Island Railroad, and then for a brewery. By happenstance he drifted into a position at the Mead, Smith & Marsh sawmill, starting as a watchman in 1856. Soon he was grading lumber and performing other tasks associated with the business. It was a typical apprenticeship; Weyerhaeuser was learning by doing.

In the nature of things, Weyerhaeuser rose swiftly; there was a shortage of individuals capable of keeping accounts in frontier Illinois. Late in 1857 he was sent to take charge of a lumberyard at the nearby town of Coal Valley. Then business disaster struck. Mead, Smith & Marsh had contracted for a supply of logs and paid for them with a note, but the logger failed to deliver. Strapped for cash and lacking a supply of timber, the firm fell into bankruptcy, and Weyerhaeuser was stranded and out of work.

Not for long. Weyerhaeuser purchased the Coal Valley facility and set out on his own. "I went around among the farmers, exchanging lumber for horses, oxen, eggs, anything they had," he later wrote. "This country produce I traded to the raftsmen for logs or to the merchants for stoves, tinware, and logging kits."

Once established, Weyerhaeuser leased an idle Rock Island mill and he reopened it. "I bought a raft of logs then lying in the eddy at Davenport for $5 a thousand [board feet], getting 10 percent discount for cash payment in gold. I hired John Potter to saw them for me, paying him $2 a thousand for sawing (including the rent on the mill) and $1 for freight to Coal Valley." At the same time Weyerhaeuser became a contractor, constructing houses and other structures.

Instinctively, Weyerhaeuser was engaged in what business analysts later would call vertical integration: controlling his source of supply, transforming the logs into lumber, and using the lumber to construct edifices that were sold. In the process he functioned as financier, manager, accountant, foreman, and salesman, along with doing whatever else was needed. It worked, primarily because Weyerhaeuser had the native abilities and experience to capitalize upon a felt need. Earnings for the first nine months came to $3,000, and for the following year, $5,000. It was 1860; the Civil War was soon to begin, bringing increased demand. Already the twenty-six-year-old Weyerhaeuser was a tycoon by Rock Island standards.

That year Weyerhaeuser formed a partnership with his brother-in-law Frederick Denkmann, and they set out to expand operations. There was plenty of room for growth, even without wartime demand. The region was still basically wild; lumberyards and mills blanketed the East, but in the Midwest they were concentrated in a few centers along the key rivers: La Crosse on the Black River, Eau Claire and Chippewa Falls on the Chippewa, and Stillwater on the St. Croix. Timber stands were rich and plentiful. The region was growing rapidly: the population of Illinois went from 851,000 in 1850 to 1,712,000 in 1860 and on to 2,540,000 ten years later; in the same twenty-year span, Wisconsin grew from 305,000 to more than 1 million and Iowa from 192,000 to 1,194,000. Rapid settlement increased the need for lumber, to the point where Weyerhaeuser became concerned about his supply.

Keeping water routes open was an important component of Weyerhaeuser's strategy. By controlling both the source of supply and the transport of the lumber to key markets, he ensured his giant company's preeminence.

Under normal conditions, logs that Weyerhaeuser and others milled were floated down tributaries of the Mississippi, where they were collected, sorted, and drawn by an organization known as the Beef Slough Company. Weyerhaeuser realized that control of Beef Slough by his upriver rivals might endanger his supply in times of shortage, so he set about purchasing stands of yellow pine in Wisconsin's Chippewa River Valley, where he also found loggers hungry for work. He then bought interests in mills located along the Mississippi, in alliance with others in the same position. In 1867 they organized the Beef Slough Manufacturing, Booming, Log Driving, and Transportation Company and began constructing a log boom and other facilities on the site. Through persistent and skillful lobbying in the state legislature, the company won the exclusive right to develop and use the slough, which gave it effective control over the region's water transport.

Further consolidation followed, culminating in 1872 with the organization of the Mississippi River Boom and Logging Company, a cooperative organization capitalized at $1 million and led by Weyerhaeuser. This consortium dominated logging and sawmill operations for an area larger than France. The amount of timber harvested by the Weyerhaeuser interests rose exponentially during this period. In 1867 about 12 million board feet passed through the slough; the figure reached 500 million by 1885.

Realizing that without the right to cut timber the Logging Company would shrivel, Weyerhaeuser initiated a large-scale land purchase program. In 1876 he bought 50,000 acres from Cornell University and continued to add large tracts until, by 1879, he controlled some 300,000 acres. Even so, operations were leveling off, and as the forests of the upper Mississippi were depleted, the loggers moved farther west.

Now Weyerhaeuser started to concentrate on the Douglas firs, Idaho ponderosa pines, Western white pines, and Engelmann spruce of the Columbia River region. In 1891 he relocated to St. Paul, Minnesota, to be closer to the virgin territories and two years later moved to a house next door to that of the railroad tycoon James J. Hill, with whom he already had business dealings.

As a result of various purchases and grants, Hill's Great Northern Railroad was the largest landholder in the region. Hill devoted much of his time to attracting farmers and others to the Northwest, offering them bounties, inexpensive land, and other assistance. The simple truth was that the Northern Pacific couldn't thrive as a carrier unless its service area was populated by people and enterprises requiring its service. Lumbering clearly was one such enterprise. So the two neighbors had a mutual interest in the land.

Weyerhaeuser had first considered purchasing timber stands from the Northern Pacific in 1885, and the following year took an option on 80,000 acres of Douglas fir near Tacoma, Washington; neither purchase was consummated. Additional options followed, with the first exercised in partnership with others in the 1890s. Now he was sending shingles cut from Washington and Oregon fir eastward — via the Northern Pacific, which granted Weyerhaeuser preferential rates during the spring season, before the harvests, when the railroad had large numbers of empty freight cars.

By this time Weyerhaeuser had decided his future was in the Northwest. Two significant moves took place in early 1900. That January he led a syndicate that agreed to buy 900,000 acres of largely unexplored timberland from the Northern Pacific for $5.4 million, of which $3 million was in cash and the rest in eight semiannual installments. This was the largest single purchase of timber in history. According to one participant, "It took practically all the lumbermen on the upper Mississippi River to raise the money." Many refused to join, and in the end Weyerhaeuser & Denkmann had to provide $1.8 million of the sum.

It was a gamble. The only way to get the timber to market was via the Northern Pacific, which meant that Hill could dictate terms if and when he decided to do so. Already there was talk of a canal across Central America which would provide an alternative to rail transportation, but at the time that was just a dream. The area itself was primitive, lacking facilities, workers, or a population that might provide a modicum of local demand; between them, Oregon and Washington had fewer than 1 million inhabitants, and growth was slow. Much of the acreage had yet to be explored, but some of what had been caused grave doubts. Weyerhaeuser knew that white fir and hemlock grew there in abundance, and at the time both were considered commercially worthless, while Douglas fir was deemed useful only for construction. The price seemed out of line, too. Six dollars an acre was high, when prime coastal timberland went for $9 an acre.

Soon after, Weyerhaeuser sent an inspector to the wilderness. "I have tried not to be at all prejudiced in this matter," he reported in June, "but cannot get away from the conviction that on the so-called unexamined lands we have been imposed upon, and that there has been given us a large quantity of isolated, scattering timberless tracts of land which it will never pay us to log." Then came a report that the Northern Pacific was offering 18,000 acres of land at $1.90 an acre. The inspector thought Hill should be approached and asked to make an adjustment in price.

By then the consortium that had purchased the land had organized itself into a new entity, the Weyerhaeuser Timber Company, with Frederick Weyerhaeuser its president. The outlook wasn't particularly inviting; some in the company were urging Weyerhaeuser to consider abandoning the property through nonpayment of taxes. But he saw in the "inland empire" of the Northwest the same kind of prospects as those available in the upper Mississippi close to half a century earlier. Rather than abandon or try to sell property, Weyerhaeuser purchased more acreage, in much the same way John Jacob Astor had in New York before the Civil War, knowing that in time population growth and increased demand would make the holdings valuable. By early 1905 Weyerhaeuser Timber owned nearly 1.5 million acres, which had cost almost $9.5 million.

The gamble paid off. In 1900 the West Coast produced 3 billion board feet of lumber, or 8 percent of the national total. By the time Weyerhaeuser died in 1914, production had risen to over 7 billion board feet, or almost 19 percent of the national output. In the same period lumber prices almost doubled. Weyerhaeuser Timber had net assets of $5.9 million in 1900; at the time of Weyerhaeuser's death, the figure came to a shade under $150 million.

The America Frederick Weyerhaeuser had come to in 1848 had an abundance of lumber; by 1914 conservationists were warning of shortages. "Is a Timber Famine Imminent?" asked Henry Gannett of the Geological Survey in the title of a 1900 magazine article. His answer: yes. Weyerhaeuser disagreed, noting that new materials were coming into use. "We have lost the wooden fence and sidewalk business," he told a group of friends soon before his death.

The Weyerhaeuser Timber Company's efforts in reforestation were inspired by the conservation movement of the late 1800s.

"We are losing the packing box business — and this is a large part of our sales — and we are being threatened with other substitutes for wood so that our market is being more and more restricted."

The steel boxcar was replacing those of wood, asbestos shingles and siding were pushing aside wooden ones, and wood-burning stoves were giving way to those burning coal and oil. In 1905 the Weyerhaeuser family purchased a car — that had a wooden body and wheels. This too would change. Nonetheless, his company started to devote considerable resources to forest conservation and fire prevention, and soon would pioneer in reforestation as well. As it happened, wood remained a major product and today is one of the largest American exports. In time Weyerhaeuser's company would find customers not only in the Northwest as well as elsewhere in the East but become one of the United States' most important exporters to the Orient.

Frederic Tudor, the Ice King

FREDERICK WEYERHAEUSER constructed his fortune upon one of the most abundant materials to be found in the Americas: trees. Frederic Tudor dominated an industry even more than Weyerhaeuser did by capitalizing on something yet more common. He saw possibilities for large profits where others saw only ice, a form of the most plentiful substance on earth. "Nothing is more useful than water," wrote Adam Smith in his classic *Wealth of Nations* in 1776. "But it will purchase scarce any thing; scarce any thing can be had in exchange for it. A diamond, on the contrary, has scarce any value in use; but a very great quantity of other goods may frequently be had in exchange for it."

Nineteenth-century marginalist economists explored this apparent dilemma and came up with the answer: while water is worth little in areas where it is abundant, it fetches a good deal in those places where it is scarce. And what was true of water also held for ice. Tudor's simple idea was to take ice from areas where it was worthless to places where it would command a high price. It was an imaginative, even audacious idea, which puzzled and amused his contemporaries.

Born into a patrician Boston household in 1783, Frederic Tudor seemed destined for a comfortable, rather conventional existence. His father, William, had studied law with John Adams and was George Washington's judge advocate general during the Revolution. William prospered with independence, to the point where he retired early to pursue a life of "literary expectations." All three of Frederic's older brothers graduated from Harvard, and he was expected to carry on the tradition. But such a life did not interest him, and at the age of thirteen he decided to leave school and try his hand at the spice business.

Little is known of his experiences at this time, but one assumes he went through an apprenticeship, perhaps at a shop where his father was known, and, given his connections and intelligence, probably did well enough, dealing in sugar, tea, candles, silk, and other dry goods and condiments. Perhaps his early involvement with spices also prompted Tudor to think in terms of food preservation. Whatever the background, we do know that in 1805 Frederic attended a party hosted by his wealthy brother-in-law, Robert Gardner, where he and his brother William speculated half jokingly about the possibility of shipping ice taken from nearby Fresh Pond to southern ports, where it could be sold at a high

price. Other discussions with William followed, along with extensive investigations of technology and markets, from which there emerged a plan.

Writing to a cousin in December 1805, Tudor sketched his ideas and what he proposed to do about them. William and another cousin had gone to Martinique to seek exclusive rights to market ice there and hoped to do as much in other Caribbean islands. "The idea of carrying ice to tropical climates will at first no doubt startle & astonish you," he wrote, "but when you take into consideration the following circumstances I think you will cease to doubt the practicality of the thing & adopt the proposal I shall presently make to you."

Others had blazed the way and demonstrated its practicality, and Tudor cited examples of such voyages. An American captain had taken a cargo of ice from Norway to London, "and realized a very handsome profit notwithstanding he was detained a long time in settling with the custom-house on account of duties." There had been cases, he wrote, of ice being transported safely to the Indies without having thawed. "Ice-creams were carried to Trinidad by the English when they were in possession of that Island in pots packed with sand from Europe." Other examples were offered, though Tudor wrote nothing of technical problems. As for costs, he estimated they would be six to seven thousand dollars, including the ice.

Tudor kept an "ice house diary," in which he recorded his thoughts and progress on the project. From its pages emerge the picture of a businessman who carefully considered risks and acted to minimize them. Tudor tried to obtain an exclusive market for ice; competition would be difficult to deal with for so perishable a commodity, which until proper insulation materials were found would have to be sold as soon as it arrived. He often traveled to his markets because he recognized that the widespread use of ice would not be automatic among people who had never used it. Tudor constantly sought methods to improve ice harvesting, knowing this was a key element. As Weyerhaeuser would do later, he took on partners so as to spread risks and obtain capital.

With the personal and financial support of a cousin, James Savage, Tudor invested $10,000 in a shipment of 130 tons of ice to Martinique. The event was noted in a Boston newspaper: "No joke. A vessel has cleared the Custom House for Martinique with a cargo of ice. We hope this will not prove a slippery speculation." Tudor followed soon after, hoping to show prospective customers who perhaps had never seen ice just how it could be used. Enough ice arrived, and there was sufficient interest, for him to make some sales. Tudor wrote of how amazed the denizens were when they saw the ice. "The man who keeps the Tivoli garden insisted ice creams would not be made in this country and that the ice itself would all thaw before he could get it home!" In response, Tudor talked him into ordering 40 pounds of ice, promising to be there the next morning to make ice cream, which he did, "being determined to spare no pains to convince these people that they can not only have ice but all the luxuries arising as well here as elsewhere. The Tivoli man recd. for these creams the first night $300; after this he was humble as a mushroom."

So there were some successes and encouragement. But not enough to turn a profit; within six weeks his inventory had melted, and all Tudor had to show for his efforts was a loss of $4,000. Undaunted, Tudor sailed for Cuba, while William tried to secure monopoly arrangements in St. Croix and Barbados. He had no luck and in addition was frustrated by international difficulties. In 1807, in an attempt to maintain American neutrality in developing European wars,

Frederic Tudor built his fortune by selling one of the earth's most abundant resources in its solid form — ice. He harvested the ice from Massachusetts ponds and transported it to the South and the tropics, where it fetched a high price.

President Jefferson instituted an embargo, which thwarted Tudor's plans. He then returned to Boston, where he learned that his father had lost his fortune.

Unable to pay his creditors, Tudor narrowly escaped debtor's prison and remained on the family farm until the embargo ended. He then returned to Cuba and obtained exclusive rights to sell ice there. But before he could capitalize on this, the War of 1812 intervened, and once again Tudor was obliged to return to the farm.

When the war was over, he again sought markets, this time not only in the Caribbean but in the southern states as well. He showed doctors how patients could be soothed by the application of ice packs. Tudor sold cold drinks at the same price as warm ones in order to accustom people to their pleasures, a marketing device that would be rediscovered later on by scores of other businessmen. He was obsessed with the idea that sometime in the future Americans would insist upon cold drinks, which, with ice selling for 10 cents a pound and assuming there were 16 tumblers to a gallon, would cost little more than half a cent per glass for cooling. Tudor proposed "to establish with one of the most conspicuous bar keepers a jar and give him his ice for a year."

> The object is to make the whole population use cold drinks instead of warm or tepid and it will be effected in the course of three years. A single conspicuous bar keeper having one of the jars and selling steadily his liquors all cold without an increase in price, [would] render it absolutely necessary that the others come into it or lose their customers — they are compelled to do what they could in no other way be induced to undertake.

Tudor was doing a good business by the mid-1820s but was still struggling. In this period some 3,000 tons of ice were shipped out of Boston annually, two-thirds of it by him. Competition was growing; the idea of selling ice, which cost around 30 cents a ton to cut, for 10 cents a pound a thousand miles away was a dazzling prospect. Tudor struggled to lower his costs and in general improve operations so as to best his rivals. Harvesting was relatively inefficient, storage could be improved, and ship captains complained that irregularly shaped chunks of ice tended to shift at sea, especially when melting began, and that this damaged hulls. All of these problems had to be resolved.

Tudor went to Havana to experiment with diverse methods of insulating the ice houses. He tested above-ground storage methods, insulating the ice with sheepskins, straw, wood shavings, tin castings — almost any kind of material he felt might do the job — and had several refrigerators built as well. He finally had some success, which enabled him to defeat rivals. Now he would sell ice for as low as a penny a pound until his competitors' supply had melted, after which he would raise the price.

Around this time Tudor met Nathaniel Jarvis Wyeth, who had inherited a hotel complete with ice house. Fascinated by the idea of selling ice in southern areas, Wyeth developed an interest in ice harvesting and in 1825 patented an invention that revolutionized the process. It was an ice cutter, whose blades were drawn across the frozen surface of the pond, cutting deep grooves. After a checkerboard pattern was cut, large, regular blocks could be easily pried apart by inserting metal bars in the grooves.

Tudor secured agreements with Wyeth whereby he obtained sole rights to the device, and in exchange the inventor became manager of the ice company. The price of harvesting now dropped to 10 cents a ton, and this, together with the improved ice depots and exclusive rights, gave Tudor an insurmountable advantage over his competitors.

Ice harvesters in California in the 1890s still used a cutter like the one invented for Tudor in 1825. The tool made it possible to remove ice from ponds efficiently, in large, regular blocks.

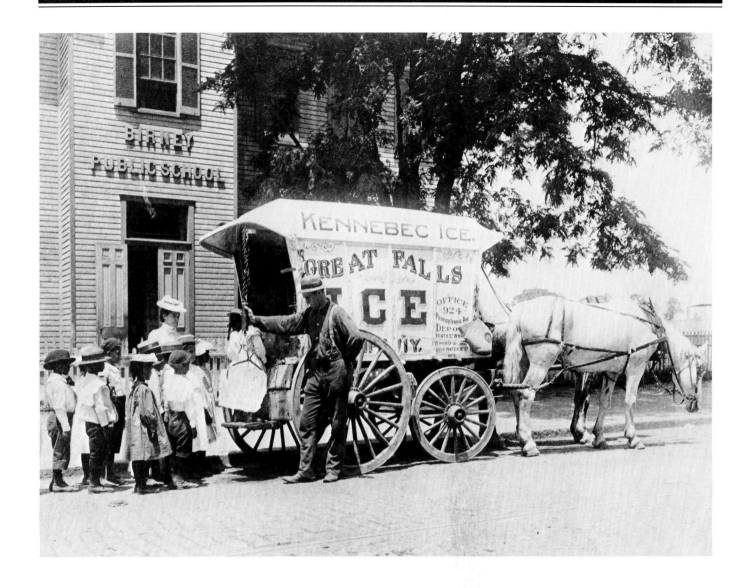

Both men benefited from the arrangement, but tensions between them soon developed. Wyeth's income from the hotel came to $1,200 a year, and he derived a like amount from the ice company. He wanted to keep both positions but lacked time and interest to run both. Besides, he was not as interested in cultivating a monopoly in the ice business as was Tudor. So he turned his sights west and soon left Massachusetts to enter the fur trade in Oregon.

Although Tudor was granted exclusive rights to the Wyeth patent, infringement ran rampant and competition flared. Harassed and discouraged, Tudor wrote in May 1832: "This is I believe the last cargo of ice I shall ever ship." Throughout his life he had dabbled in other ventures: digging for coal in Martha's Vineyard, designing a pump, attempting to grow cotton and tobacco at Nahant, where he also created what was probably the first American amusement park. Now Tudor turned to coffee importing — just as the bottom fell out of the market. He lost $200,000 on this foray, which would take him fifteen years to recover.

But Tudor's pioneering in ice was starting to pay off. The markets were developing, demand was on the rise, and shipments increased. Ever on the prowl for new customers, in 1833 he sent a ship laden with 180 tons of ice on a four-month voyage to Calcutta. There he erected a large ice depot and showed the transplanted Englishmen how to construct small, efficient refrigerators. He also brought along apples, pears, and other fruits grown in temperate climates, as well as well-preserved butter and cheeses. The shipment was a huge success, and others followed. Now Tudor turned to Persia, where he established a flourishing business.

The ice business soared. Boston shipped 1,200 tons in 1816; ten years later the figure was 4,000 tons, rising to 65,000 tons in 1846. Ice helped reinvigorate a port that had been losing trade to New York due to the success of the Erie Canal, making Tudor a local hero. By then competition had intensified, especially after Wyeth returned to Boston and reentered the business on his own, taking Tudor to court in an attempt to win back his original ice cutter patent.

By 1841, as ice merchants scrambled for harvests, it became clear that rights would have to be established at Fresh Pond. That same year Wyeth persuaded the state legislature to charter a railroad line to run between the pond and the Charlestown docks. A brochure for the railroad claimed that ice offered as much refreshment to Southerners as coal brought comfort to their northern brethren. What came to be known as the Charlestown Branch Railroad, which utilized special ice handling and loading technology developed by Wyeth, carried its first ice shipment in December.

This was none too soon, for ice merchants were scrambling for new sites to harvest. Tudor purchased extensive rights at Walden Pond, the enclave of Henry Thoreau. In fact, the new Fitchburg Railroad, which absorbed the Charlestown Branch in 1846, ran by the author's home, and it was that line's whistle that prompted him to wonder about the mechanization of the world and how it intruded upon nature. As Thoreau reflected upon the strange bustle of enterprise at his once placid site, he observed that "the sweltering inhabitants of Charlestown and New Orleans, of Madras and Bombay and Calcutta, drink at my well. . . . The pure Walden water is mingled with the sacred water of the Ganges."

Nathaniel Wyeth died in 1856, by which time Tudor's position as Ice King had been firmly established. In that year, Boston shipped 146,000 tons of ice to such places as the Philippines, China, and Australia, as well as the West Indies and the southern states. Refrigeration by means of ice was altering the way people lived, what they ate and drank. By 1860 iceboxes had become increasingly popular in upper-class urban homes. That year New Orleans imported 24,000 tons; in 1827 its consumption had been only 375 tons. While not exactly commonplace in summer, ice was becoming increasingly ubiquitous, and its use was filtering down to the middle class.

By the end of the nineteenth century, the use of ice in the home had become widespread and America had gained a new romantic figure, the iceman.

Gustavus Franklin Swift: Meat for the Multitudes

THE GROWING USE of ice had a profound impact on several industries, altering old ones while creating new entrepreneurial opportunities in others. One of these was meat packing: hardly more than a local industry before refrigeration, it was transformed into a national business with the help of Gustavus Swift, one of the first to perceive just what this innovation meant.

Refrigeration was a rarity in the United States when Frederic Tudor was doing his pioneering work in the South and the Caribbean. Despite his success, the use of ice for the preservation of food was still not widespread at mid-century. The railroads helped change this. Gradually, Americans began to incorporate more fresh fruit, vegetables, and dairy products into their diets; but no systematic method of transporting fresh meats under refrigeration had been developed. In this period cattle, pigs, and chickens were raised and consumed locally or transported live to the markets and slaughtered there.

As industrialization increased, the need for transporting meat over longer distances became evident. Larger urban populations in the Northeast had increased beyond the point at which local butchers could adequately supply them. Moreover, since meats spoiled quickly, slaughterhouses had to be located in the downtown sections, an unpleasant if not unsanitary fact of life.

Tudor's entrepreneurial coup in marketing natural ice had important consequences for other industries as well. In 1905 a meat market in Benson, Arizona, could keep its supply fresh for days under refrigeration.

During the years of the long drive, the cowboy — legendary hero of the American frontier — performed the crucial function of moving cattle from southwestern ranges to cattle towns in the Midwest.

Swift's experiments with refrigerated railroad cars made it possible to herd cattle into Chicago stockyards and slaughter them before, rather than after, transporting them east — a cheaper and more efficient procedure.

KILLING.

CUTTING.

In the 1850s a few entrepreneurially inclined businessmen experimented with ice to preserve meat, but none successfully shipped fresh meat over great distances. By the 1860s, however, western meat packers were using railroads to send cured meats to the East during the winter. But fresh meats were still confined to local distribution. This was the situation Gustavus Swift faced as he prepared to relocate to Chicago, where he would put into motion plans to alter the nation's meat industry.

Swift was born, fittingly enough, in Sandwich, Massachusetts, a small town on Cape Cod, in 1839. The eighth of twelve children born to a farmer, he attended the local schools and at the age of fourteen left to work for his brother, the local butcher. Even then he perceived the simplicity of the business. The butcher purchased a steer or pig, slaughtered and carved it up, and then sold the parts for more than he had paid for the whole. Profitability depended upon a number of variables, the four most important being the price of the animal, the speed with which it was processed (for saving labor), the amount of waste, and marketing.

Within two years Swift was off on his own, heading to parts of the state where population was larger. He dealt in cattle, opening a number of butcher shops and operating wagons from which dressed (butchered and cleaned) meats were sold from door to door. Always a hard worker and astute observer of the scene, Swift knew that beef cattle were plentiful and relatively inexpensive in the West and pondered ways of bringing meats from that part of the country to the more populous markets of the East. Soon he was extending his operations

A Cincinnati pork-packing concern is illustrated here in action in 1873, extracting everything possible from the carcass. Swift also used parts that formerly were discarded to develop such useful by-products as soap, margarine, and glue.

Gustavus Swift's old-fashioned belief in the value of hard work and his intolerance of waste transformed methods of meat packing, shipping, and storage.

It is the best thing in the World! We were fattened on it!

Many competitors joined Swift in the meat-packing business, filling America's bellies with convenient beef and pork products.

to Albany and then Buffalo. By the early 1870s he was considering the move to Chicago, then one of the most important markets for cattle on the hoof, which were sent in that form by rail to the East.

Swift was not the first or only butcher to realize the inefficiency of this method. The animals had to be fed en route. Many died due to overcrowding, and freight had to be paid for the entire steer even though more than half of it was inedible. The solution was obvious: the cattle could be gathered in Chicago, fed and butchered there, and then the dressed carcasses could be sent by rail to markets. This would mean no waste or loss from death, and freight charges would be substantially lower. The only problem was how to keep the meats fresh, and the answer was refrigeration.

As early as 1871, a Chicago butcher, G. H. Hammond, had experimented with a refrigerated freight car with some success, and three years later another Chicago butcher, Morris & Company, had sent refrigerated beef in an air-cooled freight car to Boston, but only during winter months. When Swift purchased the Moore slaughterhouse in 1875, in partnership with several New England butchers, he also planned to ship meat to the East. His ambitions were not unlike Tudor's hope of selling ice in the West Indies or Weyerhaeuser's plan to market West Coast lumber east of the Mississippi.

Initially, Swift followed the Morris strategy, sending meat in air-cooled cars during the winter. When he made his first shipment, in 1876, Swift hung the meat from simple wooden racks or frames built inside the car, and cold winter air was circulated through vents. The following year he experimented with mechanical refrigeration. Working with engineer Andrew Chase, he developed the first truly workable insulated refrigeration car. During the summers ice was packed under the car's roof; a simple plumbing system took care of drainage.

The refrigerated car solved only one of Swift's problems. Ice rights had to be secured along the route, since the supply had to be replenished at regular intervals. Then there was the matter of distribution in the markets. The meat had to be sold quickly or, failing that, refrigerated immediately. This was resolved in part by constructing depots at the terminals, cold-storage buildings whose doors fit flush against the freight cars. After observing the initial shipments, a reporter wrote that "The meat is easily transferred to the storage room which is of the same temperature as the car, without loss of time and without being removed from the hook on which it was hung when killed." In this as in everything Swift insisted upon efficiency as well as a high level of technical proficiency.

While attending to these matters, Swift had to negotiate with the railroads for rights to run his cars on their trains. This was difficult, since the carriers had a vested interest in the old methods of shipment. At the time, the railroaders felt they had more to lose than gain by accepting Swift's business, for by slaughtering and dressing the animals in Chicago he effectively cut tonnage by more than half. Since the profits to dressers like Swift were far higher than those of livestock shippers, the latter could not compete if given the same freight rates. They saw, as did Swift, that in a short period he could put them out of business, and there was no assurance the railroads would benefit.

In an ill-conceived attempt to resolve the situation to their benefit in the late 1880s, the railroads tinkered with differentials, offering livestock shippers lower rates than they did the dressers. The lines that did this — the New York Central, the Pennsylvania, and the Erie — were members of the Eastern Trunkline Association. The Grand Trunk Railroad of Canada was not a member and

At the Swift plant, the carcasses were moved along by overhead conveyer, with one task performed at each station. This "disassembly line" was a precursor of the modern assembly line — in reverse.

agreed to offer Swift the same terms it did others. Thus it secured a virtual monopoly of Swift's business. With the coming of the Interstate Commerce Commission, however, the Eastern Trunkline Association had an excuse to end differentials, which were forbidden under the law. Swift won a signal victory at a time when dressed meat was becoming the rule in any case.

Marketing his meats in the East was a more complicated problem, since Swift had to deal with so many butchers. Typically, he would offer local distributors partnerships if they agreed to handle his products. Acceptance would give them an incentive to work hard, and since Swift insisted upon retaining control, he could make certain this was the case. Those who refused his offer would face fierce competition from his better-capitalized and lower-cost operation, and before long most bowed. The owner of Lowe & Sons of Fitchburg, Massachusetts, rejected Swift's offer, telling him, "I would not sell a pound of your beef if Fitchburg was starving." Swift entered the town on his own and soon three of Lowe's sons went to work for him in Chicago, handling the business their father had rejected. Over a hundred such partnerships were formed during the first few years Swift sent meat to the East.

Swift was a fanatic regarding efficiency and time. Every second was valuable, and he carried this obsession to extremes. All of the company's employees learned to recognize his horse and buggy, often found wandering driverless through Chicago. This was because Swift could not stand waiting for slow trains to pass at a crossing. If he could not convince the engineer of a stopped train to uncouple it to let him pass, he would jump out of his buggy, climb over the train, and hail a ride on the other side.

Swift's concern with efficiency was usually beneficial. He seems to have been the first of the large meat packers to utilize overhead conveyers to move carcasses from butcher to butcher. Instead of one worker butchering an animal and then dressing it, as was the prior practice, each man on the line made a single cut as the carcass moved to his section. Long before Henry Ford introduced the assembly line in the auto industry, Swift had perfected his "disassembly line." That this cut costs and increased productivity was obvious.

Utilization of the entire animal was another of Swift's manias. Behind one of his yards ran Bubbly Creek, into which waste from the abattoir was dumped. Swift liked to visit this unpleasant site, for he knew by the amount of fat in the water just how much profit was being lost through needless waste. An inaccurate cut or a tiny bit of carelessness became a monumental loss when repeated thousands of times daily. Each morning Swift inquired as to how many hogs had died during the night. There was no excuse for these deaths, he believed, except for overcrowding in the pens (causing smothering), and this could be easily avoided.

When Swift entered the business only the meat, hides, and tongue were salable; the head, feet, and tripe were sold separately as a "set" at what amounted to a giveaway price. When an entire carcass was bought, the liver, heart, and tongue were thrown in free of charge. Swift thought these "extras" were a potential source of revenue, and he soon became the industry's leader in the development of useful by-products. First came oleomargarine, and then glue, beef extract, soap, fertilizers, and, later, pharmaceuticals. Shinbones were used for knife handles. According to Swift's son Louis, the saying about using all of a pig but the squeal was adapted from his father, who said, "Now we use all of the hog but the grunt."

Frank Perdue: The Man of 270 Million Chickens

SWIFT WAS A perceptive salesman, and during his early years as a butcher and store owner, he experimented with various merchandising techniques. To prevent spoilage, most stores kept no meat on display and would not make cuts until an order was placed. Swift placed cuts attractively arranged in glass-faced counters and noted that these sold quickly. He realized that by displaying slower-moving cuts, inventory and sales could be better controlled. But despite all of this, Swift never managed to created a branded meat that might command a premium price. Independent butchers knew he offered quality merchandise, but they were likely to make purchases elsewhere if that enabled them to cut costs. After all, customers weren't asking for a Swift steak or roast. Later on, Swift and other dressers attempted with mixed results to convince consumers that their products were superior, but they never quite succeeded in meats. To this day customers in the nation's supermarkets don't know which company is responsible for the fresh meats they buy.

Not so with chickens. In this segment of the market, Frank Perdue not only created a branded product and so obtained a powerful position in his service area but also revolutionized advertising. Like Mary Kay Ash, Perdue relies

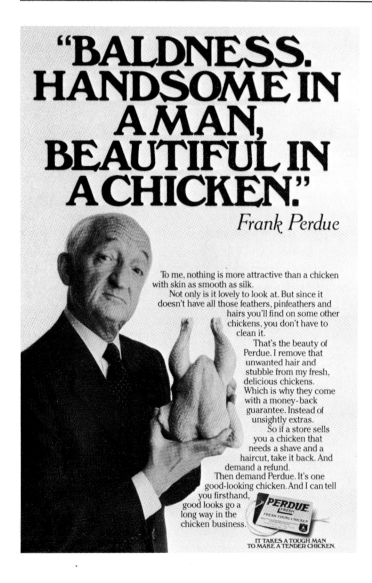

upon show business techniques to promote his products, and for that reason his contributions have tended to be overlooked or minimized. But his rivals generally concede that Perdue is a major innovative force in his industry.

The Perdue family's involvement with chickens began in 1920, when Frank's father Arthur, a Salisbury, Maryland, railroad express worker, spent $5 for fifty layer hens and entered the egg business as a small supplier to the New York City market. Begun as a part-time venture to make some extra money, it soon blossomed to the point where Arthur quit his job and committed himself to the egg business.

Arthur Perdue loved his work, taking great pride in his eggs and proclaiming their superiority to anyone who came within earshot. Knowing that profit margins were slim in the egg business, he monitored costs carefully and so managed to survive in an industry where failure was quite common. He also refused to borrow money or take on partners, fearing inability to repay loans and the loss of independence.

Arthur raised Frank to think that way, giving him some culls when he was quite young. Soon the boy's small flock was outproducing his father's. "We couldn't figure it out," Frank recalled. "They got the same feed. I learned years

Perdue's entertaining show business techniques have made his face — and his product — the most familiar in the industry.

later that there is indeed a pecking order among chickens, but before that I had concluded that the larger the pen, the happier the chickens." And he meant to have contented chickens. In 1937 he abandoned his impossible dream of becoming a major-league baseball player and joined his father in the egg business.

In 1940 the Perdues took the logical step of switching from eggs to chickens and began contracting with independent growers. Frank experimented with feeds and came up with a formula that was superior to anything on the market. In 1953 the Perdues went into the feed business, selling their product to many growers in the Delmarva area. They built a feed mill in 1958. "That was a red letter day in the history of the company," said Frank, "because it gave the farmers confidence in us." The Perdue farm was expanding, but it still was a small factor in the industry.

This was an exciting period for the poultry business. New raising techniques were increasing the yield per pound of feed and shortening the maturation period, while at the same time per capita consumption of children rose steadily. The reasons were productivity and price, the former rising, the latter declining. In the late 1920s, Herbert Hoover had spoken about "a chicken in every pot," an indication that in those days it was a delicacy, more prized perhaps than beef or pork. As late as the 1940s chicken was deemed a proper Sunday dinner.

But not for long. In the 1940s it had taken 16 man-hours to raise 100 birds; the figure was 8 in the first half of the 1950s and was down to 4 in the second half. There were no such dramatic economies in cattle and hog production, so the price of chickens declined relative to that of beef and pork products. This was felt at the marketplace, as the public purchased more chicken than ever before. Americans of the 1940s went for meat and potatoes. Their counterparts of the 1950s and beyond called for chicken and fries. Before Ray Kroc made McDonald's synonymous with fast-food hamburgers, Colonel Harland Sanders franchised his recipe and reaped a fortune with Kentucky Fried Chicken.

Believing this trend was bound to continue, Perdue talked his father into

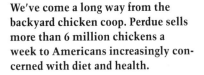

We've come a long way from the backyard chicken coop. Perdue sells more than 6 million chickens a week to Americans increasingly concerned with diet and health.

violating one of his cardinal rules by borrowing $500,000 to construct an additional feed mill. At the same time, he continued to enlarge the business, so that by 1968 he was selling 800,000 broilers a week and was expanding his market.

That year Perdue decided to start advertising in a small way. He hired a professional agency and allotted $30,000 for radio commercials. This figure was doubled the following year and doubled again in 1970, when the first television ads were run. Perdue wasn't satisfied with the campaign, and so he switched agencies, giving his account to the relatively small firm of Scali, McCabe & Stoves, which persuaded him to be the company's leading spokesman and trademark. The idea was fairly new and even daring; corporate executives in that period tended to be faceless individuals who had little concept of just how to use media to best advantage.

The strategy proved an unqualified success. Frank Perdue's homely appeal, earnest yet just a trifle haughty, captured the public imagination. Some noted that Perdue's face even resembled that of a chicken. Out of the television spots came some of the more memorable lines in recent advertising history, delivered in his distinctive voice: "It takes a tough man to make a tender chicken." "If you can find a better chicken, buy it!" "I'm not about to compromise when it comes to my legs and breasts."

By the early 1980s, Perdue's ads were reaching 22 percent of the market, and the company was earmarking for its ad campaigns 1 cent per pound of chicken sold. In the process it encouraged other company chief executives, such as Lee Iacocca of Chrysler and Frank Borman of Eastern Airlines, to take to the airwaves, and in the view of some media commentators may yet make businessmen national heroes and encourage them to seek high political office.

The Perdue strategy of advertising brand-name chickens in the lucrative greater New York market has spawned intense competition. Two brands, Showell Farms' "Cookin' Good" and Cargill's "Paramount," challenged Perdue with intensive advertising campaigns in what some commentators called the "Chicken Wars." They have made some inroads, but Perdue continues to control about a fourth of the New York market, roughly the same proportion as these other two combined.

Perdue sells more than 6 million fresh whole chickens a week, approximately 40 percent of them in the New York area. The company has become the nation's third largest chicken producer and one of the largest privately owned companies, a situation not likely to change, since Frank Perdue values his independence and profits are so large he has no need for outside financing. Moreover, growth seems almost inevitable. Chicken accounts for $14 billion a year in sales, and sales are rising so rapidly that it now appears probable that within a few years it will pass beef in consumption.

Innovation will help this along. At one time customers would purchase whole chickens, which were roasted, broiled, baked, or fried and then served whole. There was some business in chicken parts, but up to the late 1970s this tended to be considered a sideline. Noting an increase in demand for parts, Holly Farms concluded that this was the wave of the future, and developed "chicken nuggets," one of the most successful food introductions in modern times. McDonald's, which came out with "Chicken McNuggets," became the world's second largest chicken retailer. The company that made its reputation with hamburgers was finding that McNuggets sales were rising even more rapidly. Perdue responded by making a major push in the parts market; now parts account for 56 percent of his total sales.

Equally important, Perdue has chosen not to move into retailing, at least not in a big way. Since early 1981 he has successfully operated an upscale cafeteria-style fast-food restaurant in Queens, New York — which, not surprisingly, prepares fresh chicken almost every way imaginable.

Despite the impressive success of his advertising campaign, Perdue insists his firm's meteoric rise (sales have increased by more than 500 percent since he started advertising) was due more to quality than image. As he notes, "I have probably six or seven times more quality control people than anyone else." This ensures consistency in the product, which helps maintain the proper reputation and enables Perdue to charge premium prices. In addition, his feed continues to sell well and is used by many of his competitors. Efficient, integrated operations also make the farm highly competitive. The profitability of Perdue Farms is unknown, since the company is privately owned. But in 1984 the company had sales of $741 million, based upon the 270 million chickens it sold. That comes to more than 500 chickens sold each minute of each day.

Perdue Farms owns breeding stock, hatcheries, feed mills, soybean facilities, and a huge truck fleet. It is a leader in one of America's major growth industries, unaffected by cyclical overproduction and shakeouts, such as afflict electronics, or by Japanese competition. As a nation of joggers searches for foods low in cholesterol, calories, and fat, chicken, which ranks better than beef and pork in all three areas, continues to rise. In its own way the Perdue company is as glamorous as Apple Computer or Genentech, though chicken is hardly as exciting as microcomputers and gene splicing.

Perdue's operation would have hardly baffled Gustavus Swift. The two shared a passion for careful placement in the production and distribution chain, and Swift might have even admired Perdue for giving his name to a common meat commodity as he had done. Moreover, Swift always respected efficiency. Reprocessing all waste products for feed, Perdue uses "everything but the cluck."

John D. Rockefeller: The Standard

Perhaps the most famous businessman of them all, John D. Rockefeller transformed a modest refining operation into what became the world's largest industrial enterprise and, in the process, helped shape the gigantic petroleum industry. No less than Frederick Weyerhaeuser did he recognize the wealth of the land, though he was interested in what was below, not above, the surface. Like Gustavus Swift, he saw that by altering a product he could make it much more valuable and realize good profits; Swift would carve a carcass, Rockefeller would transform crude oil into kerosene. He knew how to promote: more than a century before Frank Perdue succeeded in establishing the superiority of his branded chickens, Rockefeller won recognition for the consistency of his products. The name selected for his company, Standard Oil, was not coincidental.

But of course there were differences as well. These other businessmen, along with Frederic Tudor, were dealing with renewable resources. Not so Rockefeller. In his long lifetime — Abraham Lincoln was a state legislator in Illinois at the time of his birth, and he died at the age of ninety-eight, when Franklin D. Roosevelt was president — Standard Oil metamorphosed constantly, reflecting alterations in technology, markets, and other factors. Just as Weyerhaeuser and Swift relocated to adjust to such changes, so did Standard Oil, which under Rockefeller became as much a global as a national entity.

Rockefeller was born in 1839 in a New York farming community bearing the foretelling name of Richfield. His parents were unusual. His father, William, was a traveling horse trader (there were those who said he was a horse thief as well) and itinerant medicine man, touting a cure-all elixir to susceptible farmers. He also dabbled in lumber, as did many of the period, and he taught his son a bit about that business. "Among other things," Rockefeller recalled, "I was sent over the hills to buy cordwood for the use of the family, and I knew what a cord of good solid beech and maple wood was; and my father told me to select only the solid wood and the straight wood, and not to put any limbs in or any 'punky' wood. That was good training for me." Although he taught his son a few things about wheeling and dealing, William wasn't as much of an influence on him as his wife, Eliza Davison Rockefeller. Strongly religious, Eliza strove to instill in John a belief in the virtues of hard work and thrift, and she succeeded beyond anything she could have imagined. "I had a peculiar training in my home," Rockefeller said sixty years later. "It seemed to be a business training from the beginning."

Young Rockefeller attended several schools, the last a commercial college, while working some of the time on the family farm (one job was to sell chickens his mother raised). He then became a bookkeeper, and in 1859, the year an unemployed railroad conductor named Edwin Drake struck oil in Titusville, Pennsylvania, Rockefeller and a partner, Maurice Clark, started a brokerage house in Cleveland, Ohio. The firm thrived during the Civil War, and Rockefeller started to dabble in railroads and land, while carefully monitoring the growing oil boom. He observed scores of wildcatters rushing to the fields, drilling on little more than hope and hunches and, for the most part, failing. Then too, the price of oil fluctuated wildly. At the time the first Pennsylvania fields were being explored, crude fetched $20 a barrel. Then a flood of oil came to market, and in two years the price was 10 cents a barrel. It rose again soon after, leveling out at $7 in 1869, only to fall below $3 in 1870.

For these reasons Rockefeller saw little sense in drilling; all you got was a dry hole or, if successful, crude oil that was worthless until refined into kerosene, which was rapidly becoming the preferred means of providing artificial light. It cost 30 cents to refine a barrel of crude, which contained 42 gallons. In 1870 kerosene could fetch $1 a gallon at the point of sale. The key to the industry, then, would be refining: he who controlled that could dictate prices to be paid to producers and distributors alike.

In 1863 Rockefeller, Clark and his two brothers, and chemist Samuel Andrews formed the Excelsior Oil Works, which was one of the many small refiners in the Cleveland area. Rockefeller plunged into the operation, making Excelsior the largest refinery in the area, processing over 500 barrels a day, but his partners were dubious, and two years later he bought them out. Wanting to improve on his position, Rockefeller borrowed heavily, and during 1865 and 1866 purchased 50 refineries in Cleveland and another 80 in Pittsburgh.

Rockefeller's refineries were the most modern and efficient in the industry, giving him significant cost advantages. His high volume put him on good terms with the railroads, and he virtually controlled the Cleveland terminals. Because of this strong position, he was able to secure capital from local banks, but he preferred to acquire firms through exchanges of stock rather than outright pur-

Shrewd and zealous, pious and imperious, John D. Rockefeller was a genius of an entrepreneur. He acquired phenomenal wealth and power in the oil industry by knowing where to play his hand.

In the early days of the oil business, almost anyone with a few hundred dollars could drill a well like this one in Titusville, Pennsylvania, where oil was first discovered. Rockefeller gained position in the chaotic industry by refining rather than drilling oil.

chases. Some rivals claimed they had been forced into selling, but the evidence suggests that Rockefeller offered reasonable if not high-priced exchanges, especially to many refiners close to failure.

Many did fail during the postwar depression, but some offered Rockefeller stringent competition. In order to achieve even greater economies and so price his product lower than theirs, he took several steps toward vertical integration, in somewhat the same way Swift was doing in meats: he bought timber reserves and manufactured barrels, built warehouses, and acquired fleets. In addition, he reorganized the company, forming a partnership with fellow entrepreneurs Henry Flagler and Samuel Andrews in 1867, which three years later was renamed Standard Oil Company of Ohio.

Rockefeller was not the only one to realize that the key to success in the petroleum industry — and indeed most industries — was control of a vital process or service upon which all else depended. The Pennsylvania Railroad held a monopoly on trains between the oil fields and eastern ports, obliging Rockefeller to pay what it demanded to carry his kerosene and other products to markets in the East. It was a situation somewhat similar to that Swift had to face, and the Standard leaders resolved it the same way. Rockefeller and Flagler approached the New York Central with a proposition: they would guarantee 60 carloads of oil per day and give up their shipments by water if the railroad

would grant them an especially low rate. The Central agreed, and the Pennsylvania's rail monopoly was cracked.

Rockefeller soon came up with an idea that, had it been enacted, would have given him even greater power. He organized a group of refiners into the South Improvement Company, which would divide their shipments between the Pennsylvania, New York Central, and Erie railroads at preferential rates of $2.40 per barrel — except Standard, which would be charged $1.90, in addition to a kickback (or rebate) on the shipments by nonmembers! This scheme, never put into effect, was declared illegal by the courts.

Standard Oil expanded rapidly during the 1870s, making additional acquisitions and solidifying its control over the industry, and all the while Rockefeller strove to realize economies. Accounting became a mania, with prices figured to three decimal places. He insisted that a statement of his net worth be on his desk each morning when he came to work. In order to save on transportation costs, he started to build pipelines; Standard owned 400 miles of them by 1876, along with terminals that could store 1.5 million barrels of oil. When the Pennsylvania Railroad offered another challenge during the late 1870s by entering the refining business, Rockefeller crushed what then was the country's largest company and then bought out its refining facilities.

By the 1880s it had become evident that Rockefeller could no longer afford to ignore drilling and distribution. The Pennsylvania fields were starting to run dry, and Standard, now controlling companies with assets of over $70 million, had to insure a steady supply of crude. Rockefeller purchased several regional distribution companies. His company, already known as "the octopus," overspread the industry, accounting for some 90 percent of refinery runs and dictating the prices of such products as kerosene, lubricants, paraffin, naphtha, solvents, and other products extracted from petroleum by Standard's scientists and technicians.

But Rockefeller did not seek to control 100 percent of the market with his empire. He understood that smaller, less-efficient competitors could take up this slack and be forced to struggle for survival during hard times, while Standard Oil could continue running at near-full capacity. At the same time, Rockefeller's company would avoid charges of monopoly control.

As the Rockefeller empire burgeoned, it threatened to become unwieldy, which was why Flagler and Standard's attorney, Samuel Dodd, organized a trust in 1882. It totally owned 14 companies, including Standard of Ohio, partially owned 26 others, ranging in size from the $30 million National Transit Company to the $30,000 Germania Mining Company, and was capitalized at $70 million. The trust provided for the creation of subsidiary companies bearing the Standard name, to be established in New York, New Jersey, Ohio, and Pennsylvania, each to concentrate on activities in its state.

This structure was not only powerful but highly visible, and its existence prompted the antitrust movement of the period. In *Wealth Against Commonwealth*, journalist Henry Demarest Lloyd drew up an indictment of the trust, calling for its dissolution. "We must either regulate, or own, or destroy, perishing by the sword we take." To which Rockefeller replied that "the American beauty rose can be produced in the splendor and fragrance which bring cheer to its beholder only by sacrificing the early buds which grow up around it. And so it is with economic life. It is merely the working out of a law of nature and a law of God." Lloyd had his wish: the Sherman Antitrust Act was passed in 1890, but while the trust went through several changes, Rockefeller's grip on the market continued until after the turn of the century.

There were setbacks. By the mid-1880s Standard was exploiting the Ohio fields. Through the purchase of the Ohio Oil Company and the establishment of several new companies, the mid-continent area became the primary region in the Standard territory. There was some new exploration in California and Texas, but for the moment the company rested on its oars. Besides, there was some question as to whether there was much petroleum there. One Standard executive, John D. Archbold, was dubious, offering to drink every gallon of crude discovered west of the Mississippi. And in addition there were complications in the form of an anti-Standard administration in Texas, which had its own antitrust act.

In 1894 Texas governor James Hogg initiated an action against Standard, going so far as to request Rockefeller's extradition from New York to stand trial. Nothing came of this, but the difficulties in Texas meant that Standard could do little exploration there. Consequently, it missed out on the greatest oil bo-

The gas-powered automobile brought with it a new and permanent addition to the American landscape: the filling station. This attendant works the pump at a Standard station in New Jersey in 1927.

nanza in American history up to that time, beginning with the discovery of oil at Spindletop in Beaumont in 1901. Out of this came new companies such as Gulf and the Texas Company (later known as Texaco) and the growth of others including Sun and Shell. Foreign competition was growing as well. Standard's industry position was being eroded; by 1911 its share of refining had declined to 75 percent. Rivals supplied one-third of the nation's gasoline. Standard had only 29 percent of the rich California fields, 10 percent of production on the Gulf Coast, and even in the mid-continent, where it once was dominant, it accounted for but 44 percent of production. Ironically, that was the year the anti-

trusters finally had their way: the trust was broken up, on the grounds that it had sought to "drive others from the field and exclude them from their right to trade." This did not mean that the company would vanish or that the Rockefeller power was much diluted. One of the successor companies, Standard Oil of New Jersey, was the second largest industrial firm in the nation (behind U.S. Steel).

By then, however, Rockefeller had all but retired from business and was to devote much of the rest of his life to philanthropy. Even then he was a contentious figure, alternately admired and despised. He died in 1937, at a time when business was under attack as having caused the Great Depression. The obituary in the AFL's *Detroit Labor News* began with this: "Hell must be about half full now"; the *Detroit News* proclaimed: "His wealth never grew large enough to ransom him from littleness" — all but ignoring Rockefeller's massive accomplishments. "First and last, he lived by the book and the book was small and thin in keeping with the spirit of the man."

True enough, Rockefeller lived by the maxims inculcated by his mother — "Willful waste makes woeful want" — and the lessons drilled into him the hard way by a father with strange ideas. (On one occasion William was supposed to have said, "I cheat my boys every chance I get. I want to make 'em sharp.") But

The corporate trust, initiated by Standard Oil, became a target of political attack as America grew wary of the abuses of near monopoly. Protests against it prompted the Sherman Antitrust Act of 1890.

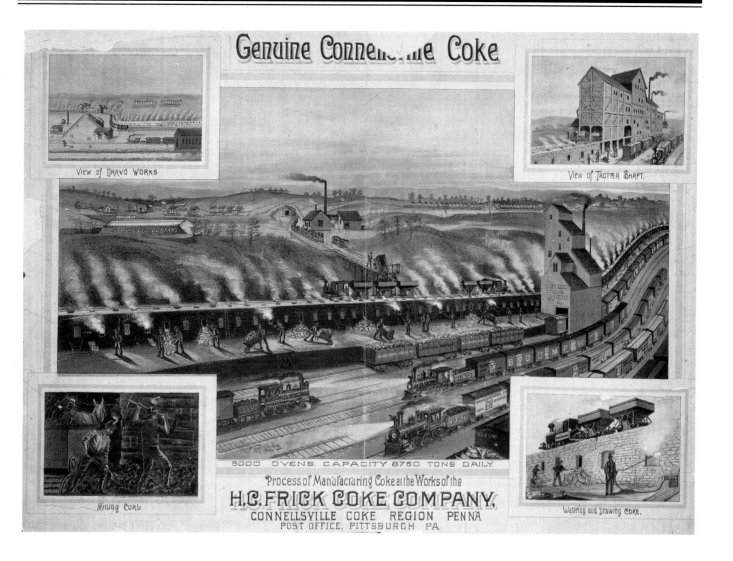

Genuine Connellsville Coke

View of Dravo Works

View of Trotter Shaft

Mining Coal

Watering and Drawing Coke

8000 OVENS. CAPACITY 8750 TONS DAILY.
Process of Manufacturing Coke at the Works of the
H.C. FRICK COKE COMPANY,
CONNELLSVILLE COKE REGION PENNA.
POST OFFICE, PITTSBURGH PA.

Like Rockefeller, other powerful industrialists made huge fortunes mining America's natural resources. In the 1870s, Henry Clay Frick, who later merged his interests with Andrew Carnegie's mammoth steel company, manufactured coke at this Pittsburgh plant.

the application of these principles by an individual of superb imagination and vision certainly worked. Several obituaries ran the text of a ditty he wrote, summing up his career — his only foray into poetry:

> I was taught to work as well as play;
> My life has been one long, happy holiday —
> Full of work and full of play —
> And God was good to me every day.

Rockefeller was succeeded at the helm of Standard Oil of New Jersey by Archbold, who, despite his miscalculation about crude in the West, was one of the industry's shrewdest businessmen. In fact, Rockefeller always considered the cultivation of personnel his most important task. "The secret of success of Standard Oil," he claimed, "was that there had come together a body of men who from the beginning to end worked in single-minded cooperation." It was that way almost from the start. In 1879 William H. Vanderbilt, head of the New York Central, praised the ability of the Standard management team. "These men are smarter than I am a great deal [sic]. They are very enterprising and smart men. I never came into contact with any class of men so smart and able as they are in their business." Besides Archbold and Flagler, there were Rockefeller's brother William, Henry H. Rogers, James Moffatt, Charles Pratt, Oliver

H. Payne, and others, who together formed what arguably was the ablest management team in the nation.

With their assistance Rockefeller pioneered the development of modern corporate organization. Most served on Standard's executive committee, charged with making strategic plans and gathering and interpreting information in addition to direct management. All appropriations over $5,000 and new construction for more than $2,500 had to be ratified by the committee, which even approved salary increases of more than $600 a year. Clearly this couldn't continue; so huge was the Rockefeller empire that in time the committee had to delegate power to middle management. Later some would suggest that the Standard structure was in part borrowed from that of the Roman Catholic Church, but Rockefeller and other industrial tycoons learned far more from the way the railroads, especially the Pennsylvania, were operated.

Francis Cabot Lowell and the Value of Labor

Francis Cabot Lowell recognized that one of America's richest resources was its workers. He was able to recruit farm girls for his New England textile factories by assuring parents that the girls would receive a morally correct education and be closely supervised at all times.

T HE MANAGERS of Standard Oil, like the railroad leaders, continued to develop and adapt new methods to maximize the output of that critical and yet often scarce American resource, labor. Not that Standard paid high wages; indeed, they were quite low — as low as Rockefeller could get them. In 1889 laborers averaged $1.50 a day. Unskilled workers could better themselves, however; superintendents received $8.33 a day. The need to locate, hire, and then properly motivate and reward labor was one of management's most important tasks. Such had been the case since the dawn of American industrialization, in the days of Francis Cabot Lowell.

There is a lot of history in the Lowell name. In 1775, the date of Francis Cabot Lowell's birth, the roster of Boston aristocrats included the Forbeses, Derbys, Russells, Higginsons, Jacksons, Appletons, and Saltonstalls. But everyone knew that these families were of the second rank, while the likes of the Tudors were far behind them, deemed arrivistes, if even that. More than a century later, John Collins Bossidy would offer a toast that put the matter into perspective:

> And this is good old Boston,
> The home of the bean and the cod,
> Where the Lowells talk to the Cabots,
> And the Cabots talk only to God.

Francis Cabot Lowell could trace his ancestry back to the first Lowell, who arrived in 1639. Francis's grandfather, John, graduated from Harvard College in the class of 1721 and became a respected minister. His son and Francis's father, also named John, was Harvard class of 1760. He married three times — to a Higginson, a Cabot, and a Russell — and was a distinguished jurist. Francis also attended Harvard and, although suspended for lighting a bonfire in Harvard Yard, graduated in 1793. The family hoped he would enter law or, failing that, the ministry. Certainly the path was open for him in either area. But Francis excelled in mathematics in college, and this prompted him to try his hand at business.

Through family connections, Lowell became supercargo on some trading vessels, opened an office on Boston's Long Wharf (in which the Lowells had an

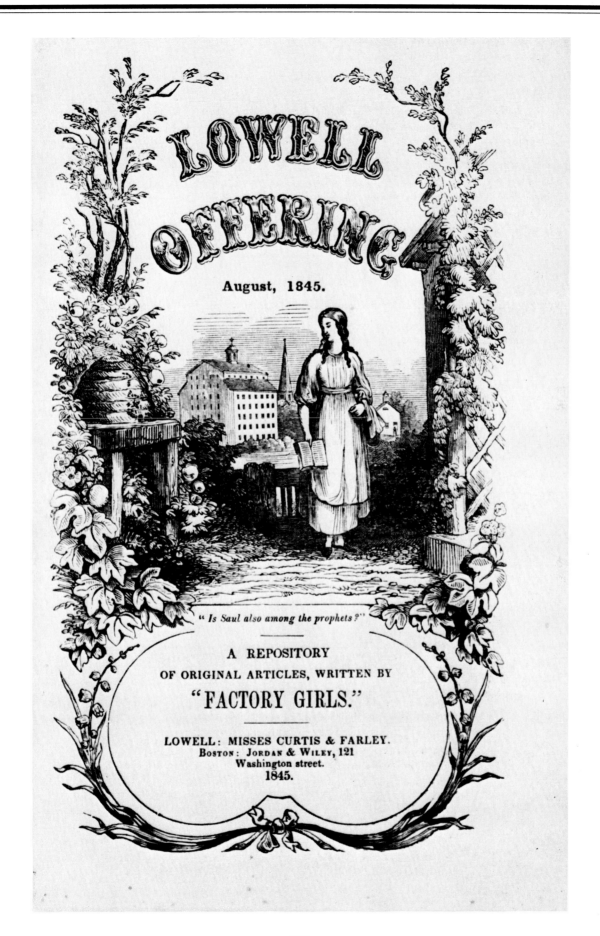

LOWELL OFFERING

August, 1845.

"Is Saul also among the prophets?"

A REPOSITORY

OF ORIGINAL ARTICLES, WRITTEN BY

"FACTORY GIRLS."

LOWELL: MISSES CURTIS & FARLEY.
BOSTON: JORDAN & WILEY, 121
Washington street.
1845.

Farm girls who came to work at Lowell's mill in Lynn, Massachusetts, shown here in 1895, found highly structured work patterns designed to increase efficiency. The mechanized tasks may have been dull, but many found them preferable to life on the farm, and the promise of regular wages continued to draw workers to factories in the East.

interest), and proclaimed himself a merchant. In those days this meant he speculated in real estate, underwrote insurance, contracted for cargos, and in general sought opportunities where he could find them, as did most sedentary merchants. He had the right name, sufficient capital and the promise of more, intelligence, and connections. As though to underline this last item, in 1798 Lowell married Hannah Jackson, also a Back Bay aristocrat, and sister of Patrick Tracy Jackson, another merchant of Lowell's generation. The two men joined forces, and their partnership flourished. But not for long: the embargo imposed by Jefferson in 1807 that hampered Frederic Tudor's ice business also foiled Lowell and Jackson's plans, so they sought new avenues for investment.

In 1810 Lowell set out for England with his family for what he said was a vacation. In fact, the trip was motivated by business reasons. In Scotland he visited several cotton mills, observing their activities and discussing what he had seen with a fellow Bostonian, Nathan Appleton. This had to be done surreptitiously: in its efforts to control this critical industry, England had legislated against the export of machinery, plans, and even artisans. Lowell's baggage was searched twice as he left England in 1812, as war seemed imminent between that country and the United States. Hostilities began while his ship was en route to America, and the family had some difficulty getting back to Boston. Apparently satisfied with what he learned in England, Lowell formulated plans to create his own textile mill.

Lowell intended to meet the demand for textiles that formerly had been supplied by the British. There already was a budding yarn business in Providence, Rhode Island, and other like facilities were sprouting there and elsewhere in New England. Lowell's hopes for his mill were more ambitious: he planned a facility at which multiple functions would be performed, on the order of the Scottish factories. Trade had been disrupted due to the war, and Lowell thought such an enterprise might fare well in the absence of competition, repelling the British textile interests once peace returned.

He soon learned it was far more complicated than that. Lowell would have to raise capital, find a site for his mill, erect it, locate mechanics capable of reproducing machinery, recruit a labor force, manage the plant, perform rudimentary market research, seek retailers willing to purchase his goods, and insure that friendly governments assisted where they could. In other words, Lowell would have to combine the talents of an entrepreneur, banker, wholesaler, retailer, and political lobbyist — all this by a thirty-eight-year-old whose only prior business experience had been as a sedentary merchant and who never managed more than an office. Out of such raw material, industrial capitalism in the United States was born.

In 1813 Lowell assembled a dozen close friends and relatives and organized the Boston Manufacturing Company, its purpose being to create a textile mill on a site he had found in Waltham. The company was to be capitalized at $400,000, a prodigious sum in those days, with $100,000 initially called. Lowell located an excellent mechanic, Paul Moody, then conformed his knowledge of Scottish factories to Moody's originality to bring forth designs for a new power loom and other machines. Moody was placed in charge of erecting the mill, while Lowell pondered the matter of a labor supply. There really wasn't much from which to choose; the problem required a leap of imagination.

In this period the vast majority of Americans were engaged in the production and distribution of agricultural products. According to the 1810 census, of the estimated 2.3 million in the labor force, almost 2 million were engaged in agriculture. There were 10,000 cotton textile workers that year — and seven times as many domestic servants. More Americans worked as miners than textile workers, and there were 2,000 more schoolteachers. Able young men in the Boston area became farmers, fishermen, or sailors, or hoped to open small businesses of their own. None had worked in a textile factory, simply because there was no such enterprise in the area. There were flour mills, to be sure, but these were small, family-owned and -operated affairs. Lowell not only had to create a new industry but hire and organize a labor force, when there were no models at hand for even such basic matters as wages and hours.

The Scottish mills employed young boys and occasional adult male labor. Early on, Lowell decided to recruit farm girls, who would work for a while to accumulate a dowry and then leave, probably for marriage. When the mill complex was almost complete, he traveled from farm to farm, inquiring as to whether any daughters of the family would be interested in working at the facility. They would live in a boarding house, supervised by an older woman who would serve as housemother and chaperon. Lowell urged the parents to visit Waltham to see for themselves that it was a healthy, moral environment. Nathan Appleton, who was an investor in Boston Manufacturing, later wrote:

> There was little demand for female labor, as household manufacture was superseded by the improvements in machinery. Here was in New England a fund of labor, well-educated and virtuous. It was not perceived how a profitable employment has any tendency to deteriorate the character. The most efficient guards were adopted in establishing boarding houses, at the cost of the Company, under the charge of respectable women with every provision for religious worship. Under these circumstances, the daughters of respectable farmers were readily induced to come into these mills for a temporary period.

The system worked for several reasons. Seeing themselves as burdens to their families, many young farm women were eager for the chance to enter a new environment in which they would not only be self-sufficient but help support their parents and siblings and accumulate dowries. The pay was low: in May 1817 there were 125 employees at Waltham, of which 36 were weavers earning 62 cents per day, 17 carders at 44 cents a day, and 12 spinners at 51 cents a day. Conditions improved, but by the mid-1830s such workers averaged only $3.25 for a seventy-five-hour, six-day work week. This seems painfully little by modern standards (less than 5 cents an hour) and was low even during the early nineteenth century. However, fees for room and board were also modest, and a mill worker could realistically expect to save as much as $2 a week. Within just a few years this could amount to a respectable dowry. Indeed, most mill girls started work at age fifteen or sixteen and quit in their early twenties. Lowell did not consider this an unreasonable turnover rate. He not only had anticipated it but hoped it would work out that way. Mill work tended to wear out laborers within a few years, making them less productive.

Lowell both managed the factory and oversaw the sale of its products. Boston Manufacturing hoped to develop a few large wholesalers rather than sell small quantities of cloth to many small retailers, but it had little success, and for a while Lowell offered his cloth through auctions. Then, as the demand for cloth rose and Lowell was swamped by other duties, Appleton took over in the sales area. In 1815 he arranged for the commission house of B. C. Ward & Company to take all of the mill's output, which it sold to wholesalers in the Boston area.

As the industrial labor force dramatically increased, managers hoped to give workers a sense of belonging and inspire company loyalty. Like the Sayles Finishing Plant in Rhode Island in 1923, many companies organized employee associations to "strike up the band" outside the factory.

Lowell's recruitment of women into the work force allowed them to venture into other positions in greater numbers after the turn of the century. This bookkeeper at the Standard Lime and Stone Company in Fond du Lac, Wisconsin, in about 1910 might have laughed at anyone who told her that a woman's place was in the home.

Lowell's Waltham mill had become the center for textile technology in the United States. From the first, the enterprise sold machinery to others, helping to create industrial pockets in the Fall River, Massachusetts, and Providence, Rhode Island, areas. It wouldn't be going too far to say that Boston Manufacturing was one of the progenitors of the American factory system. More than that, Moody, Appleton, Jackson, and others developed production line techniques far in advance of any in the world and were pioneers in matters of distribution. Lowell showed the way in finance and recruited one of the nation's first industrial labor forces.

By 1840 there were half a million workers engaged in manufacturing. The overwhelming number of Americans still worked the land — that year there were 3.6 million farmers. But the Waltham mill foreshadowed the fact that before the end of the nineteenth century the system would grow and evolve, and the factory more than the farm would set the tempo of the working lives of Americans.

By the late nineteenth century, the factory system had evolved remarkably since the days of Slater and Lowell. But entrepreneurs continued to innovate in the organization of workers. By conducting "time and motion" studies and developing techniques of "scientific management," Frederick W. Taylor and his followers sought to routinize production work in some industries after the 1890s, but such systems were seldom fully instituted and, not surprisingly, raised the ire of workers. At the same time, others, such as John H. Patterson of National Cash Register, instituted "welfare capitalism" programs to provide employee incentives and benefits. In this way, concerts, field trips, special celebrations, free lectures, and medical, housing, and dining facilities became fairly common corporate fixtures. Company owners adopted such measures as much out of their fear of unionization and labor unrest as their paternalism, altruism, and recognition that, in the words of Patterson, "it pays."

Entrepreneurs continue to innovate in a similar way. Donald Burr's ability to create a sense of belonging and caring is one of the greatest competitive assets of People Express, and some of the entrepreneurs examined here deserve a place in this tradition. Mary Kay Ash culls the resources of her salespeople as effectively as any, and Alfred Sloan's innovations in the development of new corporate forms were an important step in the effective marshaling of human resources. That good use of human resources is good business is a fact perennially rediscovered by the nation's business leaders.

III

Expanding America

IN 1815 America stood on the brink of a period of critical expansion. Then spanning the territory from the Atlantic to the Mississippi, scarcely more than a single modern-day time zone, the young nation shared many of the economic problems of the empire from which it had freed itself two generations earlier. It was difficult — sometimes impossible — for farmers and merchants in one region to move goods to market in another. America was a collection of small, isolated communities separated by mountains, deserts, and almost impassable forests.

But all of this would change within less than a century, as the United States rapidly transformed itself into the greatest economic power in world history. By 1890, the year Frederick Jackson Turner declared the closing of the American frontier, national territory had doubled and reached the full 3,500 miles from the Atlantic to the Pacific. At the same time, the continent had become a great national marketplace, united by a web of commerce. Territorial growth, which could have become an economic curse, was made into a blessing.

Transportation technologies, developed by inventors and entrepreneurs, made this possible. The first large-scale transportation projects were the canals, grand projects such as De Witt Clinton's Erie, which lowered costs and shipping times beginning in the 1820s far below those of wagon hauling. But soon another technological breakthrough — the railroad — made even greater strides. J. Edgar Thomson built the Pennsylvania Railroad into the largest system in the world, and by 1890 the United States had the largest railroad network in the world. Innovation followed innovation: within a century of the opening of the first canals, airlines such as Juan Trippe's Pan American had a similarly dramatic effect on transportation costs and speeds.

As always, change and entrepreneurial opportunity fed each other, but the business of building and expanding America had its special characteristics. Elisha Otis's safety elevators, which moved masses of people in separately controlled cars, was an exception. Most methods of transportation took the form of integrated networks that were constructed on a grand scale. The size and capital requirements of the canals were unprecedented in their day, and these were soon dwarfed by the great railroads. Not surprisingly, a few entrepreneurs, perhaps none more influential than J. Pierpont Morgan, saw opportunities in the financing of such projects.

Indeed, the United States has been peculiar among the industrialized nations of the world for the degree to which it has left infrastructure building to private entrepreneurs. The government did offer support of various sorts, but it was highly competitive individuals, seeking their own ends, who again and again supplied the driving force for development.

Transportation industries remade the fabric of the United States, creating a national economy with national markets and fostering the development of a host of important related industries, such as wood, coal, petroleum, iron and steel, glass, and aluminum. At the same time, they transformed the way business was conducted, and none did this more than the railroads. Modern corporate management was a result of the special needs of American railroads, which in the 1800s were the largest and most complex enterprises in the world. Later, when the automobile industry surpassed the railroad as the leading form of transportation in America, innovation continued: Alfred P. Sloan of General Motors recast modern corporate administration.

□

Dirt roads and turnpikes formed the first transportation network as the country rapidly expanded westward. But mud and ice often made them impassable and they were difficult to maintain. Insightful private investors recognized the role new technologies could play in uniting the country's fragmented markets.

Early systems of transportation were a hodgepodge of roads, canals, and ships. Competitors had good reason to fear the advent of the railroad, which transformed not only passenger travel but the way business in America was conducted.

In 1815 the time was ripe for these developments to begin. The Treaty of Ghent, which ended the second war with Britain, had just been signed on December 24, 1814, and although "nothing was adjusted, nothing was settled," by the treaty, as John Quincy Adams put it, a series of postwar agreements took away the barriers to western settlement by removing restrictions on Anglo-American trade and effectively demilitarizing the Great Lakes. From this time until the outbreak of the Civil War in 1860, the United States would enjoy a long and uncharacteristic peace, interrupted only briefly by the Mexican war of 1848.

New westward settlement followed rapidly. Indiana joined the union in 1816, Mississippi in 1817, Illinois in 1818, Alabama in 1819, the same year that Spain ceded Florida, and Missouri in 1821. Another wave of territorial expansion between 1845 and 1848 brought in territories from Texas, Oregon, and Mexico, adding more land than had the mammoth Louisiana Purchase of 1803.

As this expansion unfolded, America took on a new, inward-looking orientation. No longer could it depend on manufactured goods from overseas, and the first real stirrings of industrialization appeared in New England and the Middle Atlantic region. To fortify this new trade and manufacturing status, many business leaders, such as Francis Cabot Lowell, called for and soon received government protection from British competition in the form of a tariff.

The Tariff of 1816 was of a piece with the growing demand for government intervention in the economy, and not merely to keep out foreign goods. Protection of infant American industries was critical, and adequate transportation was an even more pressing issue. President Thomas Jefferson, no believer in big government or aid to business, departed from his convictions in 1805 to recommend that surplus revenues "be applied to rivers, canals, roads, arts, manufactures, education, and other great objects within each state."

The Erie Canal, built with a combination of public and private funds, opened in 1825. The waterway linked the Midwest to eastern markets and offered business opportunities along the way.

In 1806 Congress authorized construction of a National Turnpike to link Ohio to the East. Two years later, in his *Report on Roads and Canals*, Secretary of the Treasury Albert Gallatin called for the creation of a broad transportation network, knowing that some portions would be expensive and never repay their costs. "Some works already executed are unprofitable; many more remain unattempted, because their ultimate productiveness depends on other improvements, too extensive or too distant to be embraced by the same individuals." This, said the secretary, was the proper role of government.

Improved transportation would not only bind the nation closer together politically but also open commercial opportunities by enlarging markets, in this way benefitting both agrarian and manufacturing interests. The simple notion that stirred Frederic Tudor to take ice to the West Indies, moved Frederick Weyerhaeuser's timber down the Mississippi and Gustavus Swift's meats from Chicago to the East, also struck Gallatin as eminently reasonable. It made sense to provide the means to send products to market. If individual businessmen could not do the job, thought Gallatin, government acting for the common good should undertake it. Or it might be that the two could work in harmony.

There was yet another interest involved, that of landholders. Land was worthless unless it was accessible, and it gained value as access improved. Wilderness territory was there for the taking, as squatters realized. When products of frontier farms could be moved to market, the price rose. Scores of land companies in Washington appreciated this and petitioned Congress to support internal improvements.

Federal aid in this area, which came to $2,000 in 1806, rose sixfold the following year and, on the eve of the War of 1812, was $68,000 — certainly not a large amount, but an indication that interest was increasing. Expenditures continued even while the fighting was on, as President James Madison recognized the need for military roads. In fact, one of the "lessons of the war" was that additional spending would be needed to prepare for the next conflict. "Defensive measures of the United States . . . [require] the construction of good roads," read one congressional report. "A single good road from the river Ohio to Detroit . . . would have afforded complete security to that frontier, at a fourth part of the cost actually incurred in its defense, and have effectively preserved the honor of American arms."

Politics and economics were converging, as were the interests of farmers, manufacturers, and shippers, to stimulate internal improvements. Road construction boomed, and canals began to attract much attention.

De Witt Clinton and the Erie Canal

INTEREST IN CANALS was especially strong in New York, where developers had long dreamed of finding some way to unite the Hudson River to Lake Erie by means of a canal running west from Albany to Buffalo. This would make Manhattan the entrepôt between the American Midwest and Europe, and possibly even Asia and Latin America. Goods originating in Chicago might be sent through the Great Lakes, then along a canal to the Hudson, down river to Manhattan, and from there to Britain and the Continent; imports could reverse the same route to a growing American market in mid-continent. The port of New York would become the rival not only of Boston and Philadelphia but of London itself.

Could it be done? Jefferson had doubts. In 1809 he was consulted by engineers then engaged in planning the project, who knew of the outgoing president's interest in it. He offered no hope, referring to work on the Potomac Canal, which had lured many Virginians including George Washington in the 1780s, and which was still incomplete:

> Why, sir, here is a canal of a few miles, projected by General Washington, which if completed would render this a fine commercial city, which has languished for many years because the small sum of two hundred thousand

The Erie Canal remained an important source of transportation and commerce into the twentieth century. This barge is delivering goods to Clinton Square — named for the canal's founder, De Witt Clinton — in Syracuse, New York, in 1905.

dollars necessary to complete it cannot be obtained from the General Government, the State Government, or from individuals, and you talk of making a canal three hundred and fifty miles through the wilderness! It is little short of madness to think of it at this day.

De Witt Clinton was hardly mad; in fact, he was one of the hardest-headed politicians of his time. The son of a fairly prominent New Yorker, James Clinton, who had served as a brigadier general during the Revolution, De Witt graduated from Columbia College in 1789, became an attorney, and then went on to serve as private secretary to his uncle, George Clinton, who was governor of New York. George Clinton hoped to unite the landholders of central New York with the commercial interests in the city, thus forging an alliance that might take him to Washington. The way to accomplish this was to create a canal from Albany to Lake Erie, which he sketched in 1791. Funds were raised and stock sold in what was to be a private corporation. Some construction actually took place, but in general the program foundered.

Meanwhile, De Witt Clinton was elected to the state senate and, by the early nineteenth century, was emerging as a powerful figure in New York politics. Like his uncle, he had national ambitions, and he entered the United States Senate in 1802, only to resign within months to become mayor of New York, where he served until 1815. In 1812 Clinton became a presidential candidate but lost to James Madison by an electoral vote of 128 to 89. By 1817, while governor of New York, he thought about another run for the presidency.

And that canal. Always interested in transportation and aware of its importance to New York, he had as state legislator helped John Jacob Astor obtain the charter for his American Fur Company, and as mayor worked with Robert Fulton to establish a steamship line on the Hudson. Clinton had been a member of the commission that in 1810 explored the Albany–Buffalo route, and five years later petitioned the legislature for funding. This attempt had failed, but in 1817 he was prepared to try again.

For a while Clinton hoped to obtain federal support for the canal, but when President Madison vetoed a measure that would have provided $1.5 million for the purpose, he decided to finance the canal through an ingenious example of "mixed capitalism" — combining public and private funds.

Most farmers and merchants had hitherto relied on natural bodies of water for transportation or cooperated to cut and maintain paths or plank roads to serve nearby markets. The Erie would benefit entire regions, linking the Great Lakes of the Midwest with the eastern seaboard, but it would cost millions of dollars to construct — a sum clearly out of the reach of single capitalists or even groups of investors. In a nation built upon the sanctity of private property rather than public ownership, mixed capitalism seemed a viable solution to the problem of raising vast quantities of capital for a publicly beneficial yet private project like the Erie.

In April 1817 the New York legislature passed the Canal Act, which created a Canal Fund to control finances and plan for construction. The fund would obtain its income from taxes on salt, steamship travel, and land within twenty-five miles of the proposed ditch, as well as from lotteries and auction duties. This hardly seemed enough: construction costs were estimated at $7 million; the total capital in the state's banks and insurance companies was barely three times that amount. Additional funds would be needed, and these would be raised through the sale of stocks and bonds, mostly to foreigners.

Clinton assured everyone that the money would be found and threw himself into the work, knowing that success could catapult him to national prominence, perhaps the White House itself. Besides, he knew others had an equally important stake in the project and could be counted on for help. Several land companies with extensive holdings in the western part of the state would reap fortunes if and when the canal came through. The Holland Land Company alone owned over three million acres, largely unpopulated, a situation that would quickly change if Clinton prevailed.

The initial flotation was successful. With the assistance of the land companies, Clinton was able to place most of the bonds in Europe, England in particular, while the Holland Land Company announced a large land grant to the state to assist in the work. Several Manhattan banks (in which the state had important equity positions) purchased stock, selling it slowly at the New York Stock and Exchange Board. The state senate appropriated $1 million a year for two years as a supplement.

Work now began on the project, officially named the Erie Canal. The mid-

In its heyday, the canal captured the imagination of the American public in the same way the railroad would later. Much romance followed in the wake of boats that traveled the canals, although in fact most boats, like this one, were modest affairs.

dle section, connecting the Mohawk and Seneca rivers, was completed in October 1819, and traffic was admitted the following May, by which time engineers were pushing on to Lake Erie. The news encouraged investors to purchase more shares and bonds. The Wall Street brokerage firm of Prime, Ward & Sands took large blocks and wholesaled them throughout the country and overseas. Baring Brothers, the most prestigious London merchant bank, made investments, which encouraged others to do the same. John Jacob Astor not only placed a large order for new bonds but also quietly accumulated older ones.

The Canal Fund swelled, fed by investments plus revenues from tolls paid by users of that portion of the Erie in operation. The more miles that were added, the greater the use, the higher the tolls, the more attractive the securities, the higher the price of western land, and the more politically powerful Clinton became.

On November 4, 1825, Clinton celebrated the completion of construction by pouring a keg of Lake Erie water into the Atlantic at Manhattan in a ceremony called "The Marriage of the Waters." The Erie ran 363 miles and cost slightly more than the $7 million originally budgeted; even before completion, toll revenues exceeded interest charges. All marveled at the project. As a writer

for the *Buffalo Emporium and General Advertiser* put it, "They have built the longest canal in the world in the least time, with the least experience, for the least money, and to the greatest public benefit." It was a masterful accomplishment, equivalent for its time to the erection of the Brooklyn Bridge more than a half century later and the Panama Canal soon after the turn of the century.

De Witt Clinton was in many ways atypical of the entrepreneurs who would follow him in building the nation's infrastructure. His public ambitions had no counterpart among his private-sector peers, and even there Clinton could hardly judge himself successful. The closest he got to the White House was an offer from President John Quincy Adams to serve on a mission to England in 1825. He refused, remaining in Albany, and died in office three years later.

Like the more influential and successful projects of its kind, "Clinton's Ditch" in no small measure changed the face of America. Prior to the canal's opening, it had cost $100 a ton to ship freight from Buffalo to Manhattan, the trip taking twenty days; by canal the cost fell to $15 and the time to eight days. New York prospered; the construction helped spark a new wave of immigra-

The powerful, majestic iron horse became an apt symbol of America's relentless territorial and economic expansion. Unlike canals, the railroad functioned in all weather and could reach every corner of the nation with unprecedented speed.

tion, with most of the newcomers debarking in New York, which was swiftly replacing Boston as the major gateway to the interior.

As a result of the Erie's financial success, government aid to roads and canals grew rapidly, from $363,000 in 1825 to $1.2 million in 1835. A portion of the money came from increased land sales, the funds from which were deposited in local banks, making them available to the growing ranks of speculators. Foreigners, too, eagerly invested in dozens of proposed American canals. For a while in the mid-1830s, it appeared that promoters were organizing companies to dig ditches between every two bodies of water in the land, not to mention those between water and the wilderness. Credit expanded to meet the demand, to the point where the nation's financial structure badly eroded. President Jackson then issued the "specie circular" in July 1836, requiring that by the end of that year all sales of public lands (except to residents of the state in which the land was sold) would have to be paid for in gold. This put an abrupt halt to much of the speculation and precipitated a wave of bank failures, which in turn led to a depression. Politicians had made the canal boom possible; now one of them helped bring it to a close and, in the process, ruined thousands of investors, many of them Europeans who had willingly purchased any paper shoved their way.

The boom would have ended anyway. Canals were expensive highways, unusable during winter freezes and droughts and expensive to maintain, having to be dredged constantly. In the wings was another, superior form of transportation — the railroad.

J. Edgar Thomson: Master of the Pennsy

IN LATE 1825, when most in the state were celebrating the success of the Erie, George Featherstonhaugh of Schenectady, New York, took the first step to undermine the canal by announcing he would seek a charter for the Mohawk and Hudson Rail Company to carry passengers and freight between Schenectady and Albany in horse-drawn cars. The forty-mile stretch between these two cities was the most arduous part of the trip by canal. At Schenectady, where the canal merged with the Mohawk River, boats had to stop at several locks, sometimes for hours. To save time, passengers would often take a coach to Albany. Featherstonhaugh found many willing investors — among them the ubiquitous John Jacob Astor — and started construction. The line carried its first passengers in late 1831. This was the first step in the creation of what would be known as the New York Central Railroad.

Meanwhile Philadelphia struggled with its Main Line Canal, an inefficient hodgepodge of waterways and railroads. The Main Line was threatened both by the Erie and its developing railroad, which were capturing the Midwest's commerce, and by Maryland's Baltimore & Ohio Railroad, which had designs on the carrying trade of Pennsylvania's west. To prevent being crushed by these two, Philadelphia's leaders gathered in 1845 to plan a railroad of their own, and soon after the Pennsylvania Central received its charter in 1846.

The line was organized by a diverse group of sedentary merchants not unlike Francis Cabot Lowell of the previous generation. Samuel Vaughan Merrick, its president, was typical of the breed. He had established and run companies that turned out fire-fighting equipment, oversaw an iron foundry, and engaged

Engineer, manager, and determined expansionist, J. Edgar Thomson of the Pennsylvania Railroad was a key figure in the development of America's integrated transportation network.

in insurance and lotteries. He also helped found the Franklin Institute in Philadelphia. None of this provided the experience he would need to manage what was to become the world's largest railroad. So Merrick sought a professional engineer and experienced railroader, and in 1847 found him in J. Edgar Thomson.

Thomson came from an old and respected Pennsylvania family, which had immigrated in 1682 with William Penn, but he was hardly an aristocrat. His father was a farmer and self-taught engineer who helped plan at least one canal and a railroad, and who trained John Edgar in the profession. By 1830 Thomson had become an engineer on the small Camden and Amboy Railroad.

Realizing the English had developed the most advanced technology in the field, he followed the path blazed by Lowell and journeyed there to study, traveling extensively and absorbing the latest techniques. On his return, Thomson became chief engineer for the Georgia Railroad and Banking Company, in charge of expanding the line from Augusta westward to what would become Atlanta. By the time he accepted Merrick's offer of $1,000 a year, the thirty-nine-year-old Thomson was considered one of the most able individuals in his young profession.

A gruff, blunt man with a keen sense of his own worth, Thomson had no intention of permitting amateurs such as those on the board to interfere with his work. Relocating to Harrisburg, as much to be away from the directors in Philadelphia as to direct construction at the site, he started the push westward. Thomson never consulted the board and rarely informed it of his intentions. When Merrick protested in 1847, he threatened to resign and agreed to remain only after the board raised his salary to $5,000 plus expenses. There were additional clashes, but Thomson won most of them. In 1852 he was named chairman and president of the Pennsylvania Central, and for the next two decades no one questioned his policies. In this period the Pennsylvania would be dominated by the greatest railroader of the time, an engineer-businessman whose strategies and techniques were studied and imitated by others of his generation and those who followed.

Thomson completed construction from Harrisburg to Pittsburgh the year he assumed command. Complete through-service to Philadelphia was available in another year and a half. It then became possible to travel from Philadelphia to Pittsburgh in seventeen hours — less than a third of the time it took to travel from Manhattan to Buffalo by boat and railroad. New York's lead in developing the west, seemingly annealed by the Erie Canal, was now threatened, for Thomson made no secret of his ambition to take the Pennsylvania into Chicago — and beyond. Before the Far West was opened, Thomson even spoke of the possibility of erecting a transcontinental railroad to link the Atlantic and Pacific oceans.

In 1853 Thomson managed to convince the state legislature to grant him permission to invest in other railroads, intending to use this method to traverse the 450 miles between Pittsburgh and Chicago. He started by taking an interest in four other lines, one of which, the Ohio & Pennsylvania, got him as far as Crestline, Ohio. Thomson then financed the Ohio & Indiana, which laid track between Crestline and Fort Wayne, Indiana. Next he merged the Ohio & Indiana with another line to create the Pittsburgh, Fort Wayne & Chicago, a major line, which, as the name indicated, succeeded in realizing his objective.

Thomson now moved to "colonize" the Midwest with rail lines. The Marietta & Cincinnati formed a link with Cincinnati, while the Springfield, Mount

By the turn of the century, the railroad depot was a common feature of the American landscape and an important center of commerce. The placement of a depot could either make or break an existing town or create a new one at a crossroads.

Vernon & Pittsburgh took the Pennsylvania into Columbus. On the eve of the Civil War, there was scarcely a significant settlement in southern Ohio, Indiana, or Illinois that was not within a short haul of a line in which the Pennsylvania had an interest or was laying track.

In a period of ten years, Thomson had erected the largest railroad network and industrial corporation in the nation. When he had assumed the presidency in 1852, the Pennsylvania operated less than 250 miles of track and its gross revenues were not quite $2 million. By 1862, the first full year of the Civil War, the road's mileage was 438 and its revenues almost $11 million, not including those railroads in which it had an equity position.

While occupied in expanding his network, Thomson also directed day-to-day operations at the Pennsylvania, involving himself in matters of finance and management as well as construction. In this period he became increasingly aware of the need to delegate responsibilities and fashion a new kind of management organization for this large-scale enterprise. Thomson was not alone in this. Other railroads were contending with the Pennsylvania in its service area and elsewhere in the country, and managers there were also occupied with

these matters. Not much of a writer, Thomson never put down his ideas in any systematic fashion; but one suspects he would have agreed with the observations of the Erie Railroad's general manager, Daniel C. McCallum, who, in the 1850s, sketched one of the problems for his employers and offered suggestions for solving them:

> A Superintendent of a line fifty miles in length can give its business his personal attention, and may be almost constantly upon the line engaged in the direction of its details; each employee is familiarly known to him, and all questions in relation to its business are at once presented and acted upon; and any system, however imperfect, may under such circumstances prove comparatively successful.

> In the government of a road five hundred miles in length a very different state of things exists. Any system which might be applicable to the business and extent of a short road, would be found entirely inadequate to the wants of a long one; and I am fully convinced that in the want of a system perfect in its details, properly adapted and vigilantly enforced, lies the true secret of their failure; and that this disparity of cost per mile in operating long and short roads, is not produced by *a difference in length*, but is in proportion to the perfection of the system adopted.

McCallum argued for what amounted to the creation of line and staff posts. There should be, he wrote:

1. A proper division of responsibilities.
2. Sufficient power conferred to enable the same to be fully carried out, that such responsibilities may be real in their character.
3. The means of knowing whether such responsibilities are faithfully executed.
4. Great promptness in the report of all derelictions of duty, that evils may be at once corrected.
5. Such information, to be obtained through a system of daily reports and checks that will not embarrass principal officers, nor lessen their influence with subordinates.
6. The adoption of a system, as a whole, which will not only enable the General Superintendent to detect errors immediately, but will also point out the delinquent.

All of this required the development of a management structure. Thomson left much of this work to his general superintendent, Thomas Scott. In 1862 Scott entered the Union Army to take charge of the nation's transportation, but not before fashioning a management team composed of a strong headquarters staff directing managers in the field, each of whom had definite authority within prescribed areas and who reported results and requirements on a regular basis. This was the model that inspired John D. Rockefeller at Standard Oil and other industrial tycoons. With such a structure, the Pennsylvania could continue growing, always adding line managers and making certain reporting was regular and accurate and that the staff had a realistic knowledge of what was happening in the service area. In the process Thomson and Scott fashioned the Pennsylvania into an entity without boundaries to its ambitions.

What were those ambitions? Management indicated them in the first words of the 1858 annual report: "It has been the policy of your Board to seek an increase of traffic for the road by securing freight destined to every part of the world." All of which pleased the stockholders and their representatives on the board. The Pennsylvania paid good dividends, and Thomson appeared to believe that this was all they should expect for their investment.

But the modern corporate form in America was still young. There were founders on the board who remembered how it had been in the days of Boston Manufacturing, when a band of friends and relatives combined to take shares in an undertaking and not only own it but have a say in management. At the Pennsylvania the functions of ownership and management were diverging; the seeds of this had been planted during Thomson's early clashes with Merrick. As long as Thomson delivered on promises, and paid those dividends, there would be little protest from the shareholders and others on the board — which is to say he was relatively free to realize his ambitions for railroad hegemony.

The method was simple enough. The Pennsylvania would build and absorb, exploit markets and create new ones, and then build and absorb again. Shortly after the war, Thomson purchased several small New Jersey railroads and reorganized them as the United New Jersey, the clear intention being to enter the New York and Baltimore markets. He put together the Baltimore & Potomac in 1871 and the following year had a terminal in Washington, D.C. Now the Pennsylvania ran along the East Coast from Jersey City to Washington, went as far west as Chicago and St. Louis, and as far north as Canandaigua, New York, and Michigan's upper peninsula.

The Pennsylvania was hardly alone in expanding. When the Civil War began, the nation had less than 31,000 miles of track, and at its close in 1865, 35,000. With the arrival of peace, construction picked up. Slightly more than

In the early days, the railroad offered few creature comforts, and passengers would have to dash out frantically for refreshments during ten-minute stops. George Pullman seized an entrepreneurial opportunity by designing luxurious cars with such amenities as plush dining and sleeping facilities.

800 miles were added in 1865; in 1866 the figure was over 1,400, and the following year, better than 2,500. More than 5,600 miles of track were constructed in 1870, and 7,439 miles were added in 1872. By the end of that year there were more than 66,000 miles of railroad track in the United States, with plans afoot to double this amount before the end of the decade.

Meanwhile, Jay Cooke, then the nation's most prominent investment banker, was selling railroad securities, especially those of the Northern Pacific, to hoards of European investors, in an effort to create a line that would be greater even than the Pennsylvania. Cooke employed all sorts of devices to lure investors and hired publicity men to whip up enthusiasm. Sam Wilkerson, a former newspaperman, excelled at this. One of his strategies was to present newspaper publisher and Democratic presidential candidate Horace Greeley with shares, after which the *New York Tribune*'s publisher-editor ran stories of a "vast wilderness waiting like a rich heiress to be appropriated and enjoyed."

The railroad served as a vital link between farmlands and urban areas. Farmers could transport their produce to profitable markets and take advantage of depots to conduct trade.

The expansion of the railroad was not all triumph. Accidents meant wasteful wreckage and were sometimes deadly. Thomson created managerial systems that made scenes like this one less likely.

To attract German settlers, Wilkerson had the railroad name one of the cities along the route Bismarck. Newspapers ran enticing paid advertisements:

> Prosperity, Independence, Freedom, Manhood in its highest sense, peace of mind and all the comforts and luxuries of life are awaiting you. . . . Throw down the yardstick and come out here if you would be men. Bid good-by to the theater and turn your backs on the crowd in the street! How many regret the non-purchase of that lot in Buffalo, that acre in Chicago, that quarter section in Omaha? A $50 lot may prove a $5,000 investment.

The powerful speculative wave crested with the financial panic of 1873, the most severe the nation had yet known. While the Pennsylvania held firm, dozens of weaker lines were forced into bankruptcy. Still, Thomson was obliged to pay a dividend in the form of an IOU, bearing an interest rate of 6 percent redeemable in cash in fifteen months.

This was the moment dissident stockholders had awaited, and now they called for an investigation. The report, issued in 1874, corroborated the fact that Thomson had indeed put together a powerful enterprise. The Pennsylvania was almost 6,000 miles long, possessing nearly 8 percent of the nation's track, while its capital — the awesome amount of $400 million — represented some 13 percent of the entire sum invested in railroads. Nonetheless, the investigating committee recommended a respite in expansion so as to make possible a more generous dividend policy.

Thomson watched all of this with dismay. Prior to the panic, he had planned to enter the Far West through the takeover of one of the railroads then being constructed and paid most attention to the Union Pacific. With this he would have the transcontinental for which he had planned for a quarter century. Now sixty-six years old and ailing, he lacked the strength simultaneously to run the railroad, engage in a struggle with the dissidents, and plan for expansion. Thomson relinquished more and more power to Thomas Scott. He died on May 27, 1874.

Railroads continue to grip the American imagination, a strange blend of romance and sheer mechanical power. Under the guiding hand of Thomson and his industry peers, however, they became much more than this — a driving force of industrialization as well as the seedbed of the development of modern managerial practices and the corporate organization.

In addition, railroads consumed capital at an astonishing rate, so to them we largely owe the rise of what in the late nineteenth century became known as finance capitalism. Just as the railroad could be considered a symbol of industrialism, and Thomson a symbol of the railroad, so John Pierpont Morgan remains the quintessential finance capitalist.

The august and formidable J. P. Morgan, quintessential finance capitalist, was instrumental in providing the means to support the business of expanding America.

J. P. Morgan: The Corsair

IN THE MIDST of the 1873 panic, when bankruptcies were being announced almost hourly, the great Philadelphia-based investment banking house of Jay Cooke & Company closed its doors for the last time.

The news hit the business community like a thunderbolt. "No one could have been more surprised if snow had fallen amid the sunshine of a summer moon," wrote the *Philadelphia Inquirer*, while the *New York Tribune* reported that "dread seemed to take possession of the multitude" when the news was made public. Asked to comment on the failure, Cornelius Vanderbilt, who commanded the Pennsylvania Railroad's great rival, the New York Central, showed no pity. He indicated that Cooke had brought it upon himself:

> There are many worthless railroads started in this country without any means of carrying them through. Respectable banking houses in New York, so called, make themselves agents for the sale of the bonds of the railroads in question and give a kind of moral guarantee of their high quality. The bonds soon reach Europe, and the markets of the commercial centres, from the character of the endorsers, are soon flooded with them. The roads get into difficulties and bad language is heard all around.

The investment bankers Vanderbilt referred to had become the indispensable handmaidens of railroads and other large ventures. Their major function was to raise funds required in such large-scale enterprises as the Erie Canal and the Pennsylvania Railroad and then serve as financial advisers when additional capital was required. They had not been needed in the time of Francis Cabot

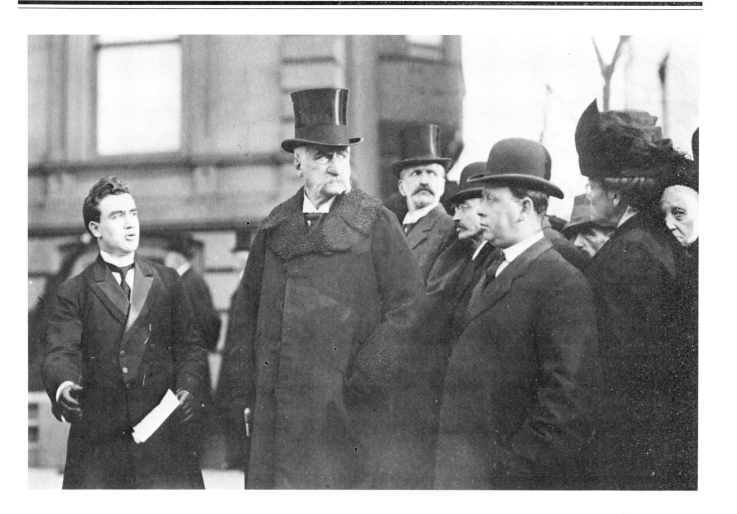

Lowell and Frederic Tudor, when businessmen called upon friends and relatives for whatever relatively small amounts were needed. But the same process of evolution that was divorcing management from ownership at the Pennsylvania was mandating an increase in investment banking activities.

During the post–Civil War period, the Pennsylvania was continually borrowing money and raising capital through the issuance of common and preferred stock, and investment bankers found investors willing to make these purchases. In 1871 the Pennsylvania had 669,000 shares of common stock outstanding, owned by 7,284 individuals, many of whom had never seen the line. Ten years later there were 1,561,000 shares outstanding and over 10,000 stockholders, more than one-fifth of whom were foreigners. Many such stockholders purchased their shares from investment bankers.

The shares and bonds were traded at the New York Stock Exchange and at other exchanges that comprised the "secondary market." Investment bankers and their clients tended to look upon stock prices as a combination thermometer-barometer-advertising device. Should the price of the company's stock rise, it might indicate that business had improved and would get better, so investment bankers could sell additional shares of common at higher prices and offer bonds with lower interest rates. That some investment bankers were therefore suspected of "rigging the market" was understandable, and occasionally the suspicions were justified. But whether they were respected or considered manipulators of the worst kind, their importance could not be denied. They were the centerpiece of finance capitalism, which was rapidly replacing the older variety of financing represented by the likes of Lowell and Tudor.

Jay Cooke, who had won fame by marketing government securities for the Union during the Civil War, had been the most famous of the investment bankers, which was why his failure came as such a surprise. Yet had Cooke managed to survive the panic, he still would have declined in power, for even then he was being challenged by John Pierpont Morgan, whose abilities at selling securities in the United States and abroad were unparalleled.

Born in 1837 the son of Junius Spencer Morgan, an American who became one of London's most prominent bankers, Morgan received a fine education, after which a place was found for him with the firm of Duncan, Sherman & Company. Together with Charles Dabney, an accountant there, he organized Dabney, Morgan & Company in 1864, a firm engaged in the buying and selling of securities and various commercial paper as well as currencies and gold. Maintaining close relations with J. S. Morgan & Company and Baring Brothers in London, it rose quickly and became a force of some magnitude in New York.

Morgan soon allied himself with Anthony Drexel of Philadelphia (second only to Cooke in that city), Levi P. Morton in New York, and several of the city's more prominent banks. But the major source of his strength was still his ability to place American securities overseas. Because of this he was able to take a portion of a $200 million Treasury issue from Cooke in 1871 and sell much of it to foreign investors, and in early 1873 Morgan and his allies won half of a $300 million Treasury issue on the same grounds. Morgan disposed of his portion with relative ease, but Cooke had trouble with his, which contributed to his downfall.

Then and later some claimed that Morgan, in a deliberate attempt to destroy his main rival, manipulated the market to bring this situation about and that his machinations triggered the 1873 collapse. Such matters are difficult to prove, but it can be noted that this was not an uncommon practice at the time, and Morgan, now a veteran, was certainly capable of acting in this way.

What by then had become Drexel, Morgan & Company emerged from the 1873 debacle the nation's most powerful investment banking firm. As such, it dominated the market for United States government bonds, still distributing prime paper in Europe. Still, the government was paying off its debt, making flotations less frequent, while at the same time the private economy was booming — and the need for investment banking services had become pressing.

Morgan's first important move in this direction came in 1879, when he was asked to sell 250,000 shares of New York Central common for William Vanderbilt. The challenge was great because Morgan would have to take the shares at an agreed-upon price and place them in such a way as not to disturb the secondary market. This last was critical for a number of reasons, not least the fact that even after the sale Vanderbilt would own 150,000 shares. Naturally he did not want to see their price fall due to the addition of so large an amount to the supply. Morgan agreed, but insisted upon conditions. Vanderbilt would have to guarantee that the Central's dividend would remain in place for at least five years, and that one of the Morgan partners would have a seat on the railroad's board to help oversee operations. Vanderbilt agreed, Morgan placed the securities as promised (receiving a commission of $1 million), and the episode was widely hailed as the opening of a new chapter in the history of investment banking and an affirmation that the finance capitalist had become the mover and shaker of the economy. This was underscored the following year,

Life insurance companies and banks across the country joined in the race to raise capital for America's huge corporations at the turn of the century.

when, as leader of a syndicate, Drexel, Morgan underwrote $40 million of Northern Pacific bonds without disturbing the market.

Morgan's position was solidified during the next financial crisis, which occurred in 1884. It began with bank failures and soon spread to the stock exchanges. Unlike the 1873 crash, however, there was no large-scale selling by European investors. This was because Morgan, at the head of a syndicate, started purchasing stocks being dumped on the market by panicky investors and speculators. From then until his death in 1913, Morgan was the most influential person in American investment banking. Some critics charged that he had more power than most presidents.

By the 1880s much of Morgan's time was being spent on railroad financing and reorganization. All the while he attempted to bring an end to what he interpreted as wasteful competition. Morgan mediated differences between the Pennsylvania and New York Central in 1885 and went on to attempt the creation of "communities of interest" to prevent what he deemed to be ruinous competition and overbuilding. It was just such an organization, the Eastern Trunkline Association, that Gustavus Swift battled in the late 1880s when he tried to ship his refrigerated dressed beef from Chicago eastward. One man's community of interest was another's combination in restraint of trade.

By the early 1890s, Morgan and other investment bankers had helped reorganize most of the nation's major lines, often arranging for mergers and take-

overs to effect economies, recapitalizing them so as to lower fixed charges, and in general doing whatever they could to make certain they stayed afloat. That Morgan remained the leading symbol of finance capitalism became clear in early 1895, when gold was leaving the country due to economic difficulties. A rumor soon swept Wall Street to the effect that the United States would have to abandon the gold backing for its currency. President Grover Cleveland issued assurances this was not so, but the sales of American paper for gold continued, draining the Treasury to the point where insolvency threatened. Recognizing the need for outside help, the president sent for Morgan, who agreed to head a syndicate to take $100 million in government bonds, paid for with gold, for sale to Europeans. The New York Subtreasury's reserves were down to $9 million, and a check for $12 million was outstanding. "If that is presented today," Morgan told the president, "all is over." Not only was Morgan able to place the $100 million issue but he arranged for an international agreement not to convert dollars into pounds sterling or buy American gold until the flotation was completed. Afterward Cleveland asked Morgan how he knew the European bankers would purchase the issue. He replied, "I simply told them that this was necessary for the maintenance of the public credit and the promotion of industrial peace, and they did it." The episode demonstrated that in business circles toward the end of the nineteenth century, Morgan's reputation surpassed that of the United States government.

In this period it was becoming evident that industrial combinations would soon rival the railroads in size. Yet several industries were involved in the very kind of cut-throat competitive practices Morgan disliked in railroads. Some, however, were evolving into trusts on the Standard Oil model, and Morgan wanted to see more of these. Accordingly, in 1892 Drexel, Morgan helped create General Electric from Edison Electric and its rival, Thomson-Houston.

By then the financing requirements of American business demanded more capital than even Morgan could command. What would become J. P. Morgan & Company in 1894 fashioned alliances with several leading New York banks, among them George F. Baker's First National and James Sillman's National City. Henry P. Davison, a Morgan partner, also helped found the Banker's Trust. In order to obtain additional funds, Morgan took a controlling interest in the Equitable Life Assurance Society, while George Perkins, another partner, became chairman of New York Life. Taken together, this was the most massive aggregation of wealth the world had known to that time. And all of it was necessary in 1901, when Morgan put together the world's largest corporation, United States Steel.

At the time, Carnegie Steel dominated the industry. Ever hoping to create a more orderly industrial climate, Morgan sought some way to control Carnegie or, failing that, eliminate him from the steel picture. J. P. Morgan & Company and other investment bankers put together more than twenty steel companies from 1898 to 1900, trying to create counterforces to Carnegie Steel. In addition, Rockefeller entered the industry, accumulating steel properties in what seemed a bid to offer a challenge of his own. A major industrial war appeared in the making in 1900, when Charles Schwab, who ran the company for Carnegie, sent a signal to Morgan: Carnegie might be willing to sell, if the price was right.

His demand was astronomical: $480 million, of which Carnegie would receive $225 million, the rest going to his partners. Schwab took the figures to Morgan, expecting to be rejected. The banker looked them over briefly and simply said, "I accept." Two days later he met Carnegie and extended his hand. "Mr. Carnegie, I want to congratulate you on being the richest man in the world."

Now Morgan started to spin his web, organizing a massive syndicate to bring in many of the other steel companies. Federal Steel, a Morgan property second only to Carnegie in size, came in, as did Rockefeller's interests. When it was all done, the Morgan group exchanged $1.4 billion in securities for the properties involved, making the new entity, United States Steel, the world's largest industrial corporation by far and the first billion-dollar corporation in history. In the process, of course, Morgan thought he had created stability in a major industry and rid it of a disruptive influence.

Morgan went into decline after this major accomplishment. He failed to create an American monopoly in the merchant marine area and was disappointed in several rail mergers, though he remained the prime force in railroads — while permitting others to become investment bankers for the developing industrial sector. Perhaps most surprising was Morgan's attitude toward the automobile. Failing to perceive any future for automobiles, he turned down a request from William C. Durant, founder of General Motors, for help in selling securities. Durant gave his banking business to Lee Higginson & Company instead. Morgan's attitude also affected the pliable Chauncy Depew, president of

Chaotic as it might have seemed to outsiders, the stock exchange, seen here in 1920, was an effective way to bring buyers and sellers together to finance the growing needs of American business.

the New York Central. On learning that his nephew wanted to invest $5,000 in Ford Motors, Depew called the young man to his office for a lecture and lesson on finance and technology. "Nothing has come along to beat the horse. Keep your money. Or, if you must spend, buy a horse and you'll have enough left over to furnish it with feed for the rest of its life."

Morgan did have one more moment in the sun. In 1907 the nation was struck by its most severe panic, worse in some regards than that of 1893. The seventy-year-old tycoon was attending an Episcopal Church convention in Richmond, Virginia, when he heard the news and rushed back to Wall Street to bring the panic to an end. For a week Morgan exercised more power than any American since Abraham Lincoln. President Theodore Roosevelt, well known for his attacks on the trusts, dispatched Treasury Secretary George Cortelyou to New York City with orders to take directions from Morgan. New York itself was faced with bankruptcy, so Morgan sent one of his aides to City Hall and took over direction from Mayor George McClellan. He called the city's leading religious leaders to his office and informed them that they were to deliver optimistic sermons that weekend. Morgan commanded the Street's major bankers to his office, locked the door, and, throwing a document on the desk, told them he was raising a fund of $25 million and that their contributions had been decided upon. One by one they rose to sign. Old Edward King of the Union Trust shook as he approached the desk. Morgan put an arm around his shoulders and placed the pen in his quavering hand. "There's the place, King, and here's the pen." He signed. When it was all done, Morgan unlocked the door, waved the bankers adieu, and returned to his desk for a cigar and another round of solitaire. This game, in which order is made of the chaos of the deck, was Morgan's favorite.

Part of the $25 million went to finance the purchase of the rich Tennessee Coal & Iron Company for U.S. Steel. Morgan had told Roosevelt that this was vital if the crisis was to be ended and demanded immunity from antitrust prosecution. The president bowed. Conditions returned to normal, and Morgan received the credit.

During the next few years, Wall Street and Washington pondered what might happen in some future panic, when Morgan would no longer be there to help. In 1908 Congress passed the Aldrich-Vreeland Act to provide for the issuance of a temporary currency and other government intervention in time of crisis. But would this be enough? Morgan provided part of the answer in congressional testimony in 1912. "Is not commercial credit based primarily upon money or property?" he was asked by committee counsel Samuel Untermyer. "No sir," Morgan replied. "The first thing is character." Untermyer pressed the point. "Before money or property?" To which Morgan responded, "Before money or anything else. Money cannot buy it."

The trouble was that any law or regulatory body was bound to lack Morgan's character and reputation. But Congress worked on, attempting to fashion some device to act as Morgan might in times of crisis.

Morgan died on March 31, 1913. A few days later, the family gathered to hear his last will and testament, and some might have been surprised that there was no reference to business but instead a strong theological message. The tone was vintage Morgan; one can almost see and hear him glowering at Saint Peter while addressing him sternly:

> I commit my soul into the hands of my Savior, in full confidence that having redeemed it and washed it in His most precious blood He will present

it faultless before my Heavenly Father; and I entreat my children to maintain and defend, at all hazard and at any cost of personal sacrifice, the blessed doctrine of the complete atonement for sin through the blood of Jesus Christ, once offered and through that alone.

"There will be no successor to Morgan," wrote the *Wall Street Journal* the day after his death. "Now Wall Street is beyond the need or possibility of one-man leadership." "There will be a coordination of effort, union of resources, but Morgan will have no successor," echoed the *New York Times*. Not quite. Less than a year later, President Woodrow Wilson signed into law the Glass-Owens Act, providing for an organization that would perform some of Morgan's functions: the Federal Reserve System.

Morgan helped finance and reshape an impressive roster of infrastructure industries in the United States — railroads, steel, telegraph, telephone, electric power, banking, and insurance — and his endeavors often intersected with those of Edison, Carnegie, Thomson, and other builders of America whose impact on the growth and spread of business enterprise was ubiquitous by the end of the nineteenth century. By 1890 the United States had surpassed Great Britain in the production of iron and steel and was operating more miles of railroad track than all of Europe and Russia combined.

But railroad networks, built by the likes of Thomson, could only do so much. They provided much of the connective tissue for the nation, tying together its urban centers and providing conduits for the agricultural products of the Midwest to be exchanged for the industrial goods of the Northeast and Middle Atlantic states. They could not, however, provide the circulatory systems cities needed to keep the flow of goods, information, and people moving. If cities were to grow as centers of population, commerce, industry, and political and cultural life, they needed to grow up as well as out.

In 1852, Elisha Graves Otis devised the first "safety elevator," which included a catch to prevent the car from falling if a cable broke. Convincing demonstrations in public places won over all the skeptics.

Elisha Graves Otis and the Rise of Vertical Transportation

B Y THE 1890s there was no more obvious physical manifestation of change than the burgeoning skyline of the American city. In New York, for example, the majestic spire of Trinity Church, which had towered above the city since the early 1800s, was eclipsed in 1890 by the Pulitzer Building, which used elevators to convey office workers to its upper floors. And after several years of an intense building boom, many of the streets of New York City were already shadowed by tall buildings.

Nor was Manhattan the only urban place in America being transformed into a modern city. In 1850 New York was the sole city in the country with more than a half million people, and only 5 other cities had crossed the 100,000 mark. By 1890 New York, Chicago, and Philadelphia each had more than 1 million citizens, and by 1910 no fewer than 31 urban centers had populations of at least 100,000. The great cities of other western societies had been dominated by cathedrals, but the American landmark became the office skyscraper.

What made this possible was vertical transportation — and the first safe elevators were developed by Elisha Graves Otis.

Like Thomson, Morgan, and a host of other entrepreneurs who helped build the urban, industrial world, Otis got his start during the mid-nineteenth century. But his rise to business history fame underscores the complex and

often ironic role of the entrepreneur. The originator of one of the greatest industrial enterprises in America as well as one of the first multinational companies in the world, he had little notion of the importance of his discovery and died before his enterprise gained a stable foothold. His achievement was a clever but simple technological adjustment, made in the routine course of his duties as a mechanic-supervisor. But his own creativity and drive, matched by those of his sons, were critically timed, for innovative iron and steel construction methods were raising buildings to new heights.

Like Frederic Tudor, Elisha Graves Otis had a venerable heritage, which he cast aside for a career in business. Born in Halifax, Vermont, on August 3, 1811, he was a descendant of the first Otis in the New World, John, who had settled in Hingham, Massachusetts, in 1631. The famed revolutionary patriot James Otis was also a direct ancestor, and Elisha's father, John, a successful farmer, had served as a justice of the peace and state legislator.

However, Elisha struck out on his own at age nineteen, changing jobs and careers frequently during early adulthood as he roamed throughout the Northeast. While such an existence might seem unsettled and transient, it was not uncharacteristic of the lot of many early-nineteenth-century Americans. Otis first settled in Troy, New York, and worked for his brother, a master carpenter. After a nearly fatal bout with pneumonia forced him to quit, he teamed horses until 1838, when his health and capital had recovered enough to enable him to construct a dam, gristmill, and house alongside the Green River in Vermont. As this venture foundered, Otis converted it into a carriage manufacture, which he operated successfully until 1845, when the local market for fine carriages became saturated. Otis then converted his facilities into a sawmill, but he failed again as his health took a turn for the worse.

Moving to Albany, Otis put in a stint as a master mechanic at a bedstead factory, where his invention of an automatic lathe earned him $500 and confidence as a practical mechanic. Prospects seemed bright, so the ambitious in-

After Otis's death in 1861, his sons took over his elevator company. Within fifty years they transformed the small family enterprise into one of the first multinational corporations in the world.

When Otis perfected his "hoisting machinery" to make it safe for passengers as well as freight, he had little idea that the elevator would become a standard feature of elegant modern office buildings like this one.

ventor again set up his own shop, soon designing and building a unique breed of water turbine. Then another blow fell. In 1851 the City of Albany took over the creek he used for his steam power supply, thereby choking off his energy source. Otis returned to the fold of his former employer at the bedstead factory, now in Bergen, New Jersey. The following year he was relocated to Yonkers, New York, to supervise the construction of a new bedstead factory.

In the course of his duties at Yonkers, Otis devised a lift for the factory that included many innovative features, the most important of which was a safety catch that prevented the car from falling in the event of a cable break. Tension on the lifting rope held in sets of teeth, which projected outward toward other teeth running down the sides of the elevator shaft. If the tautness of the cable was relaxed, the teeth would automatically lock the car securely into the shaft. This made the Otis lift the first "safety elevator" in history.

Although hoists of various sorts had been in use since ancient times, none until the Otis elevator was ever considered safe enough for passenger use. It was a critical breakthrough. Yet Otis considered the accomplishment a routine part of his job and thought little or nothing of its possible applications. As his son Charles later wrote, "I do not suppose that my father had the slightest conception at the time of what the outcome of this invention would be."

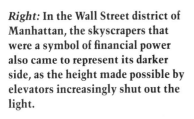

Left: The safety elevator transformed the value of urban real estate. Higher was better, and glamorous towers such as New York's landmark Flatiron Building, built in 1904, went up almost overnight.

Right: In the Wall Street district of Manhattan, the skyscrapers that were a symbol of financial power also came to represent its darker side, as the height made possible by elevators increasingly shut out the light.

Indeed, Otis was prepared to head west for the gold rush, when a local manufacturer placed an order for two elevators. So once again Otis set up a shop of his own, on September 20, 1853. But first year sales totaled only $900, entirely from the initial order. Recognizing that some serious promotional work was needed, Otis packed up a prototype and set out for New York's Crystal Palace Exhibition of 1854, where he put on a dramatic display of his contraption. Having himself hoisted above the gathering crowd in an open elevator car, he would order that the cable be cut. As observers gasped, the car would lock safely into the shaft.

The stunt and Otis's persistent efforts boosted sales somewhat the following year, but in 1855 they still reached only $5,605, and none were used to lift passengers. Acceptance of the safety elevator was slow to develop, but the firm managed to market 27 elevators in 1856 for a total of $13,448. The following year Otis finally installed his first passenger unit in the New York City glass and china establishment of E. V. Haughwout & Company.

Otis did not live to see his enterprise grow beyond modest proportions. In 1860 the company name was changed to N. P. Otis and Brother, signaling the passing of leadership to the next generation. After patenting the world's first steam elevator in 1861, Elisha Otis died on April 8 of that year, days before the outbreak of the Civil War. The total value of his factory, which employed only eight or ten men, was $5,000.

The elevator paved the way for the inner-city transportation boom in the early twentieth century. On Chicago's State Street (*left*), streetcars carried shoppers from store to store. And in New York, the remarkable technology of the Manhattan Bridge (*above*) extended the city's reach across the Hudson in 1909.

As important as Otis's invention was, his company might have foundered quickly if not for his two sons, Charles Rollin Otis (1835–1927) and Norton Prentiss Otis (1840–1905), who possessed technical and entrepreneurial abilities on a par with their father. Both were astute businessmen and mechanics, and they kept the firm alive while registering many patents related to elevator technology.

The firm hobbled along during the war and managed to survive the cholera epidemic soon after, which ravaged New York City. "The panic among businessmen seems to be over," Charles Otis recorded in 1866, "and we hear less about the cholera. There is now beginning to be some inquiry about hoisting machinery. Money matters are easier, think we can get along pretty well now." The brothers incorporated the business for $225,000 the following year as Otis Brothers & Company.

At last elevators seemed to be catching on. As the brothers invested $10,000 to build and equip a new factory in Yonkers in 1868, Norton expressed his astonishment that the public reacted to elevators "as though they were some new discovery that had just come out." It did not hurt matters, of course, that the earliest installations were in places frequented by the public, such as hotels and department stores. In later decades the first electric light companies would benefit in a similar way, when electric lighting began to be used for fairs, theaters, hotels, newspaper buildings, boulevards, and other prominent public places.

The implications of the safety elevator were becoming clear: not only did it offer convenience and even glamor but its installation could drastically recast real estate values. No longer would the upper floors of buildings, accessible only by stairs, have the lowest rents. With the best views and easy elevator access, they could increasingly command the highest fees. "Elevator buildings" of five or six stories began to appear in cities throughout the nation, as the devices repeatedly proved their ability to sustain urban growth in crowded areas. Before the first Otis installations in the congested Wall Street district during the 1870s and 1880s, many New Yorkers were convinced that the financial district would be forced out of the city.

Unlike railroads, electrical systems, and other networks, elevators could be installed individually and without great expense. To be sure, the equipment needed to manufacture them was not cheap, especially for the nonmachinist, but as Otis himself had demonstrated, the business could be conducted for a few thousand dollars. Not surprisingly, imitators were quick to enter the trade, and competition soon became fervent. To their credit, the Otis brothers were able to capitalize on their father's first position in the industry and moved quickly to secure key installations in the United States and, eventually, throughout the world.

After it struggled through the depression of the 1870s, the company grew on a foundation of continuing technological innovation and installations in key architectural landmarks. Its first hydraulic elevator went into the New York Stock Exchange in 1878, and the next year the first bank of high-speed units was installed in Manhattan's Boreel Building. Electric elevators were developed by the company in 1889. Then the first operatorless elevator was installed in a private Manhattan residence. In 1900 the Otis Elevator Company pioneered a new form of vertical transportation — the escalator — and displayed the first model at the Paris Exposition held that year.

The brothers retired for a time, selling out to a syndicate in 1882, but they regained control of the firm five years later, placing themselves in top positions as key consolidations seemed imminent. The first was the organization of the Otis Electric Company in 1892, which united Otis Brothers & Company, Thomson-Houston Electric Company, Edison General Electric Company, and General Electric in the manufacture of electric elevator motors. In this way, the interests of two supreme American builders neatly converged, and Otis Electric even installed its first "Unit Multi-Voltage" control at Edison's Pearl Street Station in New York.

In 1898 the Otis Elevator Company, capitalized at $11 million, was formed through the merger of eight other elevator concerns. Firmly in control of the market, the corporation boasted installations in virtually all of the world's tallest buildings — the Singer Building, the Metropolitan Life Insurance Company, the Woolworth Building — and was operating offices in more than a dozen cities, with major branches in London and Paris. The company even made a foray into automobile manufacturing, producing "Sultan" automobiles at a Springfield, Massachusetts, plant beginning in 1906, but this diversification came to a dead end four years later.

The global strategy paid off well. By the First World War, Otis Elevator joined the ranks of International Harvester and Singer Sewing Machine to become one of the first great multinationals in history. As annual sales topped $20 million in 1917, associated Otis companies were operating in Germany, England, France, and Canada. Elisha Otis had made his seemingly mundane innovation at a propitious time. His sons, as well as the hordes of professional managers who guided the enterprise in later decades, held strong. While for most riders it remains an uninteresting component of modern life, the elevator has become one of the most commonly used forms of transportation in America.

Alfred P. Sloan, here at the wheel during the 1933 New York Auto Show, steered General Motors into the leadership of the auto industry, usurping Henry Ford's hold on the market.

Alfred P. Sloan: Intrapreneur of General Motors

THE OTIS ELEVATOR FIRM survived the transition from small family enterprise to giant industrial corporation; but not all firms of its stature could make the same claim. It is commonly believed that, as organizations grow large, the gulf between entrepreneurship and management widens. In this way, the scenario goes, success contains the seeds of its own downfall: for once an enterprise reaches a large scale, its bureaucratic arteries begin to harden, leaving it vulnerable to attacks from smaller, more limber challengers whose entrepreneurial pulses have not yet quieted.

Recently, as we have noted, a new term has been coined, "intrapreneur," which describes managers who keep their entrepreneurial edge and act as though they were steering dynamic, upstart companies — all within the walls of giant corporations. To the extent that big business can use a dose of creative

GENERAL MOTORS CORPORATION
ORGANIZATION

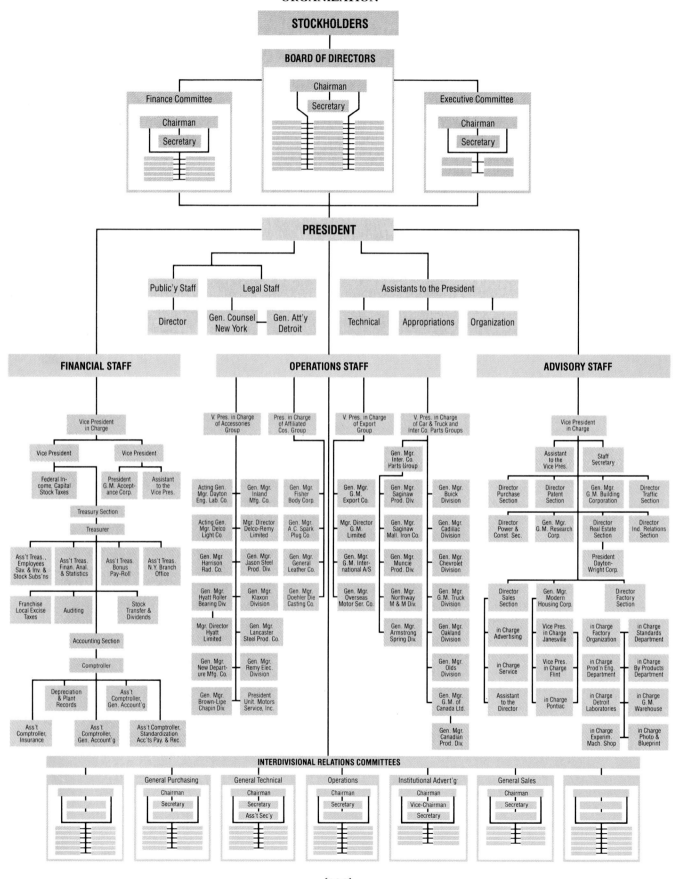

thinking and unorthodox action, these intrapreneurs are surely welcome. But when it comes to innovating within the context of a large-scale business enterprise, intrapreneurship is little more than a new name for a very old phenomenon. American business has done so well, in fact, because many of the managers of its biggest firms have acted entrepreneurially. But these influential top managers have tended to be upstaged in history, quietly working beyond the public view like "the man in the gray flannel suit."

Alfred P. Sloan is a prime example. Few students of intrapreneurship would recognize his name today, yet Sloan engineered one of the greatest coups in American business history by taking most of the automobile market from the company owned by colorful, hard-driving Henry Ford. General Motors could easily have become an unwieldy, uncontrollable colossus. Instead, Sloan kept it on course, and in so doing he helped the automobile business become a crucible of managerial innovation and the automobile the most widespread form of transportation in America.

Unlike most of the first generation automobile pioneers, Sloan was no farmboy tinkerer intrigued by the new buggies. The son of a Brooklyn-based coffee and tea importer, Alfred was born in New Haven, Connecticut, on May 23, 1875. As a boy Sloan showed no interest in machines or business; in fact, he was a classic bookworm. The elder Sloan recalled: "Alfred was everlastingly digging at some school problem. He had no inclination for shop-work or any mechanics. He wouldn't even bait his own fish-hook because he despised to get his hands dirty." Sloan entered the Massachusetts Institute of Technology, graduated in three years, and then took a job as draftsman at Hyatt Roller Bearing. In 1897, with his father's financial aid, he purchased controlling interest in Hyatt, which went on to become a prime supplier of bearings to the automobile industry.

By then the twenty-two-year-old engineer realized he had an innate talent for management. "We were nearly as scientific in our operations as a business could be — in that time," he later wrote. "Our works were highly organized. About 95 percent of the productive labor was on piecework, and I had installed an effective cost system. On the payroll were chemists and metallurgists. Every step in the development of raw materials into antifriction bearings was checked by scientific methods."

Hyatt sold its bearings to most auto manufacturers, but the firm's two largest customers by far were Ford and General Motors, and this troubled him. "One dismal fact was revealed by our accounting: more than half our business came from Ford, and our other big customer, General Motors, dwarfed the remainder. If either Ford or General Motors should start making their own bearings, our company would be in desperate situation." In recognition of this, Sloan sold the company to General Motors in 1916 for $13.5 million.

At the time, William C. Durant was buying auto manufacturers and suppliers in an attempt to cobble together the largest entry in the industry. In two periods of feverish activity (1908–1910 and 1916–1920), Durant went on buying sprees, swapping GM stock for companies. The first wave included such now-famous firms as Buick, Oldsmobile, Cadillac, and Champion Spark Plug, but also such forgotten names as Cartercar, Scripps-Booth, Welch, Sheridan, and Oakland. In the second wave came Chevrolet, Fisher Body, Frigidaire, and Hyatt, and Durant would have gobbled Ford had he been able to raise the $3 million Henry Ford demanded.

Sloan reorganized GM into a multidivisional corporation with staff managers at headquarters and line managers in the field. His "intrapreneurial" strategy kept the company on course as it grew into a leviathan.

Unlike Ford, which was built on one product, GM merged several automakers. Its divisions included Cadillac, Oldsmobile, Pontiac, and Chevrolet. Sloan understood the needs of his customers: he instituted annual model changes and offered trade-ins and purchases over time.

A vain, impetuous gambler, Durant had almost no interest in management, leaving such matters to men like Charles Nash and Walter Chrysler, both of whom left in exasperation to form their own auto companies. Rather, he accumulated companies with little thought to their utility in the larger enterprise and rarely sought economies that might have been realized had more care been given to the matter. Indeed, Durant didn't transform GM into a holding company until 1917, which provided at least the semblance of structure. Still, by 1919 he had made GM the nation's fifth largest industrial enterprise.

Sloan observed all of this from a vantage point as president of Durant's holding company of parts suppliers, United Motors, and in 1918 he was elevated to a vice presidency at GM. When auto sales slumped during the 1920

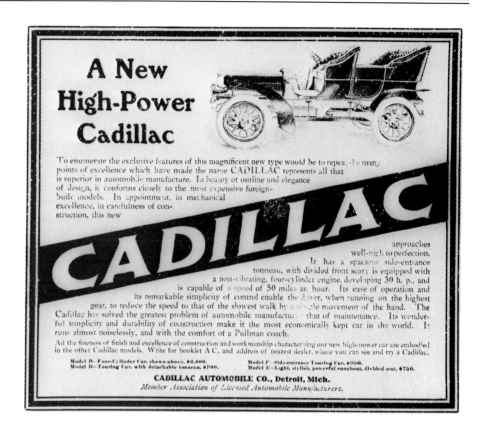

depression and Durant lost much of his personal fortune in the stock market, the Du Pont family, which owned a large stake in the company, took over and installed Pierre Du Pont as president, while Sloan became operating vice president. Du Pont knew little about automobiles and was sufficiently astute to realize this. He relied heavily on Sloan, who engineered the company's recovery and in 1923 became GM's president.

During the next decade Sloan restructured GM, in the process creating the rubric that would be studied and imitated by many others, including all the auto companies. Yet it wasn't completely original. Sloan's division of management into staff and line (the former operating at headquarters, the latter in charge of field operations) was quite familiar, having been fashioned at the larger railroads in the nineteenth century. Modern armies, especially the Prussian, had also pioneered such organization, and many concepts were developed simultaneously at industrial corporations. Indeed, Sloan occasionally used military examples to illustrate just what he was attempting at GM.

Sloan created a multidivisional structure at General Motors. He began by weeding out many of Durant's subsidiaries and gathering the strongest carmaking units into divisions. The strategy, now familiar, was elegant in conception and brilliantly executed. Years later Sloan put it this way:

> The line of products we had was very defective. General Motors had a line of cars, and of course it was in a highly competitive position. It seemed to me that the intelligent approach would be to have a car at every price position, just the same as a general conducting a campaign wants to have an army at every point he is likely to be attacked. We had too many cars in some places and no cars in other places. One of the first things we did was to develop a line of products that met competition in the various positions in which competition was offered.

Sloan thought that GM's entries should stretch downward from Cadillac to Buick to Oakland to Oldsmobile, ending up at Chevrolet, which was the lineup in the early 1920s. There would be changes: Pontiac was added in 1925 to fill the gap between Chevrolet and Oldsmobile, Oakland would be dropped, and LaSalle would be added and then discarded.

Each of these units had its own line and staff managers, and the president of each was to cooperate and compete with the others. This meant that the Buick division would share parts with Oldsmobile, but at the same time there were overlaps in price and style, so that many Buick customers were likely to be interested in some Oldsmobiles and vice versa. In this way Sloan hoped to preserve the benefits of competition while enjoying the fruits of economies of scale. Similarly, the parts, truck, finance, and other GM units were to have a large degree of autonomy, their leaders rewarded for successes and replaced when they failed. GM was to become a huge operation, but Sloan tried to make certain it retained the vitality of a smaller one.

Above all Sloan stressed marketing. When he took over at General Motors, Henry Ford, the industry leader, altered his famed Model T when improvements were developed or invented, and adjusted prices — always downward to reflect economies of scale and changes in the manufacturing process. Sloan wanted style changes on a regular basis, whether the technology called for it or not. Ford saw no need for a design department; at GM the designers often had more power than the technicians, and the dealers were prized. "General Motors fully recognizes that the dealer is the most important link in the chain that completes any transaction," Sloan said soon after assuming command. "The dealer has capital at stake; so does the manufacturer. They must work more closely together than heretofore."

Under Sloan's leadership GM was ever conscious of the customer, and he proved a brilliant mass psychologist. Sloan identified four new elements in the packaging (for that's what it really was) and marketing of automobiles introduced and perfected by GM in the 1920s and 1930s, which became the foundation for the industry afterward: installment selling, the used car trade-in, the annual model change, and the closed body. Of these the first three were the most obvious and important. Time purchases and trade-ins eased the financial pains of purchase and were the nuts and bolts of the dealer's business. Neither could compare with the sheer glamor of the model changes, which took place in the autumn and vied with the World Series for press and public attention.

Sloan claimed his plan "rested upon the concept of better and better cars, with a bigger package of accessories and improvements beyond basic transportation," but there was more to it than that. The annual model change was supposed to stir discontent in the car owner's breast, leading him or her to trade in an old but serviceable model for the latest out of Detroit. The three- or four-year-old car often was referred to as "just transportation," implying there was more to ownership than the possession of a machine whose function was to move a person from one place to another efficiently, comfortably, and safely. Such was the psychological essence of Sloanism and the concept upon which he constructed his marketing ethic. In his retirement he wrote:

> When first car buyers returned to the market for the second round, with the old car as a first payment on the new car, they were selling basic transportation and demanding something more than that in the new car. Middle-income buyers, assisted by the trade-in and installment financing, created the demand, not for basic transportation, but for progress in new cars,

This is a vacation? Thousands of Americans thought so in 1924. Free to travel when and where they wanted, they took to the highway in droves, bringing the age of the steam locomotive to a close. The Miami Causeway was one of the many new roads built to accommodate the expansion of tourism.

for comfort, convenience, power and style. This was the actual trend in American life and those who adapted to it prospered.

Sloan envisioned a young couple, starting out in life, buying a Chevrolet on time, trading it in for a Pontiac a few years later, and progressing up the GM line as financial and social circumstances permitted or dictated. At the end of the American rainbow would be the prestigious Cadillac, more a symbol of arrival than anything else, a badge of accomplishment for all to see and admire.

Sloan's strategy and its implementation worked. In 1921 GM produced 215,000 vehicles, giving it 7 percent of domestic sales; by the end of 1926 Sloan had increased production to 1.2 million cars and trucks, and GM now had over 40 percent of the market. In 1940 the corporation turned out 1.8 million vehicles, giving it almost half the total sales for the year. In contrast, Ford's market share in 1921 was 56 percent and 19 percent in 1940, not only far behind GM but in third place to Chrysler Corporation, which hadn't even existed in 1921. It was one of the most dramatic advances — and declines — in American business history.

The reasons rest in the differences between Henry Ford and Alfred Sloan. Ford was a production genius, an individual who perceived the important role the automobile was destined to play in American life and produced the first car designed for the average person. Sloan recognized that the age of pioneering had passed. Up until that time the market expanded rapidly, as many people switched from horse and buggies to automobiles. For such a market the Model T was perfect, a no-nonsense vehicle that fitted well that era's transition from rural to urban. By the 1920s, however, the market was becoming dominated by people who had already owned an automobile and desired more than just a "Tin Lizzie." As a *Fortune* writer put it, the "Model T was a wonderful car, but it certainly did not flatter your pride of ownership." The generation that bought its cars from Ford, who said the customer could have any color so long as it was black, was replaced by one demanding style, glamor, and comfort, all of which

Sloan was prepared to offer. Ford attempted to add mechanical refinements to the Model T; Sloan offered a variety of color combinations, sleeker lines, efficient heaters, and a self-starter to replace the hand crank, so that women would have an easier time at the wheel.

General Motors' triumph over Ford is one of the great morality tales of American management. Henry Ford had written, "That which one has to fight hardest against in bringing together a large number of people to do work is excess organization and consequent red tape. To my mind there is no bent of mind more dangerous than that which is sometimes described as the 'genius for organization.'" Yet it was just that, along with his view of the market, which enabled Sloan to dislodge Ford from its dominant position in the automobile industry. More so than perhaps any other American businessman, Sloan typified the union of entrepreneurial and managerial skills.

Juan Trippe: Icarus of an Airline Empire

GREAT ENTREPRENEURS and managers are impelled by a vision. The far-seeing colonial merchant John Jacob Astor envisioned and created a global trade network that linked Great Britain and New England with ports in the Pacific Northwest and the Far East. Strategies on this scale were rare in Astor's day, when transportation was still in its rudimentary stage. Today, businessmen routinely conduct face-to-face negotiations on separate continents in a single day. Air travel, of course, makes this possible.

That Americans would pioneer in the airline industry is perhaps to be expected, given our technological accomplishments and the geographical vastness of our homeland. Even so, the strategic possibilities intrinsic to the industry were not immediately obvious, even to industry insiders. Juan Terry Trippe, who headed Pan American Airways for more than four decades, was as atypical in his day for his ability to mold an intricate international transportation strategy as Astor had been centuries before. Like entrepreneurs throughout American business history, he was the first to see what later seemed obvious.

Born a year before the twentieth century dawned, Juan Trippe enjoyed the best the prewar world had to offer. His father was a wealthy New York banker and stockbroker, and Juan attended the finest private schools. There, and later at Yale, he kept company with bluebloods such as Cornelius Whitney, Percy Rockefeller, and two of Cornelius Vanderbilt's sons.

Flying and aircraft seem to have first impressed Trippe — indelibly — at age ten, when his father took him to see an air race around the Statue of Liberty between Wilbur Wright and Glenn Curtis. From that time on, Trippe displayed a consuming passion for flight, although before his college years he could do little about it but build model airplanes. In 1917 he briefly dropped out of Yale to become a Navy bomber pilot in the Great War, and although he saw no action, his childhood love of flying was consummated at last. On his return to Yale, he joined with several friends to found the Yale Flying Club (later revived by Fred Smith of Federal Express fame).

Between the Wright brothers' flight at Kitty Hawk in 1903 and the close of World War I, few people saw commercial possibilities for aircraft. The airplane's role in the war, however, along with improvements in planes' capacity, safety, speed, and endurance, led a few entrepreneurs to think otherwise. The first step

All entrepreneurs are motivated by a vision, but some think in broader terms than others. Juan Trippe's global strategy for Pan Am sent America on a flight around the world.

Ever seeking new thrills, Americans proved fickle in their continuing romance with speed. As early as 1915, they were beginning to raise their sights from the motorcar to the new technology of flight.

would be to carry the mails in order to earn income and demonstrate the airplane's safety. Only later would passenger service be added.

After graduation in 1920, Trippe worked for a time on Wall Street but soon found an opportunity to return to the air. In 1922 he bought seven war-surplus Navy seaplanes for $500 apiece and launched his first airline, a charter service that ferried socialites (not yet the jet set!) between New York and various East Coast resorts. Trippe joined with Whitney, Rockefeller, and William Vanderbilt in 1925 to form Eastern Air Transport to bid on an important mail contract. The company hoped to carry mail by air between New York and Boston under the provisions of the recently passed Kelly Act, which had authorized the U.S. Postal Service to subcontract domestic airmail to private businesses. Trippe prepared for the bid by learning everything he could about aviation economics and by grilling friends in other businesses about cost accounting and management control systems. In the end a less subtle technique turned the trick: to secure the bid, Trippe negotiated a merger with a rival bidder, Colonial Air Transport, and won the contract. Colonial began service in 1926, with Trippe as managing director.

Although Colonial's business proved profitable, Trippe was anxious to spread his wings over wider territory. On a test flight he landed in Cuba, where he promptly took advantage of the opportunity to meet the island's president. Trippe wasted no time in securing "a simple two- or three-page letter" that granted him exclusive landing rights for commercial flights to Cuba. (Years later, Trippe would admit to detesting his first name, given him by his mother in honor of her favorite aunt, Juanita; but the name proved useful to Juan in negotiating landing rights throughout Central and South America.)

When the Colonial partnership fell apart in 1927, Trippe found other investors for a new company, Aviation Corporation of America (AVCO), to exploit the route between Key West and Havana. Once again Trippe headed off competitive threats by negotiating merger agreements with potential rivals. One of these, a group that included war heroes Eddie Rickenbacker and Hap Arnold, had taken the name Pan American Airways, Incorporated. As part of the deal, AVCO became a holding company that owned Pan Am, which in turn became the operating company that ran the airmail service. At the same time, Trippe, age twenty-eight, became president of Pan Am.

At first progress was slow for the new company. To be sure, the airmail business was reasonably lucrative, but getting passenger travel started was another matter. Many people balked at the prospect of flying over water; Pan Am employees often had to offer free rides to spur usage. One paying customer was Al Capone, who, on his way to Havana, reportedly told a Pan Am ticket agent, "Better see it's a *safe* plane. If anything happens to us, it won't be so healthy for you."

Trippe's college cronies, as well as federal airmail legislation, were again common denominators on his next coup. Through a family friend of his old roommate, Trippe gained access in 1928 to Andrew Mellon, a member of the fabulously wealthy Pittsburgh family who also happened to be the United States' secretary of the treasury. Mellon arranged for Trippe to work with Pennsylvania congressman Clyde Kelly in the drafting of the statute governing federal international airmail. The ensuing legislation empowered the postmaster general to award contracts on the basis of the bidder best able to "perform the services required to the best advantage of the government." Since Trippe knew the Caribbean air routes better than anyone alive and was rumored to be a consultant to the government on international air travel, few observers were surprised when the first two contracts under the Kelly Act went to Pan Am. That Trippe came in with the maximum bid allowed by law and still got the contracts lends credence to rumors of his inside influence.

Once Trippe secured this advantage, his business grew rapidly. In quick succession Pan Am won other major routes in the Caribbean, and from there Trippe expanded his operations throughout Latin America in the late twenties and early thirties, building on his reputation, the growing scale of his operations, and his superb negotiating skills. Charles Lindbergh was appointed Pan Am's technical adviser and piloted the company's first passenger flight over Latin America in February 1929. Trippe and his wife, as well as Mrs. Lindbergh, were along for this three-and-a-half-day sojourn over Cuba, the Yucatan, British Honduras, Nicaragua, Costa Rica, and Panama.

When he announced plans to offer service across the Pacific in 1932, Trippe had no serious rivals with the resources and political clout necessary to manage such an undertaking. Regular service to the Philippines began in 1935, while regularly scheduled flights to the Asian mainland via Pan Am's China Clipper, due to start in the late 1930s, had to be delayed because of the war. Not to be deterred by war in the Pacific, Trippe opened service to Europe in 1939, to Cairo in 1941, to India in 1942, and into China from the West in 1943.

By the end of World War II, Pan Am had established in piecemeal fashion a

In 1928 Pan Am's first scheduled passenger flight, on a Fokker F–7 just like this one, took off for Havana from Key West. Pan Am's president, Juan Trippe, had been using the planes to carry the mail and had secured exclusive landing rights in Cuba.

Quarters were cramped in Pan Am's ten-seater planes, but the company did its best to make passengers comfortable.

After a bumpy stretch in the 1960s, Pan Am made a comeback in 1970, introducing the Boeing 747 with service between New York and London.

Today Americans take air travel for granted. Like Boston's Logan, pictured here, airports all over the country provide terminals for a multitude of national and international carriers.

government-sanctioned monopoly in international air travel: no other American carrier flew international routes. As contemporaries put it, Pan Am had become the government's "chosen instrument" in competition against foreign airlines backed by foreign governments.

But it was not to last. Immediately after the war, the logic of this position — which Trippe vigorously supported — faltered. Although most of the world's competing airlines had been destroyed and the ones that remained were no match for Pan Am, it was not long before competition flared. In 1945 Howard Hughes of TWA persuaded Congress to allow his company to fly across the Atlantic. Shortly thereafter, United Airlines began service to Hawaii, and as European and Asian carriers recovered, Trippe found himself presiding over a declining empire.

His early successes perhaps fed an unappealing character trait in Trippe: an arrogance that blinded him to the growth of rival international carriers in the 1950s and 1960s. Although Pan Am had emerged from World War II as the world's largest airline, Trippe contributed to the company's slow decline by failing to respond to his competitors' new strategies or to develop sound business practices or management controls. Trippe made little serious effort to resist the decline of Pan Am by increasing its competitiveness. Indeed, his temperament was more suited to exploring and opening new territories for air travel and to wheeling and dealing on a grand scale with the world's elite decision-makers than to running an established business. With the onslaught of competition, Trippe's great negotiating skills proved less effectual.

Still worse was his refusal to professionalize the management of the company. According to one account, his associates

> seldom knew what he was about to do. At staff meetings it was his practice to pull a few scribbled notes from his pocket and without warning announce the launching of a new project — whether it was to purchase a different aircraft or to extend operations across a new sea. Often the notes disappeared directly into a wastebasket at his feet, leaving no official record behind. To a remarkable degree, as one associate remarked, "he carried Pan American in his mind."

And worst of all was his infatuation with increasing the capacity and scale of Pan Am's operations. By the late 1950s, most of the desirable routes for international travel had been developed, and competition on those routes was becoming more fierce. Trippe simply failed to recognize this reality. In the early 1960s, Pan Am had placed the first substantial order for the largest and most dazzling aircraft of the day, the Boeing 747. When the planes were delivered in 1968 and 1969, Pan Am had no prospects for filling them with passengers, and the company's decline, long in the making, began to accelerate. By then, however, Trippe was no longer around to cope with the consequences of his decision. Speaking to Pan Am's annual meeting of stockholders in 1968, Trippe surprised the audience — including the executives in attendance — by announcing his impending retirement at age sixty-nine. Other managers would be left to cope with the airline's grave financial crisis. In September 1980 Trippe suffered a massive cerebral hemorrhage and lapsed into a coma. He died in April 1981.

While there is no quintessential entrepreneur, Trippe possessed a surprising number of the qualities that often characterize the breed. As an opportunist, he was never reluctant to exploit personal and family ties. (One was his wife, the daughter of a Wall Street financier and sister of Edward Stettinius, who rose to the chairmanship of U.S. Steel and later became secretary of state.) His restlessness drove him to personally scout the globe for prime landing spots and key routes. More than this, Trippe was a visionary, not only one of the first to see the commercial possibilities of air flight but also the originator of an international and then a global strategy. As a result, Pan Am was the first American airline to provide service throughout Central and South America, to fly the Pacific, and to offer flights literally around the world. But for Trippe such strategic success contained the seeds of failure. Like the mythological Icarus, whose hubris caused him to fly too high and perish, Trippe remained sanguine as competition eventually challenged his empire in the international arena.

During Trippe's tenure at Pan Am, the airline industry was transformed from a small-scale, novel, and somewhat risky form of transportation to a major industry dominating long-distance travel. In 1926, the year Trippe became head of Pan Am, domestic airlines logged roughly 14,000 revenue miles; by his retirement in 1968 they were flying more than 1.7 million aircraft and 87.5 million passenger miles per year.

Airlines are still the best answer to a long entrepreneurial search for the safest, fastest, and cheapest means of moving goods and people — but surely not the last.

IV

Made in America

AMERICANS have long shown a special ability to fashion the raw materials of the earth and sea into the artifacts of civilization. Some of the entrepreneurs who found a better way of making things — Samuel Slater, Samuel Colt, Andrew Carnegie, Henry Ford — have become American legends. But others whose contributions were equally important — Henry Leland, Arthur Vining, Joe Engelberger — are barely known or remembered.

The history of American manufacturing is a complex and fascinating story, and one which explains much of this nation's rise to worldwide industrial prominence. One can survey a good bit of this past on a single day's drive through eastern Massachusetts. A few miles to the north of Boston, a resurrected version of the Saugus Iron Works, built in 1644 by John Winthrop, Jr., features a primitive furnace, an operating water wheel that powers forging and slitting apparatus, and a resident smithy who pounds out nails one by one. Twenty miles northwest of Saugus lies the city of Lowell, the once great textile manufacturing center. Much of Lowell was recently transformed into a major National Park Service project to display this heritage, but the city also serves as the home for a variety of high technology firms.

Completing the triangle — directly south of Lowell and east of Boston — is Framingham, home of a giant General Motors manufacturing plant, where automobile chassis flow through the line like Ford's Model T's decades earlier

In the 1820s, this bucolic scene in Green Brier, West Virginia, was typical in a nation that was still dominantly rural and agricultural. The first factories to be built were anomalies, "machines in the garden" that only hinted at the onset of industrialization.

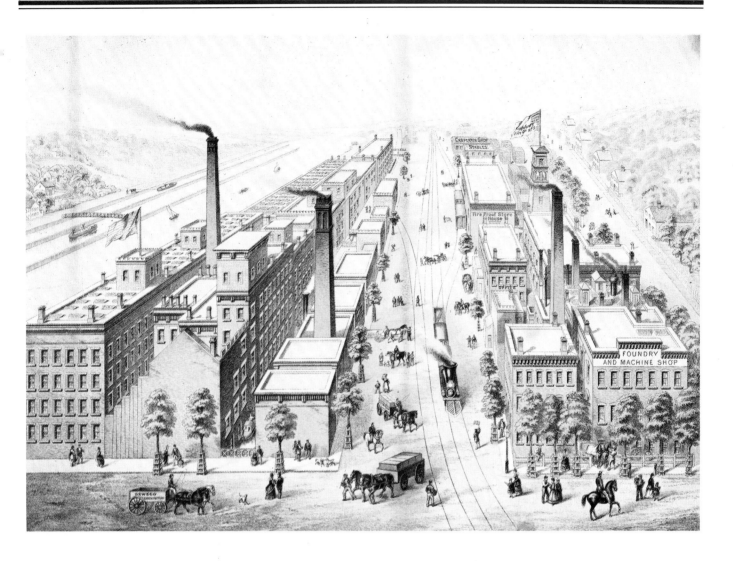

In less than a century, advances in technology and transportation made the factory town a commonplace sight, and America rose to worldwide industrial prominence.

but are assembled by both robots and human workers. Finally, crossing Route 128, the "silicon valley" of the East, one may visit the Massachusetts Institute of Technology in Cambridge, a center of research and development in robotics, computer science, and many other forms of applied technology.

Such a view of the evolution of American manufacturing methods seems hurried, uneven, and even awe-inspiring. Yet it is not a perspective much distorted. Nearly three and a half centuries have passed since Winthrop's enterprise began operating, but most of the significant changes in the way goods have been manufactured in America have occurred in the last century or so. "In the Bible Commonwealth, the Saugus iron works," noted its historian, "stood out as atypical, anachronistic and wonderful." Even the early textile mills of Samuel Slater in Pawtucket, Rhode Island, or of Francis Cabot Lowell in Waltham and Lowell, Massachusetts, were "machines in the garden," strange manifestations of industrialization in a society still overwhelmingly rural and agricultural.

While the machinery at these mills was "modern," complicated, and capable of producing textiles at an unprecedented rate, it was temperamental and, more important, made and repaired at the hands of mechanics who lived and worked on-site. If machines were to produce thousands of different products for millions, or "masses," of Americans, something more was needed. Parts had to be reproduced precisely to make them interchangeable, and for this, machines had to be developed that could fashion other machines.

It was not until the mid-1800s that entrepreneurs made the first significant gains in this direction, contributing to what became known as the "American system" of manufacturing and what ultimately evolved into a full-fledged system of "mass production." Thus it has not been much more than a century since the United States rose to industrial prominence in the world, largely on the basis of its production technology.

The career of one entrepreneur, Henry Leland, reflects the revolutionary quality of this change. During his early years, Leland put in stints at the Springfield Armory in Massachusetts and Colt's armory in Hartford, both seedbeds of American manufacturing techniques, before transferring to the Brown & Sharpe Company of Providence, a firm that was a pioneer in the use of machine tools and the development of interchangeable parts. In his later years, as automobiles became the apotheosis of mass production technology, Leland became the driving force behind the development of the Oldsmobile and the Cadillac. Leland's life and contributions spanned an impressive era. More than this, the mass production system was largely dependent upon the technological progress made by lesser-known entrepreneurs such as Leland.

Such progress was seldom smooth and easy, however. In small arms manufacture, for example, interchangeability came well before it was justified by economics, because soldiers welcomed the ability to replace gun parts in the midst of battle. Nor was Colt the only entrepreneur in the business to become alternately destitute and rich. The rapid pace of development in this industry as in others — from bicycles and aluminum to automobiles and robots — could make even the most innovative entrepreneur obsolete.

The pace of technological change first quickened in the West during the second half of the eighteenth century, when England experienced the first faint stirrings of what later would be called the "industrial revolution," a term popularized by British historian Arnold Toynbee. The phrase is really a misnomer, however, since the changes embraced every aspect of society, not only industry. Nor was it a true revolution but rather a process that began slowly, gathered momentum and accelerated sharply in the 1760s and afterward, and continued to our time and is still in progress. Were it not rather cumbersome, a better term might be "societal evolution," although that doesn't capture the flavor of the development. Complex and convoluted though it was, the process was clear enough: it involved the application of imagination and energy to the manufacturing of goods, which required the marshaling of labor and capital toward the end of mass production. In England it started in mining and smelting early in the century and soon was applied to the first of the new "industries" to be refashioned: textiles.

The names of those Englishmen involved are familiar to all concerned with the process of industrialization. In 1733 John Kay invented a device that enabled a weaver to work on larger sections of cloth, which he called the "flying shuttle." Before he could do much about it, however, Kay was driven into exile by laborers fearful the shuttle would put them out of work. In 1769 Richard Arkwright, an itinerant barber and dealer in human hair, developed a spinning frame powered by a water wheel. The following year James Hargreaves came up with his "spinning jenny," an improvement over the old spinning wheel. In 1779 Samuel Crompton, a weaver, combined the frame and the jenny into the "spinning mule." Reverend Edmund Cartwright's power loom, driven initially

In the early days of manufacturing, a single factory might produce a variety of goods for a wide range of customers clamoring for new and better devices.

by horses and then by steam engines, was patented in 1785. Others, too, originated, refined, and perfected devices to expedite the production of textiles. These men were not scientists, and most were not what we today might consider businessmen. As we noted, the movement from handcraft to machines came slowly; but within the span of a single lifetime, English textiles moved inexorably into the industrial age.

Arkwright was one of those able to assay the move from tinkerer to inventor to entrepreneur. In 1771, at the urging and financial backing of inventor and businessman Jedediah Strutt, he constructed what might be considered the first textile factory, at Cromford in Derbyshire, in the process also giving Strutt claim to the title of the original modern venture capitalist. Arkwright's mill was devoted solely to the spinning of yarn, and he was a master at it. But he and Strutt had to spend some $60,000 before making a sound start.

The machines were carved from wood and hand cast from iron, and they were powered by a water wheel. The labor force was comprised of children gathered from the countryside. The market, first local, soon spread throughout the nation and overseas as well. It happened quickly; in 1771 Arkwright had 300 workers and was lobbying Parliament for tariff protection, which he obtained in 1774. Within seven years the number employed in his string of mills had grown to nearly 1,000. Arkwright was knighted, and he and Strutt were wealthy and famous — and secretive. The basic patents ran out in 1785, which meant that anyone would be free to copy the designs and start rival operations. But first they would have to study them, and Arkwright did all he could to prevent this. Visitors to his facilities were carefully screened, and even then, few were permitted in the work areas.

In an eighteenth-century version of today's spy capers, attempts were made to steal the secrets. Since the former American Colonies had been a prime market for yarn, many of the plots originated there, backed by would-be manufacturers eager to create a domestic industry. Indeed, the Pennsylvania legislature offered £100 to anyone able to "design" a workable textile machine — with no questions asked. American agents would attempt to bribe British textile workers, going so far as to purchase machines and have them sent to Paris, to be shipped back to the United States in crates labeled "glassware." Some of Arkwright's workers and others conversant with his techniques tried to slip out of the country with plans and models, but customs agents and the Royal Navy managed to intercept all who tried. Britain was well on its way to becoming workshop of the world, and the government well realized that this status was based upon the lead in new technology, which had to be safeguarded.

Samuel Slater and the Seeds of American Manufacturing

SAMUEL SLATER, a management trainee at one of Arkwright's installations, was among those considering making a run for it. The son of a timber merchant and real estate investor who was a neighbor and business associate of Strutt's, Slater was able to obtain a position at the Arkwright works, performing bookkeeping, ciphering, and some administrative duties. It was 1782, and Slater was fourteen years old and well positioned to rise rapidly in the new industry. This he did, learning all he could of textile technology under terms of a seven-year indenture he signed with Arkwright.

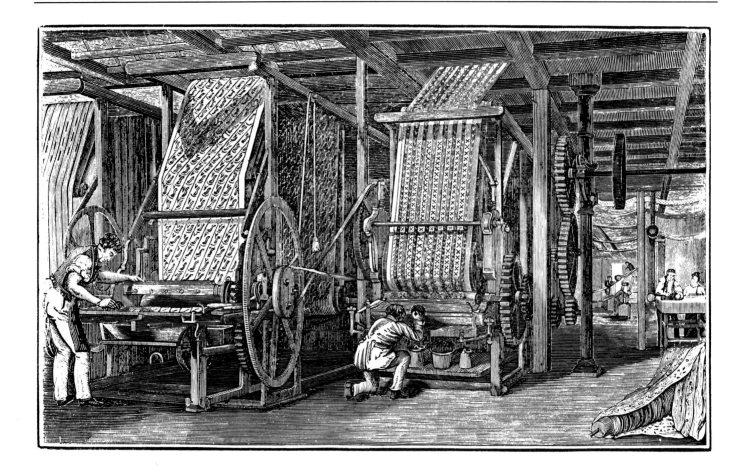

Slater had a knack for things mechanical, a natural talent that would later be seen in such individuals as Samuel Colt, Thomas Edison, Henry Leland, and Henry Ford. He lived in Strutt's house and went to the plant every day, even after church services on Sundays, to work on the machines and attempt to improve their performance. Ambitious as well as intelligent, he would have liked to strike out on his own. The prospects were good: others in his position had done so, and there were hundreds of factories churning out yarn within a hundred miles of the Arkwright plant.

Twenty-one years old in 1789 when he completed his indenture, Slater possessed skills, technical knowledge, and even some capital he had inherited after his father's death in 1782. When he came across an advertisement placed by the Pennsylvania legislature, he became determined to go to the United States, obtain additional financing there, and start a yarn factory of his own. He went about preparing for the move deliberately and cautiously, starting out by asking Arkwright to permit him a role in supervising the erection of one of his new factories, which was granted. Slater watched, learned, and memorized, intending to use this knowledge in America. Atomic spies of the 1950s operated in much the same way. Times change, but the idea was the same.

It was to be done in secrecy. Slater drew up no plans, made no models, and told no one of his intentions. Soon he was ready for flight. He informed his mother he was making a trip to London, and, taking nothing with him but his indenture papers, he left Derbyshire. After a few days in London, he boarded a ship bound for New York, telling the customs people he was an agricultural laborer. It is not certain whether he was searched on departure. English stric-

Samuel Slater's machines for manufacturing cotton yarn were based on modern patents he'd brought from his native England. By 1830 factories like this one in Massachusetts were supplying both America and England with yarn and cloth, and textiles had emerged as the nation's leading industry.

A forerunner of the modern factory system, textile manufacturing was one of the first industries to benefit from the industrial revolution. Long before this mill in Adams, Massachusetts, was operating, advanced machinery was used to do the job of hundreds of workers.

tures against the emigration of skilled artisans and mechanics were on the books but not always carefully enforced.

Slater intended to go to Philadelphia to answer the advertisement, but when his ship docked in New York November 1789, he learned there were textile operations in that city and decided to make inquiries at some of them. At one of these, the New York Manufacturing Company, he obtained a job making yarn on what he recognized as outdated copies of English machines. Slater might have stayed on had he not soon learned about Moses Brown from the captain of a coastal packet. A wealthy retired Quaker merchant from Providence, Rhode Island, Brown had become interested in textiles and constructed a mill containing Arkwright-type equipment, but he was frustrated in attempts to manufacture cotton yarn sufficiently strong to be used by his weaving machines. Deciding to contact Brown, Slater wrote one of the more important letters in the history of American business:

New York, December 2d, 1789

Sir,

A few days ago I was informed that you wanted a manager of cotton spinning, etc., in which business I flatter myself that I can give the greatest satisfaction, in making machinery, making good yarn, either for stockings or twist, as any made in England, as I have had opportunity, and an oversight of Sir Richard Arkwright's works and in Mr. Strutt's mill upward of eight years. If you are not provided for, should be glad to serve you; though I am in the New York manufactory, and have been for three weeks since I arrived from England. But we have but one card, two machines, two spinning jennies, which I think are not worth using. My intention is to erect a perpetual card and spinning. If you please to drop a line respecting the amount of encouragement you wish to give, by favor of Captain Brown, you will much oblige, sir, your most obedient servant.

Samuel Slater

N.B. Please to direct me at No. 37, Golden Hill, New York.

This letter, innocent enough, contained a code phrase Slater believed Brown would be able to decipher; had he not been able to do so, Slater might have had to dismiss him as a dabbler not worth meeting. The reference was to the "perpetual card and spinning," meaning the Arkwright patents. Unlike the spinning jenny or Crompton's mule, the Arkwright equipment was superior for operating with continuous, rather than stop-and-start, motion. Slater was indicating that he knew how to create the most modern spinning machines and would do so for Brown under the proper circumstances.

Brown had no difficulty understanding just what it was Slater had to offer and fired back his response. He was "destitute of a person acquainted with water-frame spinning" and was prepared to make Slater a generous offer, assuming he was, as claimed, an expert in the field. Brown was willing to offer Slater all profits on operations after deducting costs of machinery, capital, and depreciation, and shrewdly appealed to what he discerned was Slater's pride and streak of vanity. "If the present situation does not come up with what thou wishes, and from thy knowledge of the business, can be ascertained of the advantages of the mills, so as to induce thee to come and work ours, and have the credit as well as the advantage of perfecting the first water-mill in America, we should be glad to engage thy care so long as they can be made profitable to both, and we can agree."

Slater accepted with alacrity and within a month was in Providence to survey the situation. What he found made him understand why Brown could afford to be so generous. Brown had accumulated a heterogeneous collection of ill-made and obsolete machines that were of little use. Hoping to salvage something from his investment, Brown urged Slater to make do with what he had but in the end gave in to Slater's demand that new machines be constructed. Under the agreement, Slater would receive nothing but room and board while he designed and several mechanics constructed devices based upon the Arkwright patents Slater had memorized.

Slater spent the winter setting down the plans for construction. These were completed by April, when he and Brown drew up a partnership agreement. At this point Brown withdrew in favor of his son-in-law, William Almy, and a cousin, Obadiah Brown, to form the company of Almy, Brown & Slater, and the three men set about constructing their factory. The work proceeded through the spring and summer and was completed by autumn 1790. After some failed trials, the carding machines were made to operate efficiently. On December 20, 1790, Slater produced cotton yarn in what might be said to have been America's first factory.

The expansion of American manufacturing had its darker side as well. These boys operating the machinery in a North Carolina textile factory in 1900 were among the thousands of children who formed a good part of the work force.

In the first ten months of operation, the mill turned out sufficient yarn to supply local home weavers with enough to produce almost 8,000 yards of cloth. Indeed, the market could not absorb so much product, and Almy, Brown & Slater were obliged to shut down operations for a while until demand caught up with supply and to seek markets elsewhere.

During 1791 and 1792, Slater taught his partners how to manage the business profitably by efficiently coordinating materials, machines, and labor and

keeping careful records for analysis. He had been tutored in these skills at Strutt's mill, and this contribution in Pawtucket was at least as important to the success of the mill as was Slater's technical knowledge.

Meanwhile, agents were dispatched to Salem, Baltimore, New York, and Philadelphia, where placements were made with little difficulty. Now the company faced the opposite problem: demand became so great the small mill couldn't produce sufficient yarn, and Slater was obliged to start construction on a larger facility nearby.

Unlike Francis Cabot Lowell — whose integrated textile factory of the next generation drew upon Slater's experiences — Slater utilized the labor of young boys, rather than daughters of local farmers, since this had been the practice at Arkwright's. As Lowell would do in his time, Moses Brown petitioned Secretary of the Treasury Alexander Hamilton to support a tariff on yarn to protect this infant American industry. If this were done, said Brown, the company would expand to the point where it could supply sufficient yarn for the entire nation. Impressed, Hamilton cited the mill in his famous "Report on Manufactures," in which he discussed "the manufactory at Providence [which] has the merit of being the first in introducing into the United States the celebrated cotton mill."

Brown did not receive his protection, but the mills thrived nonetheless. Like Arkwright, Slater tried to prevent others from imitating his machines, to little avail; other yarn mills sprang up in the area and then elsewhere. Slater's business prospered, however. At his death in 1835 he was worth more than $1.2 million, an enormous sum in that period. By that time, too, textiles had emerged as the nation's leading industry. In 1790, when Slater opened his mill, cotton production came to around 3,000 bales; in 1835 the output was in excess of 1 million. Samuel Slater was one of the two men who made this possible. The other was Eli Whitney, credited with having invented the cotton gin.

Samuel Colt and the American System

IN SLATER'S DAY, machine-making was still a long way — not so much in time as in method — from what became known as the "American system of manufactures." During the early days of the industrial revolution, machines were constructed by hand, from crude plans, and each was different from the others. Metal parts were forged by hand and wooden ones carved with care, and all were laboriously fitted together, always by trial and error. When one part broke, another would be forged or carved, while the machine sat idle. This was considered both natural and unavoidable. The pace of life was still slow, and businessmen were prepared to accept these inconveniences as part of the price that had to be paid for the incredible productivity of these new devices.

But not for long. Within a few years manufacturers became both accustomed to the wonders of mechanization and irritated by the now-perceived inefficiencies such practices engendered. The solution to the problem was uniform parts for identical machines, so that spares could be kept in an inventory and substituted whenever needed. This wasn't an original thought; the desirability of interchangeable parts was almost self-evident. Anyone working with machines soon realized just how important this could be.

In the mid-nineteenth century, Samuel Colt's Patent Fire Arms Manufacturing Company in Hartford, Connecticut, became the cradle of the "American system" of manufacturing, which relied on the use of machines to produce parts that could be used interchangeably.

Handcraft workers couldn't accomplish the feat. By the early nineteenth century, inventors and mechanics were coming to realize that, just as human beings had crafted machines for Arkwright, Slater, and Lowell, so in the next generation humans would have to design and create machines to develop other machines. This was a major leap. It would require imagination as well as technology.

For generations, American schoolchildren have been taught that Eli Whitney, whose name will forever be associated with the cotton gin, was also the originator of interchangeable parts manufacturing. Historians have recently relegated this notion to the realm of myth, although by 1801 Whitney was interchanging assembled musket locks (not lock pieces) for a government arms contract he was struggling to fulfill. Other inventor-businessmen performed better than Whitney, who may not have reached his goal but saw it clearly. After securing the arms deal in 1798, Whitney wrote, "One of my primary objects is to form the tools so the tools themselves shall fashion the work and give to each part its just proportion — which when once accomplished will give expedition, uniformity, and exactness to the whole." There was little doubt that the techniques would be developed and perfected and then transferred to other products, and indeed this is precisely what was happening. The fiery, colorful, and independent Samuel Colt was arguably the most important popularizer of the technique of employing interchangeable parts, in Europe as well as in the United States.

Colt was born in Connecticut in 1814. His father, Christopher, was a farmer who engaged in the West Indies trade and, failing in this, turned to the raising of silkworms. In time Christopher Colt would establish one of America's earliest silk mills, in Ware, Massachusetts. Here his son Samuel went to work when he was ten years old, happily leaving school to do so. Sam was no scholar; his spelling remained abominable throughout his life, and he found intellectual pursuits boring. But he had a quick wit, was imaginative, and discovered and cultivated an interest in chemistry and mechanics. Bored by the sedentary life in Connecticut, he went to sea in 1830 at the age of sixteen, bound for London and Calcutta.

According to one version of the story, while in England Colt visited the Tower of London, where he saw a display of several repeating firearms, among them a revolving pistol invented in 1813 by Elisha Collier of Boston. Colt pondered the design while aboard ship and fashioned a crude wooden model. Others claim Colt got the idea from watching the action of the ship's wheel, realizing that if a pistol had a cylinder with spaces for several balls and charges, which would revolve after each shot, it would be a weapon far superior to any in use. In any case, in 1831 he returned to America with a model of his "revolver" and a desire to develop it further, obtain a patent, and go into production — but little in the way of funds.

In order to finance these efforts and make a living, Colt hired himself out as a traveling lecturer and "practical chemist." Calling himself "the celebrated Dr. S. Coult of New York, London, and Calcutta," he toured the United States and Canada for the next three months, giving demonstrations involving the use of nitrous oxide — "laughing gas" — which would be administered to amazed and amused audiences, who paid fifty cents a head for the privilege.

With some of his earnings, Colt employed John Pearson, a Baltimore mechanic, to produce a model of his revolver. With this in hand, he obtained patents in the United States, France, and the United Kingdom, and in 1836 sought financial support to begin production. A cousin, Dudley Selden, and several others invested $200,000 in what became the Patent Arms Manufacturing Company, located in Paterson, New Jersey, where Colt prepared to manufacture a five-shot revolver, and aggressively sought government contracts.

The going was slow. The pistols did poorly at a competition staged at West Point and were rejected by Colonel George Bonford, head of the Ordnance Department, as being too complicated and bulky. More disappointments followed, but finally army officers fighting the Seminoles in Florida became interested in the six-shooter. Colonel William S. Harney ordered 100 revolvers saying, "I am . . . *confident* that they are the only things that will finish the *infernal war.*" In the summer of 1840, Colonel Bonford ordered 100 repeating carbines at $40 each; but by then Patent Arms was so bogged down in debt that it no longer could continue, and Colt closed it down two years later.

Colt had few prospects, and friends suggested he use his government connections to obtain a post. He vehemently rejected the idea, writing to a relative:

> To be a clerk or an office holder under the pay and patronage of Government, is to stagnate ambition. . . . However inferior in wealth I may be to the many who surround me I would not exchange for their treasures the satisfaction I have in knowing I have done what has never before been accomplished by man. . . . Life is a thing to be enjoyed . . . it is the only certainty.

To underscore this he added, "I would rather be at the head of a louse than at the tail of a lyon! . . . If I cant be first I wont be second in anything."

Rather than seek employment, Colt turned to other inventions. He had already devised a waterproof cartridge and did some work on underwater batteries that seemed promising. Then there was a device to blow up enemy ships by means of torpedolike mines. The government was sufficiently interested in this to fund experiments to the extent of $6,000, but although the mine was dem-

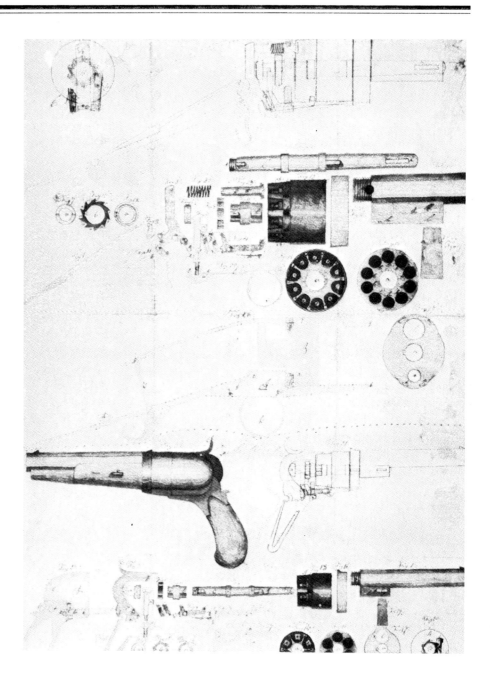

Colt's 1835 patent drawing for a repeating pistol. Modified, the "revolver" became standard equipment in the Mexican War of 1846.

onstrated successfully, both the army and Congress rejected it. Representative John Quincy Adams called it "an unChristian contraption." Colt fared better with his waterproof cartridges, receiving sufficient small contracts to keep him going.

There were also forays into related areas. Colt met Samuel F. B. Morse, who, as we will see later, was lobbying for congressional support for his telegraph, and Colt supplied Morse with the batteries and wire for the line between Washington and Baltimore. Encouraged, Colt established the New York and Offing Magnetic Telegraph Association and planned to erect a line from Long Island to Manhattan and then on to New Jersey. Little came of this, however, and he once again turned his attention to ordnance.

Orders for his revolvers began arriving in a steady stream, but not from the army, which Colt had been convinced would be his prime market. Rather,

Colt's dream of producing inter-changeable parts for firearms was fully realized only in the twentieth century, when America mobilized for war. By World War II, this ma-chine-gun factory could turn out tens of thousands of guns every week.

westerners saw in his five-chamber weapons what Colonel Harney did, namely a near-perfect weapon for fighting the Indians. Using bows and large supplies of arrows, Indians could keep up an almost continuous fire while riding their horses. A rifle or pistol that needed reloading while its users galloped at high speed in pursuit or retreat was of little use. The Texas Rangers particularly liked Colt's five-shooter. In 1844 sixteen Rangers clashed with eighty Comanches along the Pedernales River and killed half of them with Colt firearms. Ranger Captain Samuel H. Walker wrote to Colt: "Without your pistols we would not have had the confidence to have undertaken such daring adventures. . . . With improvements I think they can be rendered the most perfect weapon in the World for light mounted troops. . . . The people throughout Texas are anxious to procure your pistols."

The Mexican War broke out in 1846, and the thirty-two-year-old inventor, who, despite increasing business, confessed he was "as poor as a churchmouse," sought a captaincy in a rifle regiment as a way out of his financial troubles. Fortunately for his business, he was not accepted: he soon received an order for 1,000 revolvers, which he subcontracted to Eli Whitney, Jr., who had inherited his father's operation. Captain Walker also wanted pistols — heavier ones, a .44 caliber six-shooter. Colt obliged, producing the Walker gun, which enjoyed tremendous success. Encouraged, he borrowed $5,000 from another cousin and friends and opened a new factory in Hartford, Connecticut, and started to plan for production.

Orders for the Walker gun were pouring in, from not only Texas but California as well, now that the gold rush was under way. Colt realized that they could not be filled unless improvements in manufacture were achieved. In addition, like other arms makers, he was intrigued with the idea of interchangeable parts. "With hand labour it is not possible to obtain that amount of uniformity, or accuracy in the several parts, which is so desirable" he would write in 1851. "Nor could the quality required be produced by manual labor."

Knowing he would need expert mechanics and recognizing his own deficiencies in management, Colt hired one of the best in both areas, Elisha K. Root, and placed him in charge of operations. For years Root had been manager at the Collins Company, for which he designed and manufactured machines to turn out farm instruments. Root had turned down other jobs in the ordnance area, including one at the Springfield Armory. Now Colt offered to double his salary, or offer any "such compensation as you think fair and reasonable," but more important give him a free hand at the factory. Intrigued by the challenge, Root accepted the post. He designed the new Colt Armory, created machines, hired other mechanics (including Horace Lord, the leading machinist at the Whitney Armory), and trained the labor force, while Colt provided overall direction and sought sales. The business prospered, and Colt became wealthy at last; at the time of his death in 1862, there were more than 1,500 workers at Colt's armory, and he was considered one of the nation's richest men.

But he had not been able to create true interchangeable parts for his revolvers. The parts were molded and machined, fitted, and then stamped with a serial number. After hardening they were reassembled, with care taken that all had the same number. "There is nothing that cannot be produced by machinery," Colt had claimed, and he had gone far to demonstrate this. But Gage Stickney, one of Colt's superintendents, was skeptical regarding interchangeability: "I have heard of it, but I defy a man to show me a case."

Colt's armory achieved a high degree of uniformity, largely thanks to Root's work. It became the showcase for what by the 1850s was coming to be known as the "American system." In 1851 Colt went to the Crystal Palace Exhibition in London to demonstrate his wares and set up a factory to safeguard against imitators in the European market. The catalogue description claimed that his rifles were manufactured so that "the various parts [were] made to interchange," but this wasn't so. Colt delivered a paper entitled "On the Application of Machinery to the Manufacture of Rotating Chambered-Breech Fire-Arms and the Peculiarities of Those Arms," which was more to the point of his achievement. Even so, the British were impressed. To them, the American system meant the use of machines to manufacture goods, and in his time it was almost synonymous with Colt's work.

Boots, brogans, slippers, gaiters — unlimited footwear could be yours for the asking, thanks to American ingenuity and know-how. By the 1890s, America's manufacturing prowess made it the world leader in mass production, having surpassed all other industrialized nations in just a few decades.

This is not to denigrate Colt's achievements. No businessman in his lifetime did more in this regard or contributed so much to the continuing attempt to create interchangeability, and the advance he represented over people such as Samuel Slater was impressive. Slater couldn't conceive of interchangeable parts in 1790; Colt was reaching for it a half century later.

Samuel Slater, Eli Whitney, and Samuel Colt were inventor-businessmen, which is to say they were direct lineal forerunners of many of today's entrepreneurial scientists, who are pioneering in electronics and biochemistry. That they took this path was more the result of necessity than choice, for they lived at a time when the same individual had to develop a new product or service, raise funds for development and manufacture, and then create the organization to bring it to potential customers. But change was in the air; an ever more complex society demanded specialization of functions, and hosts of individuals with new ideas saw their shortcomings in making them commercial successes. Like Samuel Colt in the late 1840s, they had the sense to leave management of that to others.

Andrew Carnegie and the Age of Steel

ANDREW CARNEGIE entered the steel business at a time when the metal's use was already great and soon to become still more widespread. He foresaw that railroads would convert from iron to steel, which was stronger and less brittle, for their rails, and later that skyscrapers and bridges would use the superior metal for their infrastructures. More than this, Carnegie carried the logic of high efficiency in metals processing much further than anyone in the world.

Carnegie's life was an enactment of the success story rehashed dozens of times by one of America's best-selling authors, Horatio Alger. From humble, poverty-stricken beginnings in Scotland, Carnegie grew to build an empire of the steel industry and become one of America's wealthiest citizens. He was born in the village of Dunfermline in 1835, the son of a relatively prosperous linen weaver named William. Within seven years, however, the first steam-

When Andrew Carnegie entered the steel business in 1872, the metal's use was already widespread. Carnegie became the leading steel manufacturer in the world by devising ways to make his processing plants more efficient.

driven mill was opened in the village, throwing William out of work. As Britain strained under the weight of the "hungry forties," William and several other weavers joined the Chartist movement, which not only faltered but failed to put food on the table. Her husband broken and despondent, Margaret Carnegie took charge of the family, bringing in a modest income by cobbling and tending a store. Two of her sisters had immigrated to the United States in 1840 and had since sent back increasingly encouraging reports. So in 1848, the year Europe was rocked by a series of revolutions and Karl Marx published the *Communist Manifesto,* the Carnegies — William, Margaret, Andrew, who was thirteen, and his brother Tom, five, boarded ship for America.

Scottish friends and acquaintances in the States softened the shock of transplantation for the family. Margaret resumed cobbling, and Andrew was hired to work in a textile mill at $1.20 a week by a Scot named Blackstock. The job consisted of dipping bobbins into hot oil and firing the factory boiler, and was unpleasant to say the least, yet Carnegie reveled in his first gainful employment. Years later he wrote, "I have made millions since, but none of these gave me as much happiness as my first week's earnings."

In this group picture taken at the White House in 1863, Andrew Carnegie (*far left*) poses with three other members of the power elite. Next to him (*left to right*) are famed political reformer William Jennings Bryan; J. J. Hill, president of the Northern Pacific Railroad; and John Mitchell, president of the United Mine Workers of America.

Carnegie was diligent and hardworking and was rewarded with occasional stints of office work, which exposed him to accounting methods. He promptly expanded his knowledge by attending a night class in double-entry bookkeeping after fourteen-hour shifts at the mill. Soon his upward climb accelerated.

Horatio Alger's stories were more than just parables encouraging hard work and virtue; success came from a combination of "pluck" *and* "luck." Carnegie had plenty of the former, and during the next few critical years, he was blessed with an ample portion of the latter as well. The first break came when David Brooks, the manager of O'Reilly's Telegraph in Pittsburgh, hired Andrew as a messenger boy. As Carnegie later wrote, "My Good Fairy Found me in a Cellar." His weekly wage doubled and then climbed to $4 when he was appointed full-time telegrapher in 1851.

More than this, the telegraph brought Carnegie to the epicenter of commerce and business. Tapping out and receiving messages, telegraphers of the day were clued in to how business was conducted, where it was moving, and who its key players were. Edison had a similar early education, as did a host of other upstart entrepreneurs. All of this Carnegie absorbed with enthusiasm, at the same time becoming a staunch advocate of capitalism American-style. "I am to have $4.00 a week and a good prospect of getting more," he wrote back to the old country. "In Scotland, I would have been a poor weaver all my days, but here, I can surely do something better. . . . If I don't it will be my own fault, for anyone can get along in this country."

The next opportunity followed quickly. In 1852 Tom Scott, head of the western division of the Pennsylvania Railroad, offered Carnegie a post as his personal secretary and telegrapher. Carnegie didn't hesitate. The wage of $35 per month was attractive, but more than this Carnegie recognized that working

This 1886 engraving gives an apocalyptic glimpse of the converters at work, making Bessemer steel at a Pittsburgh factory.

An awe-inspiring look inside the Carnegie factory in 1905. These gargantuan "ladles" poured molten steel into huge molds that were conveyed on moving flatcars.

A train passing over a railroad bridge offers a lesson in entrepreneurial insight. Having made a fortune producing steel for rails in the late 1800s, Carnegie found a new market in the construction of bridges in the early twentieth century.

at Tom Scott's side at the great Pennsy would provide an education far superior to even the telegraph business.

He was right. Seven years later, when Scott was promoted to the vice presidency, Carnegie was well enough seasoned to take over his boss's job, and five years after that, Scott offered his protégé the superintendentship of the railroad. This time Carnegie declined, choosing instead to set out on his own as an "investor."

During the next seven years, Carnegie completed the education upon which he would draw in becoming the world's greatest steel maker and its richest citizen. Under Scott, he had learned the importance of careful cost accounting, a practice in which the railroads had pioneered. With millions of dollars of moving stock, hundreds of employees, and thousands of passengers, the railroads — and the Pennsy was the largest — were impelled to keep careful records in order to make operations, investment, and personnel decisions or even to determine if profits were being made. This realization Carnegie would later forge into one of the basic rules of business: "Watch the costs and the profits will take care of themselves."

Scott had also initiated young Carnegie into the wonders of nineteenth-century investment. In 1856 he loaned Carnegie $600 and encouraged him to invest it in the Adams Express Company. Always diffident to his mentor, Carnegie made the move despite his almost innate revulsion toward debt but was soon rewarded with a $10 dividend check. "Here's the goose that lays the golden eggs," he exclaimed, amazed that earnings could come without toil. Similar investments, and rewards, followed. In 1862 Carnegie borrowed $1,250 to invest in the Keystone Bridge Company; this yielded dividends of $7,500 a year later, by which time his income from such investments had climbed to $45,000. Once when asked how he was, Carnegie replied, "I'm rich, I'm rich!"

It was hardly all luck. Conflict of interest laws still lay far in the future in Carnegie's day, and the executives at the Pennsylvania made it a common practice to exploit their inside information at the railroad. Pennsylvania railroad men made Keystone Bridge investments with the knowledge that their company would soon award generous contracts to Keystone for railroad bridges. Eventually Carnegie grew weary of this trade, sensing that the line between solid investing, which he believed in, and speculation, which he purportedly scorned, sometimes grew too thin. Liquidating his holdings, Carnegie entered the steel business in 1872 by investing $250,000 to construct a modern plant south of Pittsburgh.

Again the timing was propitious. The next year a severe panic shook Wall Street, sweeping away many investments in its tide — but not Carnegie's. More important, railroads such as the Pennsylvania were making the conversion to iron rails, and other uses for the metal were blossoming. (Perhaps to reinforce his ties with the Pennsy, Carnegie named his plant the J. Edgar Thomson Steel Works.) On the other hand, capital requirements were extremely high in the business, and Carnegie was a novice. He would need something special to survive.

His railroad experience told Carnegie that there were serious flaws in the way the steel business was conducted. For one thing, different processes were fragmented: smelting was conducted at some facilities, forging and rolling at others, cutting and even founding elsewhere. As Lowell had done with textile spinning, weaving, and dying — but on a much grander and more complicated scale — Carnegie would integrate all the processes of steel manufacture under a single roof.

Steel producers were also behind railroad managers in cost accounting. Most continued to rely on simple double-entry bookkeeping, a method that had not changed since the Italians had devised it for their merchant trade in the thirteenth century. Some plants simply divided expenses by total output in order to determine profits, a method that gave no indication of overall operating costs, much less those for specific processes, equipment, or personnel. "I insisted on such a system of weighing and accounting being introduced throughout our works as would enable us to know what our cost was for each process," Carnegie later explained.

Cost considerations spurred Carnegie toward practices that astonished, perplexed, and angered industry experts. Hiring Alexander Holly, an expert on the Bessemer process, Carnegie became the leading advocate of "hard driving," the practice of running equipment and men full-out for maximum productivity. While other steel makers would have winced at burning out a furnace in weeks or months instead of years, or scrapping new equipment long before it was obsolete in order to replace it with state-of-the-art models, Carnegie charted cost and output numbers and rejoiced. His first ton of steel had been produced at a cost of $56. By 1900 the cost was $11.50 and Carnegie had profits of $40 million a year. In one special furnace, named Lucy after Tom Carnegie's wife, his practices increased output from 13,361 to 100,000 tons per year. Raw materials flowed into Carnegie's carefully designed plant, and finished products poured out at the other end with almost balletlike precision.

Carnegie integrated operations during the late nineteenth century, acquiring quarries and mines to insure a steady supply of raw materials and constructing open-hearth furnaces and coke furnaces to update and integrate production processes. As demand for steel rails waned, other uses for the metal increased. In the 1880s Carnegie steel was used to build the first skyscraper, Chicago's Home Insurance Building, and the Brooklyn Bridge. Carnegie's position seemed unassailable, although many a rival tried to merge or enter into cartellike agreements with the steel master. "I can make steel cheaper than any of you and undersell you," he once told them. "The market is mine whenever I want to take it. I see no reason why I should present you all my profits."

Carnegie was even successful at fending off merger attempts by J. P. Morgan. Only long after his partners had grown weary did Carnegie acquiesce to the U.S. Steel merger and turn to his next occupation — giving away his hard-won fortune. "The man who dies rich, dies disgraced," he had said in 1889. And he meant it: before his death in 1919, he had donated about $350 million to philanthropic causes.

Henry Leland: Interchangeable Parts and the Auto Industry

HENRY MARTYN LELAND was one of several generations of farm boys who went on to become industrial tycoons. Like Carnegie, Leland helped accelerate the drive to urbanize and industrialize the nation. Rather than rationalize the production of an existing commodity, however, Leland found ways to manufacture goods for urban dwellers in the quantities they required by means of his greatest achievement, the development of interchangeable parts.

Born in the town of Barton, Vermont, in 1843 and named after an English missionary to India, he maintained strong religious conviction throughout his life. (This was a pattern followed by others as well, including Rockefeller and Morgan.) His father, Leander Leland, was a failed farmer and cattle driver barely able to keep his large family together. The search for work took him to Worcester, Massachusetts, where at the age of eleven Henry obtained a job making shoes for a factory that supplied southern slaves. Seeing little future there, he cast about for something else. Through the intervention of the local Adventist minister, Leland was taken on at the Crompton Works as an apprentice mechanic, working ten-hour shifts for 50 cents a day. Crompton produced textile machinery for the industry, which was growing rapidly. Leland disliked the job, and town life in general, and hoped some day to scrape together enough money to purchase a farm. Yet he was good at the work and discovered an affinity for precision manufactures that derived, perhaps, from his extraordinary discipline and mania for perfection.

The Civil War erupted before Leland could complete his apprenticeship. He tried to enlist in the Union Army but, like George Westinghouse, was rejected when his mother informed the recruiting officer he was under age. His brother Edson was accepted and died on the battlefield in 1863. Grief stricken,

This happy-go-lucky cyclist in Medford, Massachusetts, in 1906 most likely was unaware of Henry Leland's contribution to the revolution in interchangeable parts, which made the bicycle craze possible.

Leland remained at the factory, finding an outlet for his patriotism in obtaining an assignment to make lathes for the federal armories to use in producing gun stocks. Intensely anti-Confederate, he left for a lower-paying position at the Springfield Armory, turning out rifles for the Union Army, and remained there until the war ended. At that time, the armory laid off hundreds of workers, and Leland was one of them. He had no trouble finding new employment twenty miles away at Colt's armory in Hartford, but that didn't last. Now he drifted from job to job, taking whatever he could, even working for a brief period as a policeman.

In 1872 Leland learned of an opening at the Brown & Sharpe Company in Providence, not far from the original Almy, Brown & Slater factory. At the time, Brown & Sharpe was one of the foremost manufacturers of machine tools, led by Joseph R. Brown, who designed and manufactured calipers capable of measuring down to a thousandth of an inch. Using these and other instruments turned out at the factory, Brown could make machine parts to far greater tolerances than ever before known. Brown also patented the first micrometer and is considered one of the great innovators in precision machining and design.

Leland was assigned to the screw machine division, where he blossomed under Brown's guidance and became fascinated with problems related to interchangeable parts. He quickly rose to management positions and in 1878 became head of Brown & Sharpe's most important division, the sewing machine department. "My visions of the possibilities of manufacturing broadened," he later wrote. "My interest became intensified. I realized that manufacturing was an art and I resolved to devote my best endeavors and my utmost ability to the Art of Manufacturing."

Leland perfected several machines and designed new ones. He was deemed an exacting but fair manager, who would conduct Bible readings during lunch time and lecture the workers on theology and morality. Leland's devotion to moral causes had one interesting side effect. Thinking it un-Christian to clip horses' hair in winter, he refused to accept an order to manufacture a line of cutters but relented when told that if Brown & Sharpe didn't provide them some other factory would get the order. Faced with this situation, Leland decided to do the second best thing: design and offer a clipper more precise than those on the market so that the horse's hair would not be shaved too close to the skin.

The Leland clipper won immediate acceptance and was soon altered for use on humans, in this way revolutionizing the barbering trade. By the early 1880s Brown & Sharpe was producing over 300 barber clippers a day and sending them throughout the world. Leland was gratified by the acceptance, but not by his reward: Brown & Sharpe merely gave him a raise of $3 a week. He later remarked that "a thank you and fifty cents a day more in my pay envelope" was hardly proper recompense. "That was one of the times when I thought I ought to quit making other men rich and go to work for myself."

In 1883 Leland contracted typhoid fever, and although his recovery was complete he could no longer work in a factory. Wanting to retain his services, Brown & Sharpe made him its traveling representative, covering the area west of Pittsburgh. Lacking funds to start out on his own, Leland contented himself with the new position.

Leland met Charles A. Strelinger, a traveling salesman who had great success in selling bicycles, in 1889. Strelinger convinced him that there was great opportunity for a machine shop operator in the Detroit area. He also introduced Leland to Robert C. Faulconer, a Michigan lumber tycoon who was seeking investment opportunities and offered to provide financing.

It was a pleasing prospect: Leland liked Detroit, for among other reasons it was an antiunion city and he had no use for such "socialistic" organizations. So on September 19, 1890, Leland, Faulconer & Norton was organized as a machine shop and tool maker, with offices in the Strelinger Building. (The third partner was Charles F. Norton, a machine designer for Brown & Sharpe.) Leland's previous employers granted their blessings; Lucien Sharpe even loaned Leland $2,000 as part of his investment of $3,600. The firm was capitalized at $50,000, most of that coming from Faulconer.

Leland, Faulconer & Norton was an immediate success, turning out a wide variety of industrial equipment as well as typewriters, pencil sharpeners, and other products. The bicycle craze that made Strelinger wealthy continued, and the firm prospered when Leland invented a device for fine-grinding the gears that made the company's wheels the best on the market. Norton left in 1894, and the following year the newly named Leland & Faulconer moved to large new quarters. A gray-iron foundry was added in 1896, by which time Leland & Faulconer was one of the city's largest industrial concerns.

One of the reasons for this success was Leland's relentless perfectionism, which made his machines among the most trusted in the industry. "There always will be a conflict between 'good' and 'good enough,'" he told some sullen workers whose output displeased him, "and in opening up a new business or a

Henry Leland, the force behind the development of Cadillac and Oldsmobile, poses with his grandson in this charming photograph — a sympathetic portrait of this moral and religious man, who set high standards of workmanship.

new department one can count on meeting this resistance to high standards of workmanship. It is easy to get [worker] cooperation for mediocre work, but one must sweat blood for a chance to produce a superior product."

It was to be expected that, with his expertise, interests, and geographic location, Leland would enter the automobile industry, which was blossoming at the turn of the century. In 1901, when there were barely 7,000 sales and total registrations were under 15,000, Ransom E. Olds was manufacturing 5 motors per day and had orders for 15. Needing power plants, Olds placed an order at Leland & Faulconer for the additional units. Relations between Olds and Leland were good, and the order was for 2,000 engines, at a time when Olds had sold only 200 cars.

The Leland engines, based on Olds's designs, were the best of the period. Leland worked to tolerances of one-thousandth of an inch, while the Dodge brothers, who also had an Olds contract, were content with sixty-fourth of an inch tolerances. At the Detroit Auto Show of 1902, Olds demonstrated two Cadillacs, and as it happened one had a motor that had been produced in his own shop, the other by Leland & Faulconer. The differences were obvious to all — and to Olds's embarrassment, for he had to retard the L & F engine so it would idle as roughly as his own. It was, simply, a marvel of the time. Wilfred Leland, who worked with his father, recalled the time when Olds drove one of his early machines to their home to demonstrate its qualities. "Mr. Olds worked quite awhile cranking it, muttering something about each car having an individuality of its own. But after we began making motors for him, father took the individuality out of them."

Although Leland continued to manufacture engines for Olds, he was unhappy with the design. He spoke with Olds about designing a new power plant to replace the three-horsepower engines then in use. Irritated, Olds replied that he had been manufacturing engines since 1885 and was quite pleased with what he had. Undeterred, Leland designed a one-cylinder, ten-horsepower engine and demonstrated it to Olds and others at his shop, only to have it rejected as being too expensive.

Now Leland looked for others who might be interested in his power plant. At this time William F. Murphy, a Detroit lumber dealer fascinated with automobiles, headed a syndicate that backed Henry Ford, who at that time was deeply involved with racing cars. Murphy wanted to manufacture cars to order, while even then Ford was interested in mass production. The two men separated in 1900, and soon after, Murphy called on Leland to discover whether he was interested in turning out motors for passenger vehicles. Leaping at the chance to utilize his motor, Leland agreed. The directors wanted the new car to be called the Leland, but, more modest than most then in the industry, Leland opted to name it after the French explorer who founded Detroit, Antoine de la Mothe Cadillac.

Three models of what was called the Model A Cadillac were produced in 1902 and were demonstrated at the New York Auto Show early the next year. The car was an instant hit, with orders placed for over 1,000 of them. Within nine months, Cadillac had two cars — the "A," which sold for $750, and the larger "B," for $900 — and these were offered through forty-eight sales agencies in all parts of the country. A year after the show, Cadillac was the nation's best-selling automobile and Leland was a major force in the industry.

Automobile companies proliferated in 1902. Henry Ford started a new enterprise, James W. Packard moved his plant to Detroit, and David Buick chartered his company. These men did not actually manufacture cars; like Murphy, they designed and ordered parts from suppliers like Leland and then assembled the various parts in their shops. Because they were fabricators rather than manufacturers, the automobile companies required relatively little in the way of capital. But they were often in difficulty, for if one supplier failed to deliver his order on time, the entire process was delayed. In addition, the assemblers had to be concerned with fit and quality control, which varied sharply in the industry.

Leland recognized this almost immediately, finding that supplying parts was a difficult, frustrating, and poorly paid business. He was considering ending his association with the company when the Cadillac factory burned to the ground. Murphy soon reorganized it and asked the Lelands to take charge. They accepted, merging Leland & Faulconer with Cadillac, and now became fully committed to the industry. Orders rose, going to 4,300 in 1906. The entire industry suffered through the panic and depression of 1907, when Cadillac sales fell to under 3,000 and the company faced bankruptcy. Many automobile firms failed, but Cadillac survived and two years later was sold to William C. Durant, who had recently organized General Motors, for $4.15 million.

Henry Leland was more than an innovative and meticulous machine maker who also made an important contribution to the automobile industry. As much as anyone, he brought the dream of interchangeable parts to fruition. He demonstrated this in striking fashion at the Royal Automobile Club's stan-

In its early days, there were few barriers to entering the automobile business, and small-scale operations proliferated. Like REO Auto, many grew out of carriage or bicycle manufacturing companies.

dardization trials in 1907. Three Cadillacs were completely disassembled at a racetrack some twenty miles from London, and the parts were painted red, yellow, and blue, with a fourth pile of spares. Then the judges selected parts at random and reassembled the cars, after which each was driven five hundred miles. It was as dramatic a performance as might have been imagined and secured Leland's place in the history of manufacturing. With interchangeable parts, mass production became possible, indeed inevitable, and it was to be demonstrated most convincingly in the automobile industry.

Henry Ford and His Famous Flivver

LELAND CONTINUED on as a force in the automobile industry for another two decades. Together with Charles Kettering, he invented the self-starter in 1911, and it appeared in the following year's Cadillacs. He organized the Lincoln Motor Company to build "Liberty" engines during World War I, the name selected to honor the president for whom Leland cast his first vote in 1864. Lincoln was deliberately operated at a loss, since Leland felt it was his patriotic duty to participate in the war effort.

After the war, Leland decided to go into the automobile business on his own. His associates wanted to name the new car after him, but just as he had rejected the honor for the Cadillac, so he did for the Lincoln, the first models of which went on sale in 1920. Ironically, America's two most luxurious cars were both the product of the same man and are driven by individuals who probably don't even know his name.

Sales of Lincolns were sluggish, due more to the weak postwar economy than to any mechanical deficiencies. Indeed, by almost any measure the Lincolns were the best-crafted automobiles on the road. In financial trouble, Leland approached Henry Ford and offered to sell the firm and all of its holdings. Ford was interested and purchased Lincoln for $5 million. Under the terms of the agreement, the Lelands were to have a role in managing the company, but they soon left, unable to work with Ford, whose approach to automobiles was quite different from their own.

They were not the only individuals who found themselves in this position. The imperious Ford was already the leading figure in the industry, well on his way to becoming a legend. Leland soon faded into relative obscurity, insofar as the general run of Americans was concerned, while Ford became an industrial demigod. "The Ford and Charlie Chaplin are the best-known objects in the world," said Will Rogers in the 1920s, and the legend persists to this day.

As do the paradoxes. The Henry Ford who died in 1947 was a fabulously wealthy man, whose company was in shambles, the most famous American businessman, whose bigotry made his very name anathema to millions of his countrymen. Considered a progressive, even radical, businessman, he was a major opponent of Franklin D. Roosevelt's New Deal and of unions. Uncertain about historical and geographic facts known to most ninth graders, in 1930 he spoke of a time when underdeveloped countries would manufacture their own autos and urged Detroit to prepare for such an eventuality. "A moment's thought will make clear why the future must see nation after nation taking over its own work of supply. And we ought to be glad to help the work along."

Many small car companies appealed to Americans ever intrigued by novelty and eager for new ways to travel. Leland's Oldsmobile company outdid its competitors by exercising strict quality control.

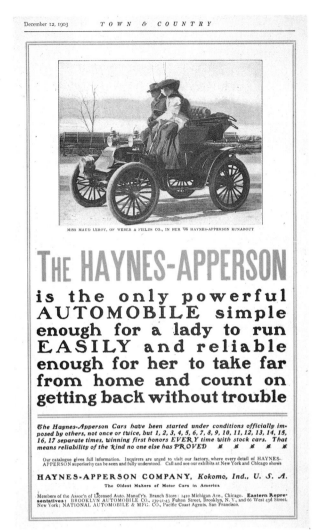

The man who did so much to alter the face of the nation devoted considerable
time and energy to re-creating the rural town he had known as a boy and died
by candlelight during an electrical storm.

Ford's parents were farmers of modest means, who worked the land in
Greenfield Village (now Dearborn), Michigan. Henry attended public schools in
the district at a time when the area was the seedbed for future auto pioneers.
Among Ford's schoolmates were J. Dallas Dort, a founder of Durant-Dort and
one of the organizers of General Motors, and Alanson Brush, who worked with
Ford at his factory and later produced his own car, the Brush Runabout.

Ford wasn't a particularly good student, but he did show mechanical apti-
tude. When his father gave him a watch, young Henry took it apart and put it
together out of curiosity, and later on he worked as a watch repairman. For a
while Ford attended business school, but he left for a job at Westinghouse,
where he learned about steam engines. In 1888 his father persuaded him to try
his hand at farming, but Henry was soon back at machines. By 1891 Ford had
moved to Detroit to join the Edison Electric Illuminating Company as a night
engineer at $45 a month. Quickly proving to have talents in this area, he was

elevated to chief engineer at $100 a month. Ford worked with and greatly admired Edison, whom he considered the greatest American of his time, and hoped to emulate him.

By then Ford was tinkering with gasoline engines. Intrigued by a magazine article on automobiles, in 1896 he developed a four-cycle motor, which was then mounted on a buggy frame. Ford called this, his first car, a Quadracycle, indicating some connection in his mind with the new motorcycles, and sold it for $200. The Quadracycle was a small, unpretentious machine, easily lifted by two men, featuring a simple and dependable motor, which Ford had designed — or perhaps it would be more accurate to say pieced together. Ford was a "cut and try" inventor, somewhat in the Edison tradition, though he never progressed to the older man's level of sophistication. More than Edison, however, Ford had an uncanny knack for all things mechanical. W. J. Cameron, one of his associates, remarked that "they were living things to him, those machines. He could almost diagnose the arrangement by touching it." Lacking formal training in engineering and disdaining the concept, Ford would identify problems and then try to solve them through trial and error. He could not draw up a set of blueprints and read them with some difficulty. Always quite proficient at improvising solutions to problems, and with an imagination that was fresh and often startling, Ford nonetheless was hardly a modern management philosopher's model of a strategic thinker.

This early experience led Ford to think seriously about entering the automobile business. Three years later, at the age of thirty-six, he left Edison Illuminating, and with the backing of several prominent Detroiters, including Mayor William C. Maybury and William Murphy, formed the Detroit Automobile Company, capitalized at $150,000. Although the company built and sold scores of autos during its brief existence, it collapsed in 1900 when the partners had a falling-out. After another company failure in 1901, but successes with racing cars, Ford obtained backing in 1903 for the Ford Motor Company, also capitalized at $150,000. At the time he told an associate that "the way to make automobiles is to make one automobile like another automobile, to make them all alike, to make them come from the factory all alike — just like one pin is like another pin, when it comes from a pin factory."

Much has been written and said of what came to be known as "Fordism," but this was the central and guiding principle: uniformity, which would lead to universality. All else was variation on the theme, the major one being mass production, a concept with which Ford is intimately identified. Yet Charles Sorenson, one of his closest associates, wrote:

> Henry Ford had no ideas on mass production. He wanted to build a lot of autos. He was determined but, like everyone else at that time, he didn't know how. In later years he was glorified as the originator of the mass production idea. Far from it; he just grew into it, like the rest of us. The essential tools and the final assembly line with its many integrated feeders resulted from an organization which was continually experimenting and improvising to get better production.

Ford Motors produced a variety of automobiles, most of them well received, and all the while Ford experimented with new materials and construction methods. In 1907 he perfected the first version of the Model T — the Tin Lizzie — and it was marketed the following year. In 1909 Ford declared that, thereafter, his company would manufacture only the Model T, which would be available in any color the customer wanted — "so long as it is black." In his autobiography Ford wrote:

The legendary Henry Ford sits jauntily at the wheel of his first car in 1918. A controversial man of many contradictions, Ford capitalized on his mechanical inventiveness to become the most famous — if not the most well-loved — businessman in America.

GENTLEMEM
OUR
COUNTRY

HENRY FORD AND HIS FIRST CAR.

I will build a motor car for the great multitude. It will be large enough for the family but small enough for the individual to run and care for. It will be constructed of the best materials, by the best men to be hired, after the simplest designs that modern engineering can devise. But it will be so low in price that no man making a good salary will be unable to own one — and enjoy with his family the blessing of hours of pleasure in God's great open spaces.

Ford also set down the principles upon which his operations were based, in what reads like a manifesto for the industrial America of the new century:

1. An absence of fear of the future or veneration for the past. One who fears the future, who fears failure, limits his activities. Failure is only the opportunity more intelligently to begin again. There is no disgrace in honest failure; there is disgrace in fearing to fail. What is past is useful only as it suggests ways and means for progress.
2. A disregard of competition. Whoever does a thing best ought to be the one to do it. It is criminal to try to get business away from another man — criminal because one is then trying to lower the personal gain and the condition of one's fellowmen — to rule by force instead of intelligence.
3. The putting of service before profit. Without a profit, business cannot extend. There is nothing inherently wrong about making a profit. Well-conducted business enterprise cannot fail to return a profit, but profit must and inevitably will come as a reward for good service. It cannot be the basis — it must be the result of service.
4. Manufacturing is not buying low and selling high. It is the process of buying materials fairly and, with the smallest possible addition of cost, transforming those materials into a consumable product and giving it to the consumer. Gambling, speculation and sharp dealing tend only to clog this progression.

Ford borrowed innovations from several entrepreneurs before him. From Gustavus Swift came the idea of the assembly line, which limited the worker to one task at every station. Combined with Henry Leland's advances in interchangeable parts, the assembly line made Ford's name synonymous with mass production.

The guiding principle behind Ford's success was *uniformity:* by standardizing every part of every car and making them all exactly alike, his factory could turn out a Model T every 40 seconds.

Later, a student of the industry suggested that all this meant, simply, that Ford intended to offer an honest product at a fair price.

Ford managed to accomplish this by changing the manufacturing process, and he did so by building upon the accomplishments of others. Take interchangeability of parts. Whitney and Colt had championed standardization, which was of paramount importance in mass production, and Henry Leland deserves much of the credit for creating new standards that made the famous Ford techniques possible. Max Wollering, one of Ford's early superintendents, who came to the company after working at International Harvester and Hoffman Hinge and Foundry, recalled that "there was nothing new [about interchangeability] to me, but it might have been new to the Ford Motor Company because they were not in a position to have much experience along that line." But Ford quickly and instinctively recognized its paramount importance. "One of Mr. Ford's strong points was interchangeability of parts," Wollering continued. "He realized as well as any manufacturer realized that in order to create great quantity of production, your interchangeability must be fine and unique in order to accomplish this rapid assembly of units. There can't be much hand work or fitting if you are going to accomplish great things."

Ford prided himself on success in this field, in effect taking what Leland was doing on a small scale and expanding it to the point where a new Model T could come out of the factory every forty seconds. "We are making 40,000 cylinders, 10,000 engines, 40,000 wheels, 20,000 axles, 10,000 bodies, 10,000 of every part that goes into the car . . . all *exactly alike,*" Ford advertised as early as 1906. He noted elsewhere that the Model T contained some 5,000 parts — counting nuts and screws — and in time all were standardized.

The assembly line was another borrowing. Gustavus Swift and others in the meat-packing industry had "disassembly lines," in which carcasses were

What more pleasant way to spend a lovely afternoon than to drive to the country in your very own automobile. With motorcars affordable and readily available, Americans found it easy to get away from it all.

Motorists had to be prepared for all eventualities. A flat tire could easily put the kibosh on a festive holiday outing.

carried by conveyers from one butcher to another, long before Ford applied the concept in reverse to car chassis. And the technique was used by George Westinghouse at least a generation before it appeared at the Ford plant. Even then, there is evidence that Sorenson, not Ford, had primary responsibility for introducing the concept and that Ford elaborated upon ideas Sorenson presented to him in 1908. In his autobiography Ford wrote: "In our first assembling we simply started to put a car together at a spot on the floor and workmen brought to it the parts as they were needed in exactly the same way one builds a house." But he soon realized this was inefficient. "The undirected worker spends more of his time walking around for materials and tools than he does in working; he gets small pay because pedestrianism is not a highly paid line." This was changed in 1913. "The step forward in assembly came when we began taking the work to the men instead of the men to the work."

Of course, it was more complicated than that: starting the assembly line was one thing; perfecting it through trial and error was another. The effects of the system were striking. In 1912, the last year during which traditional methods were employed, Ford built 78,440 vehicles; the next year, with the assembly line in place for magnetos and chassis, 189,088 vehicles were produced; in 1914, with the system further along, 230,788 Model T's rolled off the assembly lines. In the process, costs and prices plummeted. When the T was introduced in 1908, it sold for $850; by 1916, when Ford manufactured more than half a million cars, the price was $350, and by 1925, $240. During each year of its run — which ended in 1927 — the T was improved and its price dropped. "Every time I lower the price a dollar we gain a thousand new buyers," Ford said in the mid-1920s, when his reputation was at its apogee. Over 15 million Tin Lizzies were sold, more than any model in the world until the Volkswagen Beetle, which to many seemed a post–World War II resurrection of Ford's dream of "building them good, simple, and inexpensive."

In his classic *Wealth of Nations*, Adam Smith wrote strikingly of the division of labor, how pin workers could be employed more efficiently if each concentrated on a single process. "One man draws out the wire, another straights [*sic*] it, a third cuts it, a fourth points it, a fifth grinds it at the top for receiving the head; to make the head requires two or three distinct operations; to put it on is a peculiar business; to whiten it is another; it is even a trade by itself to put them into paper." Smith went on to observe that ten workers, functioning in this fashion, "could make among them upward of forty-eight thousand pins a day. . . . But if they had all wrought separately and independently . . . they certainly could not each of them make twenty, perhaps not one pin a day."

That was in 1776. Francis Cabot Lowell and Samuel Slater knew of the need for this kind of division of labor, as would Eli Whitney, Samuel Colt, and Henry Leland. Henry Ford added a twist. Each worker would perform a different task, but unlike Smith's pin workers, they would not be able to set the pace; that would be done for them by the assembly line. Thus Fordism connoted more than even the triumph of interchangeable parts and mass production; it was the transformation of the workplace, in which the worker had less control over his activities than ever before.

Almost from the start, Ford's engineers and managers attempted to maximize production by studying and perfecting the assembly line. They did so by shifting parts from place to place, attempting to eliminate waste motion, and in other ways making the worker an integral part of the line. The result was a sharp increase in labor productivity and standardization, which made those price reductions possible.

While all of this seemed admirable to the managers and was a source of pride to Ford and his executives, it had a devastating impact on the labor force. Unaccustomed to this kind of pressure and resentful at being treated like machines, they quit in disgust, often to accept lower-paid jobs with Ford's rivals. By 1913 the turnover rate reached 380 percent. Ford all but conceded that in order to obtain 100 workers he had to hire 963. While this was distressing, even more so was talk of unionization, as the workers banded together to oppose the constant speed-ups on the line.

Ford responded by raising the minimum daily wage to $2.34 in October 1913 and then offering bonuses to those who stayed on the job for three years. When these measures proved inadequate, he upped the minimum wage to $5 per day in 1914. This won Ford a great deal of favorable publicity and even now is cited as a sign of his affection for the working man and an indication of his belief that the market for his cars would be factory workers themselves. But the real reason was that, if Ford wanted an efficient assembly line, he had to pay premium wages.

The $5 day did attract scores of workers to the Ford factory, where the work continued to be intense and nerve-racking. The wife of an assembly line worker put the matter squarely and poignantly to Ford in an anonymous letter written

The spirit of independence on private wheels, poised above the unbounded prospect of the Grand Canyon — a classic image of the American entrepreneurial dream.

less than a month after the new pay scale went into effect. "The chain system you have is a *slave driver! My God!*, Mr. Ford. My husband has come home and thrown himself down and won't eat his supper — so done out! Can't it be remedied? . . . That $5 a day is a blessing — a bigger one than you know but *oh* they earn it."

The assembly line made it possible for Ford to produce his Model T's in large quantities at a price many consumers could afford — but it meant the subordination of the worker to the machine. Since then, engineers and psychologists have attempted to find some way to maximize the benefits of the assembly line while minimizing its negative effects. Today the relatively new technology of robotics — the replacement of human beings by machines that manufacture other machines and end products — may soon provide the solution that workers and their spouses yearned for almost three-quarters of a century earlier.

Joe Engelberger and the Robotics Revolution

ROBOTICS ISN'T A NEW IDEA. Statues that come to life have been the subject of Western myths and legends since the Greeks, and ingenious mechanical toys and devices have an equally venerable tradition. At one time there was talk of "automatons," mechanical devices that would perform many functions now done by humans, and this was deemed a beneficial development. But during the 1920s, when the negative implications of Fordism were becoming more apparent, the term was replaced by "robots."

The word is derived from the Czech *robota,* which translates loosely into "forced laborer." It entered the English language via Karel Capek's play *RUR.* (The title's initials stood for "Rossum's Universal Robots.") The play deals with a society in which labor is performed by humanlike machines. The robot also played a central role in Fritz Lang's classic 1926 film *Metropolis,* the theme of which was the transformation of humans into machines by a heartless and unfeeling society. Ten years later in *Modern Times,* Charlie Chaplin showed how man had become wedded to — and driven by — the machine. Today robots still have two faces — beneficial and threatening. In *2001: A Space Odyssey,* a runaway computer, HAL (the name derived by using the letter immediately preceding each letter of IBM), is the villain of the piece; in *Star Wars,* the robots R2D2 and C3PO help the heroes and are endowed with pleasant, human personalities.

Both kinds of robots appeared in science fiction tales at the turn of the century, and the possibilities of such machines have intrigued scientists to this day. The transformation of fiction into fact began after World War II, although robotlike devices were manufactured as curiosities in the 1920s and 1930s. At the 1939 New York World's Fair, "Elecktro" and his dog "Sparko" were favorites at the Westinghouse Pavilion, which was part of what the fair's promoters called "The World of Tomorrow."

At about that time, the term "robotics" was created by science fiction writer Isaac Asimov, though there is no indication he was influenced by the Westinghouse marvels. Asimov steered a neutral course, looking upon robots as simply machines, neither inherently good nor evil, which with adequate safeguards could mark the next step after Fordism in the industrial evolution. He started writing on this subject in 1939. Three years later, in a story entitled "Runaround," he set down "The Three Laws of Robotics," which are well known to those in the industry:

1. A robot may not injure a human being, or, through inaction, allow a human being to come to harm.
2. A robot must obey the orders given it by human beings, except when such orders would conflict with the First Law.
3. A robot must protect its own existence as long as such protection does not conflict with the First or Second Law.

That these formulations, set down in a science fiction tale published in a pulp magazine, are taken seriously by entrepreneurial engineers engaged in robotics research indicates the nature of this relatively young industry: at times its pioneers sound like a cross between fictional characters out of one of Asimov's stories and high technology managers operating in some Silicon Valley think tank. In any case, robotics is now considered a serious area of industrial endeavor, with activities in the field being conducted by such major firms as IBM, GE, GM, Cincinnati Milicron, Fanuc, NEC, Fujitsu, Olivetti, Volkswagen, and the like, as well as scores of smaller ones, such as Unimation, Prab Robots, DeVibliss, Graco, and hundreds of young start-up operations. Most belong to the Robotic Industry Association (formerly the Robot Institute of America), which defines an industrial robot as a "reprogrammable, multifunctional manipulator designed to move materials, parts, tools, or specialized devices through variable programmed motions to perform a variety of tasks."

That robotics will grow exponentially during the rest of this century and beyond is taken for granted. Yet its outlines are not sharply delineated. Robotics draws upon such diverse areas as computer technology and psychology, ma-

The idea of machines building machines has been brought into the future in the field of robotics. This welder performs a dangerous job with no risk to life and limb.

Joe Engelberger's Unimates (*left*) were among the first "reprogrammable, multifunctional manipulators" to free workers from boring, mechanical tasks.

Robots like this giant mixer (*right*) have become indispensable in nearly every heavy industry.

Following the lead of the Japanese, automakers worldwide have replaced highly paid workers with robots on the assembly line to gain a competitive edge in the market. *Left:* Robots assemble a Fiat in an Italian plant.

chine tool manufacture, and the sociology of the workplace. Robots today are assembling and painting cars at Ford; tomorrow they may be cleaning offices and homes and saving lives in burning buildings.

While no single individual can be said to have been the founder of robotics, Joe Engelberger was one of those who can truly be said to have been present at the creation.

Raised in Connecticut during the Great Depression, Engelberger received a degree in physics from Columbia in 1946. While there, he took the university's first course in servomechanisms, which are systems in which small amounts of power control and automatically correct the operations of machines. An avid science fiction fan, Engelberger had read Asimov and could see important linkages between servomechanisms and robots. In addition, he recognized the potential of using such machines in the workplace. Commenting upon *Modern Times*, he said, "He [Charlie Chaplin] really saw the poignant thing that was wrong — that the human was now being paced by the machines." Robots might change this.

After serving in the navy and obtaining a graduate degree in physics, Engelberger found work as a general manager of the aerospace division of Manning, Maxwell & Moore, a Connecticut-based industrial firm. In 1956 he met George C. Devol, Jr., an engineer who was one of the few working solely on robots and who then headed his own firm, Devol Research Associates. Devol had developed a machine that could be programmed and was working on others that operated in tandem with the new computers being turned out by IBM, Univac, and others. Engelberger would tell an interviewer almost thirty years later that Devol's ideas "happened to land on fertile ground. I was there. I was ready."

Intrigued, Engelberger convinced his employers to take out licenses on some of Devol's patents and started manufacturing machines, soon securing several important defense contracts. But interest in industrial robots did not develop as hoped, even though Engelberger created several prototypes and received expressions of interest in them from Detroit.

Manning, Maxwell & Moore remained skeptical, and in 1957 decided to close down the robot project, while offering Engelberger a promotion and raise if he remained. "I balked," he recalled. "I [told them I] don't think you know what you are doing, liquidating this business." Engelberger drove to New York, purchased several finance texts, read them, and decided to start his own company. Seeking funding, he met Norman Schlafler, founder of Consolidated Diesel Electric (Condec), who was willing to back the project, and went to work at a Condec subsidiary, Consolidated Controls, formed for the purpose.

Consolidated Controls' first product, the Unimate, was placed at General Motors in 1959, but no other orders were received for almost two years. Meanwhile Engelberger sought additional financing. After being turned down by several of the nation's most prominent high technology firms, he was able to interest Champ Carry, chairman of the industrial equipment manufacturer Pullman Corporation. At a time when Condec was reconsidering its commitment to Engelberger's projects, Carry offered to back him in a new company, in which Pullman would have a 51 percent ownership and Condec 49 percent. Schlafler agreed, and in 1962 Engelberger chartered Unimation Incorporated, in which Devol was to play an important role.

Improved versions of the Unimate were now developed. One of these used servomechanisms to shift it from place to place while it tended die-casting machines, injecting molten zinc or aluminum into steel dies — a dirty, unpleasant, unhealthy task for which machines were well suited. It seemed an ideal device, performing tasks humans rightly rejected. Yet by 1964 Unimation had sold only thirty robots, most of them to General Motors. While they worked well, GM held back from ordering many more, fearful of opposition from its unions. Unimate had trouble finding other customers, since many machines turned out by competitors performed poorly. "We would have been much better off at that time if we'd had successful competitors," claimed Engelberger.

Business picked up later in the decade, due more to social changes than any radical new technological breakthrough. The well-publicized difficulties at several plants, including GM's Lordstown complex, where workers complained about assembly line boredom, contributed to a drive to use machines to perform repetitive tasks. Developing concerns about occupational safety and health dictated the use of robots to perform dangerous tasks in unhealthy environments. GM started using Unimates for spot welding in 1964 and two years later ordered 66 of them for the Lordstown plant.

Along with this came growing interest from overseas, Japan in particular. "While we were agonizing in '66, the Japanese were . . . looking at what was happening and they came over, company after company," Engelberger recalled. Soon he was in Japan, touring the country and lecturing on robotics. In 1968 Unimation licensed Kawasaki Heavy Industries to build Unimates, and several joint operations followed. When the time came for American companies to intensively study the "Japanese miracle," they saw robotics as one aspect of that country's industrial thinking. Ironically, a number of American manufacturers became interested in robotics through exposure to their Japanese competitors, who themselves learned much from Unimation and other American companies.

The robotics breakthrough came in the early 1970s and continued into the 1980s, as hundreds of American companies explored their uses and scores placed orders. As before, the automobile industry was one of the major customers. Now that the Japanese challenge had materialized, the unions were becoming more willing to accept work changes, and this helped matters. Paradoxically, the loss of jobs due to foreign competition made the unions more willing to replace workers with machines so as to salvage the jobs that remained. Labor contracts permitting robotization in return for guarantees of job security became popular in the 1980s, and this, too, served to spur the industry.

A GM study at that time indicated that armies of small, programmable machines could replace highly paid labor. Industrial robots priced between $40,000 and $100,000 cost approximately $6 per hour to operate, less than a third the cost of the workers they replaced. The machines did not take vacations, qualify for fringe benefits, or apply for worker's compensation if injured on the job. At one Chrysler plant 50 welders working two shifts replaced 200 workers. The economic benefits were overwhelming and assured robotics a bright future in the automobile industry.

Robotics also played a role in aerospace and in machine tool manufacture; in the production of microcomputers, one micro helped turn out others. Even barbering was affected: just as Henry Leland invented clippers for horses, so Engelberger was asked by several Australian ranchers to develop a Unimate to shear sheep. The ranchers estimated that in time they might need 130,000 robots — which would have taken nearly two hundred years to produce at the rate Unimation was operating at the time. How far might this go? Several Japanese scholars have suggested that soon after the turn of the century only 5 percent of the labor force in advanced industrial countries will be engaged in manufacturing jobs. Perhaps that is too far-fetched, but there are sections of American and Japanese automobile companies where machines perform all of the work.

With all of this, the industry is subject to serious risks and challenges, two of which hit Unimation in 1982. That year GM organized GMF Robotics in partnership with Fanuc. At the time, GM was Unimation's largest customer. Two years earlier it had placed the first of several orders for a programmable universal machine for assembly (PUMA), to be produced by Unimation's Vicarm subsidiary; now it would appear that GM will soon be producing machines of its own. The second problem was the 1982 recession, which hit almost all firms in the industry. Engelberger looked to Condec and Pullman for help, but neither was in a position to offer much. There was a public stock offering, which raised $17 million, but Engelberger realized a stronger parent corporation was required. Discussions followed with Litton, General Electric, IBM, Westinghouse, and several others, and in the end the company went to Westinghouse for $107 million.

Westinghouse was eager to retain Engelberger's services, but he had little taste for working in so large a company and left the following year. Soon after, Engelberger helped organized Technology Transitions, a venture capital firm with special interest in robotics. He talks now of creating robots to mine coal, of developing new "seeing robots," utilizing them in meat packing, and, most often, of a robot that would be a household slave, preparing meals, cleaning up, stacking and washing dishes, vacuuming when necessary — in fact, taking care of all household chores.

This was the kind of vision that animated Karel Capek more than half a century ago. It is worth noting that in *RUR* the robots revolt and destroy their human creators until only one survives. Since none know how to construct additional machines, the human suggests that he dismantle a representative robot of each sex, but those selected refuse, having developed a romantic interest in each other, and go off, presumably to become the Adam and Eve of a new species.

Human beings are hardly in danger of this kind of fate. Rather, the movement that began with John Kay and Richard Arkwright and can be traced through Joe Engelberger will continue to enable Americans to produce more and better goods in less time and at lower human costs.

V

Giving 'Em
What They Want

"IF A MAN write a better book, preach a better sermon, or make a better mouse-trap than his neighbor," wrote Emerson, "tho' he build his house in the woods, the world will make a beaten path to his door." Making something new, or inventing a new way to make something as old and common as the mousetrap has always been an entrepreneurial obsession. But sheer innovation is not enough. The best product in the world is worthless to the entrepreneur who has no customer, and customers, alas, seldom beat a path to the proverbial door.

Marketing can make the difference. Yet most entrepreneurs show little imagination or vigor when it comes to this critical function. Those who have — Lydia Pinkham, P. T. Barnum, A. T. Stewart, Montgomery Ward, William Procter, Helen and Stanley Resor, and others we will explore here — owe much of their success to their ability to market things a better way.

What is marketing? Most think of it as selling, especially using advertising, but the concept is much larger than that. The standard dictionary definition, "buying and selling in a market," shows that the word evolved from the place where trading is done, the marketplace. It also includes "the commercial functions involved in transferring goods from producer to consumer." Thus, beyond promoting and trading one's wares, marketing is the act of physically moving — or distributing — them to the final consumer.

And more than this, it is persuasion. In recent decades marketing efforts have become increasingly geared toward the *creation* of needs, not just their fulfillment. "Give them what they want" has also become "Give them what you want them to think they want," and there are compelling reasons why this is so. As we will see, large manufacturing companies moved into the business of marketing because their survival could no longer be left to the vicissitudes of a freely operating marketplace.

Some critics have noted this change with alarm. In our consumer goods society, they charge, demands are manufactured by corporate advertisers, who employ any technique that might prove effective, from psychology to slick media graphics. In 1957 pop-sociologist Vance Packard, in *The Hidden Persuaders*, inveighed against the "large-scale efforts being made, often with impressive success, to channel our unthinking habits, our purchasing decisions, and our thought processes by the use of insights gleaned from psychiatry and the social sciences." The following year John Kenneth Galbraith, the eloquent spokesman for the economic left, echoed similar themes in *The Affluent Society:* "One cannot defend production as satisfying wants if that production creates the wants."

Still, the creation of demand has been an important part of marketing for most of American history, a phenomenon linked not only to postwar affluence and the growing power of mass media. Frederic Tudor the "Ice King," for instance, created demand for his product when he visited foreign ice depots and introduced locals to the pleasures of chilled drinks and frozen delicacies.

More than this, the theory of forced selling gives short shrift to the other side of marketing: understanding and fulfilling customer needs and desires, or what Marshall Field, proprietor of Chicago's grandest nineteenth-century department store, called "giving the lady want she wants." General Wood of Sears studied the *Statistical Abstract of the United States* in order to track shifts in the national market, and other American businessmen have helped hone these insights into a precise science by preaching that the seller should know the buyer better than he knows himself. At the very least these entrepreneurs, like

It did not take America's businesses long to recognize that successful marketing required an aggressive combination of promotion, distribution, and understanding the customer. In 1909 *Life* magazine disparaged the Age of Disfigurement with a sardonic look at "Picturesque America."

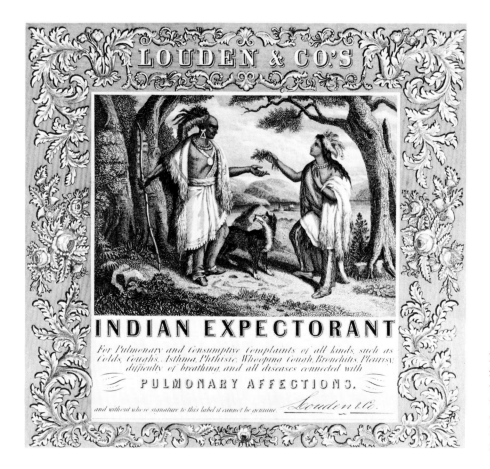

Patent medicine makers were among the first American merchants to specialize in the art of persuasive selling. Proclaiming the wondrous healing powers of potent elixirs and ointments, their ads used the lure of the exotic and appeals to special markets to draw customers.

other successful marketers in the American past, have remained alert to the wishes of the consumer, and at best they have made a careful study of the process. Even within the current ranks of powerful corporate giants, marketing is recognized as a feedback process. It is not just that it is critical to keep public tastes in mind; often this is the easiest and most practical strategy.

So marketing remains a complex and often colorful collaboration of activities: developing and pricing goods, promoting them through advertising, moving them through the distribution chain, and understanding the customer in order to provide input for product development. In formal study and practice, marketing has never been more complex, but its roots run deep in the American experience.

Colonial merchants were the most passive marketers in our national past. Much of this was an unavoidable consequence of the Colonies' crude transportation and communications networks, which did not improve significantly until the mid-nineteenth-century rise of the railroad, telegraph, and steamship. On the eve of independence, for example, news of the battles of Lexington and Concord — relayed by the fastest express carriers of the day — took four days to reach New York, hit Charleston a week later, and took about forty days to arrive at Savannah. In such a business environment, merchants were more concerned with simply getting goods than promoting them cleverly.

In 1776 the great Scottish classical economist Adam Smith, in *The Wealth of Nations*, described the atomistic, capitalistic economies of his day as being guided by the self-regulating "invisible hand" of the marketplace. In many parts of the world, however, including the American colonies, this hand was atro-

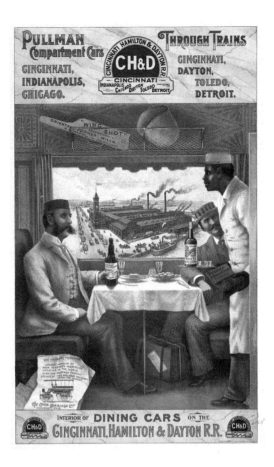

An early example of cooperation in advertising, where everyone gets a word in. An ad like this would be hard to find today.

phied by poor circulation; true competition thrives on market information and product availability, and where transportation and communication infrastructures are poor, so are these.

The general store, for instance, was normally a monopoly, more strangling than the industrial giants targeted by antitrust legislation at the turn of the twentieth century. Within a few larger cities (there were about four dozen general stores in New York City in 1776), retailers began to specialize, but at most locales general store owners were the only retail merchants for dozens or even hundreds of miles. These country merchants "bought everything that had market value," so naturally their inventories were broad and shallow. Barrels brimmed with spices, flour, grains, and other foodstuffs, kegs with molasses, whiskey, vinegar, and wine; walls were garnished with laces, pots, plows, toys. Snuff, brimstone, indigo, chocolate, and buttons were stocked, and so it went.

The general store proprietors' greatest contribution was distributive. Once or twice a year, when conditions permitted, they would make the long trek to nearby urban centers to replenish their stocks, and during the year they would secure groceries, shoes, drugs, dry goods, and books from itinerant peddlers. Because customers were captive, prices varied widely, bartering was common, and markups ran as high as 75 percent. A few general merchants, especially in larger cities and towns, published inventory lists or notices of "fresh goods" or "new stocks," but most relied on customer need to sell their wares.

Luxury items were especially appealing to those who could afford them. Imports from exotic, faraway lands held a particular fascination, perhaps none more than the treasures of the China trade. These delicate ivory carvings, hand-crafted furniture, beautifully embossed silk garments, and paintings of mystical nature scenes graced the homes of American China merchants, who kept the best artifacts and sold the rest to affluent collectors and other elite citizens during the early 1800s.

Some Colonial and early American merchants did promote their wares actively, however. The first to specialize in the art of persuasive selling were the itinerant hawkers, peddlers, and patent medicine makers who roamed the land in colorful wagons, setting up stage wherever they could find an audience. More than this, at a time when disease and epidemics frequently ravaged communities, patent medicines filled the shelves of retail establishments of every sort, from pharmacies, grocery stores, and book dealers to jewelers, tailor shops, and even post offices.

The promotional methods used by the patent medicine makers, especially after about 1800, created an enduring legacy in the history of advertising. Catchy brand names and distinctive bottles were the primary means of product differentiation. The federal government, in fact, unwittingly reinforced this trend with its first patent law in 1790, which granted patents to medicine makers — not for unique recipes but for their trademarks and the shapes of their bottles. In other words, it was literally the form instead of the content of these products that mattered. This is not surprising, given the broad range of curative properties most of the brews claimed. Dr. Robertson's Vegetable Nervous Cordial, for example, was said to alleviate "all nervous complaints, attended with inner weakness, depression of the spirits, head-ache, tremor, faintness, hysteric fits, debility, seminal weakness, gleets, and various complaints resulting from secret impropriety of youth and dissipated habits, residence in warm climates, the immoderate use of tea, the unskillful or excessive use of mercury, so often destructive of the human frame, diseases peculiar to females at a certain period of life," and more.

Patent medicine makers disseminated their messages through a variety of channels. Ambitious hawkers published their own "blazing handbills," special books, and pamphlets with names like "Every Man His Own Physician" and "The People's Common Sense Medical Advisor in Plain English" to promote the use of particular medicinal brands in home treatments. Newspaper advertising, encouraged by the proliferation of the periodicals during the nineteenth century, became an important strategy. Not only did the number of daily newspapers rise from 20 in 1800 to about 400 by the Civil War, but postal rates fell drastically during the 1840s, encouraging the spread of the media. The patent medicine makers became astute newspaper advertisers, borrowing or developing effective selling techniques, such as repetition. Some ads were carried week after week or many times in a single issue; one advertiser, for example, ran 37 ads for his product in a single issue of a paper, hoping to drill the brand name into the minds of readers.

The most enduring legacy of the patent medicine hawkers, of course, was the medicine show and wagon. Still, these did not become common until after the Civil War and were preceded by other important uses of nonprinted advertising. Soon after 1800, painted signs for patent medicines appeared on walls and rocks throughout the nation, and these were soon followed by the ubiquitous strolling men sandwiched between wooden placards. Lithographed posters joined painted signs, and both grew to menacing proportions, characteristic of the scale of the Gilded Age, which, as a result of these intrusions, was also referred to as the Age of Disfigurement.

As for the traveling salesmen with their brightly colored wagons, a phenomenon that peaked between 1880 and 1900, it is hard to overemphasize the scope of these promotional spectacles, which satisfied the public's need for entertainment as well as medicine. In the words of showman Nevada Ned, "Full evenings of drama, vaudeville, musical comedy, Wild West shows, minstrels, magic, burlesque, dog and pony circuses, not to mention Punch and Judy, pantomime, movies, menageries, bands, parades and pie eating contests, have been thrown in with Ho-Ang-Nan, the great Chinese herb remedy, and med shows have played in opera houses, halls, storerooms, ball parks, showboats and tents, large and small, as well as doorways, street corners and fairs."

Lydia E. Pinkham and Her Vegetable Compound

LIKE MOST EARLY AMERICAN merchants, artisans, and tradesmen, patent medicine manufacturers were small-scale operators who invested little capital in their ventures, used techniques not radically different from their competitors', and had business careers that were spotty at best. There were exceptions, however, perhaps none more instructive from the standpoint of marketing than Lydia Estes Pinkham, who in 1875 developed a special vegetable compound for the treatment of "female complaints" and, because of her outstanding marketing skills, became the most well-recognized woman in nineteenth-century America.

Born the tenth of twelve children of a Lynn, Massachusetts, farmer on February 9, 1819, Lydia Estes endured a difficult early life. Both of her parents were earnest Quaker reformers; intense discussions about slavery (which they adamantly opposed) and other moral issues were common in the household. Not surprisingly, while attending the Lynn Academy, Lydia became secretary of the

Using ingenious marketing strategies, Lydia Pinkham turned her home remedy for "female complaints" into a booming nationwide business. How many of the testimonials printed in this ad were actually written by the manufacturers has never been documented.

Freedman's Institute, as well as an advocate of a variety of contemporary self-improvement movements: phrenology, homeopathy, mind cure, Grahamism, temperance, and feminism. Upon graduation, she became a schoolteacher, married Isaac Pinkham in 1843, and bore five children.

Economic hardship spurred Mrs. Pinkham's entrepreneurial impulses. Her husband, who worked at various times as a laborer, farmer, trader, builder, kerosene salesman, and produce dealer, among other jobs, provided unstable financial support at best. And especially after the devastating panic of 1873 drove the family into poverty, she began to think of selling one of her home remedies.

Like many women of her day, Pinkham attended to most of the health needs of her family and friends, consulting her copy of John King's *American Dispensatory* and devising a variety of her own potions. Her special remedy was a concoction supposedly given to her by a man named George Clarkson Todd, who defaulted on a note her husband had endorsed. In partial payment, Todd offered a recipe for a compound to cure "female complaints" (the popular term for any discomfort, pain, or injury related to the female anatomy, from menstruation to a prolapsed uterus or a difficult pregnancy). The recipe (for 100 pints) read as follows:

> 8 oz. Unicorn root (*Aletris farinosa*)
> 6 oz. Life root (*Senecio aureus*)
> 6 oz. Black cohosh (*Cimicifuga racemosa*)
> 6 oz. Pleurisy root (*Asclepias tuberosa*)
> 12 oz. Fenugreek seed (*Foenum graceum*)
> Suspended in alcohol.

In proper proportion, the mixture was comprised of about 19 percent alcohol, included, of course, as a "solvent and preservative." Thus would the staunch spokeswoman of the temperance movement tout a remedy that was nearly 40 proof.

Pinkham gave away, and occasionally sold, bottles of this vegetable compound, which soon proved to be her most popular brew. As the family struggled to make ends meet, Pinkham and her sons Daniel (born in 1849) and William (1852) decided to try manufacturing and selling the mixture commercially. Agreeing on the name "Lydia E. Pinkham's Vegetable Compound," they began brewing the first batch on the basement stove. While their mother attended to production and wrote copy, Dan and Will marketed the compound. Their brothers contributed a portion of their wages to purchase supplies, and even their father, now wheelchair-bound, folded brochures.

At first the family marketed the compound by printing thousands of special four-page "Guide for Women" circulars, which they hand delivered in and around Lynn and soon in Boston. In 1876 Dan headed for New York, where he distributed more than twenty thousand pamphlets in ten days. Charles Crittenton, a leading pharmaceutical dealer, began handling the product, but sales remained sluggish. Dan, chronically broke, had to repair his shoes after every day's trek and was painfully aware of his shortage of pocket money. In desperation, the family tried to broaden the appeal of the compound by adding a few male ailments, such as "kidney complaints," to its roster of curables.

The turning point came soon. One day after filling a large order, Dan returned to Boston to rest, and while there he decided to gamble $60 on running a reproduction of the four-page handout on the front page of the *Boston Herald.* Sales picked up considerably, and the Pinkhams devoted more and more of their resources to newspaper advertising, even mortgaging their house for the pur-

Who could distrust the woman whose grandmotherly countenance adorned every one of her products? At the height of her company's success, Lydia Pinkham was the most well-known woman in America.

Lydia E. Pinkham's Remedies

THE GREAT EAST RIVER SUSPENSION BRIDGE.
CONNECTING THE CITIES OF NEW YORK & BROOKLYN.

The Bridge crosses the river by a single span of 1595 ft. suspended by four cables 15½ inches in diameter. The approach on the New York side is 2492 ft. the approach on the Brooklyn side is 1901 ft. Total length 5988 ft. From high water to roadway 120 ft. From roadway to top 157 ft. From high water to centre of span 135 ft. Width of bridge, 85 ft. Total height of Towers, 277 ft.

This promotion joined two American institutions: Lydia Pinkham's Vegetable Compound and the Brooklyn Bridge. A stroke of advertising genius, the ad linked patriotism, progress, and product.

pose. The ads had a special appeal because they were still addressed primarily to "female" problems, a category of complaint that the medical establishment either ignored or shrouded with mystery and guilt. Through Lydia Pinkham, women could find empathy and relief from one of their own. Always ingenious in their advertising strategies, the Pinkhams even started running ads in a well-known Protestant journal to maintain respectability after the frankness of their text began offending public sensibilities.

Without the need to canvass on foot, Dan was free to pursue his political ambitions and won a seat in the state legislature in 1878. The following year he suggested that his mother, now sixty and remarkably healthy, use her portrait as the trademark for their product. Soon her likeness appeared on thousands of bottle labels, newspaper and magazine ads, and billboard and streetcar signs. It was another stroke of advertising genius. Within six months sales were booming, the family confidently declined an offer to sell the company for $100,000, and Lydia Pinkham was on her way to becoming the most recognized woman in America. She was one of the few women regularly featured in American papers, where her face was sometimes used as a stand-in for Queen Victoria's.

In the end the business took its toll on the family. Just as sales were skyrocketing in 1879, Dan contracted tuberculosis in New York. His illness lingered for a year, unabated by a trip south and a variety of Lydia's health treatments and recommendations. In early 1881, the year annual sales topped $200,000, Will fell ill with the disease shortly after it claimed his brother; he was dead by October. For a few months, at least, the brothers had enjoyed success. Shattered, Lydia retreated further into spiritualism, then suffered a severe stroke just before Christmas in 1882. On May 17, 1883, she died at age sixty-four.

The medical profession did little to improve gynecological practice during the late nineteenth and early twentieth centuries, and the 1920s proved to be a heyday for the compound, as sales climbed to $3 million in 1925. But changing times spelled the decline of Pinkham's products. The compound, like virtually all patent medicines, was increasingly coming under attack by muckrakers and government regulators. Medical science had made significant gains against ravaging diseases such as cholera and yellow fever during the nineteenth century. As the public became more critical of patent medicine dealers, refusing to subject themselves to unfounded claims, and the government began more strongly to regulate both advertising and foods and drugs, the industry declined dramatically. In 1938 the American Medical Association prompted the Federal Trade Commission to cite the Pinkham company for its advertising claims, but the company was easily able to fend off the attack.

The Lydia E. Pinkham Vegetable Compound Company survived long after its founders; indeed, the product is still manufactured by Cooper Laboratories of Palo Alto, California. In recent decades, however, as family members have struggled for control of the organization, Pinkham's remedies have clearly become viewed as outmoded and old-fashioned, and sales to loyal users have fallen to a trickle. In its day, however, the compound and its gentle, persuasively understanding spokeswoman had no real rival on the national scene.

P. T. Barnum and the Business of Hype

As a group, the makers of patent medicines developed many enduring sales techniques, but few achieved the large-scale success of Lydia Pinkham. The same was true of general store owners, the most wealthy of whom seldom topped $60,000 in total sales per year. The century's most successful salesman, however, Phineas Taylor Barnum, made millions from promotional skills he had acquired during early stints as an unsuccessful promoter of a wonder cure for baldness and a general store clerk.

The quintessential salesman and a world celebrity in his day, Barnum is still remembered for the hoopla and hype he practiced so well. Keeping one hand on the pulse of the nation and the other on his swelling purse, Barnum focused his attention on meeting the challenges of marketing, a craft in which he reveled.

Barnum's early years prepared him well for a career as a master huckster. Born in Bethel, Connecticut, on July 5, 1810, to Philo Barnum, a general store owner and a farmer, and Philo's second wife, Irena Taylor, he worked at a variety of jobs as a young man, including clerk; bartender, publisher, ticket agent, and small store owner. Young Phineas was strongly influenced by his maternal grandfather, who, in Barnum's words, "would go farther, wait longer, work harder, and contrive deeper to carry out a practical joke, than for anything else under the sun."

Indeed, Barnum was the brunt of one of the most elaborate and long-lasting of these pranks. From the day the boy could speak, his grandfather told him of a tract of immensely valuable farmland called Ivy Island, which he had pur-

Though chiefly remembered for his world-famous circus, P. T. Barnum was first and foremost a museum man. Opened in 1842, his American Museum in New York's Madison Square featured such freaks and frauds as the Bearded Lady, the Feejee Mermaid, and the ever-popular Tom Thumb.

P. T. BARNUM.

chased for the boy's inheritance when he came of age. The holding was said to be the finest in the state; Phineas would be an important and powerful land baron. Other members of Barnum's family, as well as local townspeople, often chatted with Barnum and his grandfather about Ivy Island.

At age twelve Phineas was taken by his father to inspect the rich spread, only to discover it to be a virtually worthless swamp. His father, grandfather, and soon the entire community, laughed at the boy, now the victim of a decade-long hoax. Perhaps this grandiose prank contributed to Barnum's later resolve to bamboozle the public just as he had been fooled; in any event, it helped gear his thinking toward trickery and practical jokes, which he enjoyed exchanging with friends. During the early 1830s, for instance, Barnum was almost lynched by an angry mob after his friend Aaron Turner, as a joke, convinced them that Barnum was a well-known but uncaptured murderer.

Distill Barnum's brilliant marketing strategies into a formula and the first axiom might read: It is better to capture the interest and attention of the public — even if it is negative attention — than to be ignored. Consider the way Barnum managed his very first attraction at his American Museum in 1835. Joice Heth was an old black woman, who Barnum claimed was the 161-year-

General Tom Thumb and his equally diminutive wife were one of Barnum's star attractions — and proof of the master huckster's genius for convincing exaggeration.

Barnum merged his circus with competitor James Bailey's in 1871. The "greatest show on earth" drew thousands of people wherever it went, delighting them with glamor and glitter for more than 100 years.

old former nursemaid and slave of George Washington. Heth, blind and twisted, would rock gently as she related anecdotes about baby George and dazzled ministers with her knowledge of archaic church hymns.

After a time, however, crowds began to wane, so Barnum went into action. Anonymously, he published a newspaper editorial that claimed Heth was actually not human but an ingenious mechanical contrivance. Thousands who had not seen her flocked to Barnum's museum, while others who had came for a closer inspection.

Barnum used a similar ploy to stir up interest in his bearded lady. In this case, an anonymous newspaper editorial, probably composed by Barnum, declared her a fraud, prompting investigations, a trial complete with expert witnesses, and, of course, lots of press coverage.

Himself a lifelong target of negative publicity, Barnum well understood its value, recording in his autobiography: "As for the cry of 'humbug,' it never harmed me, and I was in the position of the one who had much rather be roundly abused than not to be noticed at all." Some present-day marketing analysts have speculated that the 1985 Coca-Cola formula change, resulting in a full-blown national controversy, was just such a ploy. If so, it was a tactic with a long history.

The investigation of Barnum's bearded lady concluded that she was authentic, but the same could hardly be said for a number of other Barnum attractions. His Feejee Mermaid was comprised of the torso and head of a monkey attached to the tail of a fish; Jumbo the Elephant's dimensions were constantly exaggerated, while those of tiny General Tom Thumb were diminished. Although an autopsy of Joice Heth revealed that she died at barely half her asserted age, even this seemed to work in the great showman's favor. These and other examples demonstrate the truth of perhaps a second Barnum marketing axiom: People spurn chicanery but are also fascinated by it. In a sense they want to be conned.

Barnum himself was no exception. Before becoming a promoter, he was conned by a man named Proler, who talked him into setting up a cologne manufacturing business and then disappeared one night with all the assets of the partnership. On a much grander scale, in fact, Barnum was completely bankrupted in 1855 by Chauncey Jerome of the Jerome Clock Company. In exchange for a loan of $110,000 from Barnum, Jerome agreed to move his clock plant to the site of a fifty-two-acre residential, commercial, and industrial community in Bridgeport, Connecticut, which Barnum was developing. During the next several months, complicated financial transactions ensued, through which Barnum was embezzled out of more than half a million dollars. Ruined and incredulous, he had been, in his words, "cruelly swindled and deliberately defrauded." Many citizens must have enjoyed a good laugh at the great hoaxster's expense.

Barnum was conned many times during his career, but he was also deft at turning these deceptions to his advantage. (He used the worthless Ivy Island property as "valuable" collateral for the purchase of the American Museum.) His gullibility seemed a by-product of his own curiosity and wonderment, as well as his eagerness to believe in oddities like Joice Heth, which he, in turn, would foist on the public. It is still not clear, for example, whether he believed Heth really was 161 years old, nor does this matter so much as the fact that he was intriguing people. Is it possible? they wondered. And if not, how good a scam is it?

Barnum's target, his audiences came to understand, was the public itself, which generally came to accept and even welcome the role. On one occasion, Barnum thought visitors were dallying too long in his museum, so over a rear exit he erected a large sign that read "TO THE EGRESS," knowing that many would think the egress a strange beast or some other bizarre phenomenon and go for a look. No doubt some of those who suddenly found themselves out on the street were outraged to have to pay another admission fee, but many must have chuckled to themselves and admitted that Barnum had done it again.

Still another pillar of Barnum salesmanship was the use of a variety of advertising techniques — giant, flashy signs, newspaper spots, handbills, and the like. One Barnum specialty was the ad campaign, used with astounding effectiveness to presell many of his attractions. The predisplay promotion of the Feejee Mermaid was a brilliant example of this: as Barnum held possession of the curiosity, he ran fictitious stories in New York City newspapers describing its discovery, shipment, inspection, and display throughout distant cities. By the time the mermaid "arrived" in New York for a one-week show at Concert Hall and permanent exhibition at the museum, public curiosity had reached fever pitch.

Investments that might have represented tremendous risks to other entrepreneurs were often shrewd and conservative in the hands of Barnum because of his outstanding promotional skills and instincts. In 1850 he spent $150,000 to outbid other promoters for the rights to the first American concert tour of Jenny Lind, the "Swedish Nightingale." A smashing success throughout Europe, Lind was virtually unknown on this side of the Atlantic, but by the time she arrived, nine months after Barnum had deluged the press in preparation, the first 3,000-seat performance of her sixty-concert tour was sold out at prime rates, and a crowd estimated at 30,000 gave her a hero's welcome.

"It will be seen," wrote Barnum, "that very much of the success which attended my many years' proprietorship of the American Museum was due to advertising. . . . I studied ways to arrest public attention; to startle, to make people talk and wonder; in short, to let the world know that I had a museum." Although better remembered for his circus shows, he was at heart a museum man. But whatever he was promoting, Barnum always kept in mind that the successful showman "must have a decided taste for catering for the public; prominent perceptive facilities; tact; a thorough knowledge of human nature; great suavity; and plenty of 'soft soap.'"

The central, enduring feature of Barnum's enterprises was the showman himself; millions followed his every move, and his autobiography has gone through several editions. To many, especially foreigners, Barnum seemed the quintessential nineteenth-century American — boastful, clever, entrepreneurial, and somewhat overblown. It is said that President Grant, after returning from a world tour, said to Barnum, "Your name is familiar to multitudes who never heard of me. Wherever I went, among the most distant nations, the fact that I was an American led to constant inquiries whether I knew Barnum." Barnum died, with due fanfare, in 1891, but the circus he founded in 1871 and merged a decade later with that of James A. Bailey, and his impressive insight into the inner workings of showmanship and promotion, have kept the great museum-showman's name alive for a century and should for a long time to come.

Barnum's success inspired scores of imitators and provided opportunities for one of the oldest business practices — outdoing the competition.

A. T. Stewart's grand Marble Palace, opened in lower Manhattan in 1846, forever changed the way retailing in America was conducted. The huge dry-goods emporium offered vast quantities of merchandise at low prices in splendid surroundings.

A. T. Stewart's Marble Palace

LYDIA PINKHAM AND P. T. BARNUM stood out among the thousands of hawkers and peddlers of their day because they were masters of the art of selling, who understood their customers exceptionally well. But the enterprises they built were specialized and, as marketing organizations, somewhat limited. Barnum neither produced nor distributed products in a conventional way and created no formal organization to carry on his work. Pinkham appealed to a national market with newspaper advertising but relied on the mails to distribute her limited line of goods.

Great changes were taking place in the way goods were moved from producer to consumer, however, noticeable even during the lifetimes of Pinkham and Barnum. As the Civil War tempered the steel of political nationalism after 1865, key transportation technologies — the railroad, the telegraph, and the steamship — truly united the American states as a national market for the first time. By rail, goods could cross the continent in a matter of days instead of weeks or months, and business information coursed through telegraph wires at the speed of light. And as those who made products were no longer forced to sell them locally, distribution on a national scale became a new arena for entrepreneurial rivalry.

Outside the nation's largest cities, retailers carried on business as usual well into the railroad age. The old country store remained the far-flung monopoly and satisfier of every rural need on the American frontier, while barter and local trade remained strong. But in urban centers, densely packed with customers possessing every imaginable need and desire, a transformation in retailing was under way: specialization. More and more, merchants catered to special needs and narrow market niches.

MARSHALL FIELD & CO.
RETAIL DRY GOODS, CARPETS, UPHOLSTERY, ETC.
STATE ST. WASHINGTON ST. & WABASH AVE.
CHICAGO.

In 1853 a writer for the *United States Economist* fretted over this trend in New York: "The tendency is to a still more minute division, and thus we have a dealer in hosiery, a dealer in lace, a dealer in perfumery, a dealer in pocket handkerchiefs, a dealer in shawls, and a house just starting to keep nothing but suspenders! We suppose in ten years more there will be an establishment for spool cotton, and another for corsetlaces, if such instruments of torture shall then be in vogue."

While specialization seldom reached the absurd heights predicted, during the second half of the nineteenth century several entrepreneurs developed a new kind of retailing institution — the department store — which, because it was an assemblage of small specialty stores under a single roof, combined the virtues of specialization with those of convenience.

But it was more than this. Given the scale of the department store, its owners could purchase large quantities of goods from regional and national suppliers at relatively low prices, something its small, local competitors could not hope to match. This made the department store a "mass retailer," one of a special breed of institutions — including the mail order house, the chain store, and,

Marshall Field's Department Store, opened in 1858, was Chicago's answer to the Marble Palace.

GROVER & BAKER SEWING MACHINE Co.

495 BROADWAY

NEW-YORK

LITH. & PRINTED IN COLORS BY

CROW, THOMAS & CO, 57 PARK ROW, N.Y.

Other businesses were quick to emulate the standard for commercial architecture set by the Marble Palace. In the same neighborhood, the ornate façade of the Grover and Baker Sewing Machine Company led into elegant, spacious interiors.

later, the supermarket — that sold large volumes of goods at low markups.

Historians have debated for more than a century about who founded the first department store. The verdict depends upon one's definition, of course, but most would agree that A. T. Stewart occupies a central place in the institution's history. Stewart sold only "dry goods" in his Marble Palace in New York City and did not diversify his product lines, but he did introduce nearly every other aspect of the department store a full generation before more well-known retailers like Macy and Sears entered the business.

Little is known of Irish-born Stewart's early life; indeed, even the year of his birth is uncertain; it was probably 1802. His father, a lace maker, died three days after his son's birth, and Stewart was raised by his maternal grandfather, who sent him to seminary school in preparation for the ministry. After his grandfather's death, Stewart traveled to America a couple of times, taking with him a few thousand dollars he had inherited from his father and grandfather. Accounts differ, but apparently Stewart had invested some of the capital in a stock of fine Irish linens and was forced to take over the operation of a small New York dry goods shop when an associate failed to meet his obligations.

What began as a speculative investment turned into an occupation; with no experience in retailing, Stewart found himself in the business.

That was in 1823. Stewart operated a 12 by 30 foot shop at 283 Broadway. The store was indistinguishable from dozens of other small, dimly lit, owner-operated dry goods shops. Another nearby, called Lord & Taylor, opened in 1827. Still, Stewart distinguished himself as a shrewd and honest merchant, and he expanded and relocated his store nearby several times during the next few years. He became known as a hard-driving merchandiser with a special knack for catering to customers, nearly all of them women.

Stewart made it a practice to buy in large lots for cash only, often at auctions of European goods, which were common in New York during these decades. Then he would sell these goods at very low markups. Today this practice is the central characteristic of mass merchandising, but it was a breakthrough in Stewart's day, when retailers sought profits by charging the highest markups traffic would bear. Stewart put it this way: "I study to put my goods on the market at the lowest price I can afford and secure a reasonable profit. In that way I limit competition and increase my sales; and although I realize a small profit on each sale, the enlarged area of business makes possible a large accumulation of capital and assures the future."

At first necessity drove Stewart toward this policy. Once, after being forced to meet a note, he drastically reduced prices and noticed how quickly the goods moved. During the panic of 1837, Stewart purchased and sold $50,000 worth of silks within a few days, reaping a profit of $20,000, a sales strategy that was perhaps the antecedent to the modern "bargain basement." The ensuing depression ruined many but made Stewart a millionaire.

In the early 1840s, Stewart began formulating plans to take a major gamble, which would forever change the history of retailing. Choosing a site on Broadway between Reade and Chambers streets for his next and largest store, he paid between $90,000 and $100,000 for the property under and adjacent to Washington Hall, which burned to the ground in July of 1844, and began designing a lavish shopping emporium. Most of Stewart's contemporaries considered the choice of location foolhardy. At the time, it was at the very borderland of city life. Broadway was not paved above Chambers, and Philadelphia merchant John Wanamaker pointed out that Stewart had even chosen the wrong, or "shilling," side of Broadway for the project. But Stewart's emporium was to transform the area into the center of Manhattan fashion retailing, and it remained so for decades.

On September 18, 1846, three days before the store's opening, James Gordon Bennett of the *New York Herald* deemed it the "Marble Palace." To allay his readers' fears that the "beauty and splendor" of the building's interior had been "exaggerated by popular report," Bennett described the scene:

> The visitor enters a spacious hall, on each side of which are low counters of mahogany and shelves of maple. The entrance hall opens into another circular hall, over which rises a graceful dome, the apex of which is about ninety feet from the ground. Round this circular hall are counters of highly polished mahogany and . . . drawers of maple. The wall opposite the visitor on his entrance, is to be lined to the height of the ceiling with mirrors. . . .
>
> The ceiling is supported by columns, with stuccoed capitals of exquisite design. The main arch dividing the entrance from the circular hall before mentioned, is supported by Italian marble columns, consisting of a single shaft, fluted and polished to the highest degree of finish. The design of

A rare photograph of A. T. Stewart, the first great merchant prince, who introduced most of the practices of the modern department store. A shy and superstitious man, Stewart refused to pose for portraits and paid to have existing pictures of himself destroyed.

Many of Stewart's retailing innovations were adopted by merchants across the country. Fixed prices, salespeople at every station, and male clerks to entice women into the store were all in evidence on the main floor of the Gamble-Desmond Department Store in New Haven in 1915.

the capitals, which are not as yet finished, is of the most chaste graceful character, consisting of a cornucopia intertwined with the caduceus of Mercury, the god of commerce. This beautiful device is apparent in all the ornamental painting and other embellishments of the building. The walls and ceilings are painted in fresco, and the tinting and design are exquisitely chaste, classic, and tasteful — There is one large chandelier in the main hall, that is not surpassed in beauty by anything we have ever seen. . . . The gas fixtures are of a new and beautiful pattern. . . .

The building contains five stories, including the basement. A portion of the basement is used as a carpet room, and the remainder for the reception of goods. The lower story will be used exclusively for the retail trade. The main entrance and the central hall are designed for the sale of miscellaneous and fancy articles. The north room is to be a shawl room, and the south room is to be used as a linen and furnishings room.

Carriages lined up in front of the new landmark on opening day, and thereafter crowds thronged in at an estimated 1,000 visitors per hour. The store was stocked with $600,000 worth of goods and was designed to sell over $2 million of merchandise per year and turn over its stock every three months. Such scale and style had never before been seen in America.

The exterior of the building, which was designed by the noted architects Joseph Trench and John Butler Snook, probably with significant input from Stewart, also served as the prototype for virtually all the grand emporiums since built throughout America and the world. Its frontage along Broadway was 60 feet and the structure ran 40 feet along Reade, but several additions expanded the building until it covered nearly the entire block, about 35,000 square feet. Its popular title was appropriate because, along with John Notman's Athenaeum in Philadelphia, it was one of the first buildings in the nation with a marble façade and perhaps the first such commercial structure.

Highlighting the Italian Renaissance façade, appointed with Corinthian pillars, were the huge plate-glass windows, which Stewart, impressed by the

concept in Europe, had specially imported. New York merchant Philip Hone, among others, was struck by the novelty of the panes. "My attention was attracted, in passing this morning, to a most extraordinary, and I think useless, piece of extravagance," Hone recorded. "Several of the windows of the first floor, nearly level with the street, are formed of plate-glass, six feet by eleven, which must have cost four or five hundred dollars each, and may be shivered by a boy's marble or snowball as effectively as by a four-pound shot." Stewart's innovation is now ubiquitous, of course. Still, Hone was not entirely off the mark in his criticism, since Stewart used the glass only for windows and failed to go a step farther and use them for display purposes.

For buildings, then, the basic pattern was set by Stewart. Recognizing the genius in his strategy, imitators appeared in New York and other major American cities: Arnold Constable opened a Marble Palace on Canal Street in 1857; Potter Palmer of Chicago did the same in 1858 (later Marshall Field's), earning him the title "A. T. Stewart of the West." John Shillito became the A. T. Stewart of Cincinnati; and John Wanamaker and R. H. Macy created lasting American landmarks. Stewart was first to recognize that the glamor of a building, especially on such a large scale, could be a powerful draw. In fact, he was so assured of the notoriety of his shopping palaces that he never graced them with signs.

After he completed a grand "Iron Palace" farther uptown in 1862, Stewart declared to Peter Cooper, founder of the Cooper Union: "My store will vie with your museum, and people will throng to it as they do an exhibition."

A. T. Stewart's contributions to retail operations were equally influential. Because he was doing business on an unprecedented scale, he had to be something of an administrative wizard in solving operating problems. But he also helped transform the way Americans did their shopping, helping to create buying habits that now are taken for granted but were almost revolutionary in 1846.

Consider the world of retailing in the mid-nineteenth century. The typical fancy goods shop, for instance, was small — ten or twenty feet wide and less than twice as deep. A simple sign would be posted above the entrance, but no large windows beckoned in passers-by. Once inside, a customer, probably female, would face a confusing array of merchandise, stacked with little regard for proper presentation and hard to see in the dim lighting. Most goods would be piled behind long counters, accessible only from the clerk.

Then began the buying ritual. The clerk, who was often the proprietor as well, would lead the customer around the tiny store to discuss the merchandise, the less reputable of the breed trying to sell the lady far more than she desired. There were no price tags on goods, nor did they sell for uniform prices. Haggling was the standard practice, and the clerk was always careful to size up the social and economic status of his customer before quoting figures.

Inside Stewart's palace, shopping was radically different. Customers browsed freely among the lavish departments as light poured in from the Tiffany dome and ornate gas chandelier above. Each department was staffed by a clerk, rooted at his station, who sold goods marked with fixed prices. While it is not clear that Stewart was the first to practice these important policies — known as "free entry" and "one price" — he was the first to do so consistently on a large scale.

The one price policy emerged from administrative need as well as from Stewart's sensitivity to the needs of his customers. With so many clerks — from 400 to 500 by the Civil War — selling such a large volume of goods, the Merchant Prince feared leaving price setting to their discretion. In addition, he recognized that women, who comprised the vast majority of his clientele, spurned the process of haggling over price. Always an imaginative marketer, Stewart also reversed common practice by hiring mostly men for clerk positions, realizing that many of his female customers liked to flirt. Soon, female shoppers were coming to see "Stewart's nice young men" as much as his grand emporium.

With time, Stewart implemented full vertical integration as well, owning and operating entities at every level of the distribution chain. At first he concentrated on wholesaling in addition to retailing; indeed, by 1865, only $8 million of the firm's $50 million in sales were retail. In 1845 he set up a foreign purchasing office, eventually operating offices and warehouses in Germany, France, Ireland, Scotland, England, and Switzerland. As for manufacturing, he purchased woolen mills to manufacture uniforms during the Civil War, and by the end of his career, Stewart was operating textile mills in New York, New Jersey, and parts of New England. Still, the company purchased most of its goods from foreign and domestic manufacturers, and in some cases, as with the elegant and popular Alexander kid gloves, Stewart wielded his power to secure exclusive contracts.

And it was power in retailing on an unprecedented scale. After opening the Iron Palace in 1862, which covered the entire block bordered by Broadway and Fourth Avenue and Ninth and Tenth streets (each of its eight floors, accessed by six elevators, covered 2.25 acres), Stewart was responsible for a tenth of all the goods entering New York harbor. Duties on these imports ran about $9 million annually, making Stewart the largest individual contributor to the U.S. Treasury during the Civil War. By the 1870s he had become the first merchant to sell over $10 million of retail goods per year.

Social status never seemed to follow on the heels of Stewart's financial success, however. Although he was known for standing inside the main entrance of his store to greet customers, Stewart was never very comfortable in public situations. A shy, diminutive, and superstitious man, he consistently refused to pose for portraits, and at one point even tried to buy all of those in existence. An impressive fine arts collection lined the gallery of the grandiose mansion he built next door to the Astors, but he was never fully accepted into the ranks of New York's social elite.

Stewart died during America's centennial year, following by a few months the passing of another of the nation's richest entrepreneurs, Cornelius Vanderbilt. Stewart's death brought wide but mixed press coverage. The *Galaxy* complained that it was an "incredible thing in America, neither Stewart nor Vanderbilt left one poor dollar of his fifty or sixty millions to any municipal or charitable purpose," while *Frank Leslie's Illustrated Newspaper* rallied to the defense of the deceased moguls: "An Astor, a Stewart, a Vanderbilt is a blessing in another sense; for each gives honorable, renumretive [sic] and permanent employment to an army of men and women."

In a macabre and drawn out episode, Stewart's body was exhumed by grave robbers and held for ransom, then falsely reported to be recovered more than a half dozen times. Because Stewart was childless, his business fell into the hands of an incompetent, apparently anti-Semitic associate named Henry Hilton, who ran it to ruin, dashing also Stewart's plan to create a utopian community at Garden City, Long Island.

As a result, few people today recognize the Stewart name. Yet he was the first great proponent of mass merchandising in America and a man who, in his day, held one of the largest fortunes in the nation, built a palatial mansion at Thirty-fourth Street and Fifth Avenue, at the time the largest residence in North America, and owned probably more Manhattan real estate than anyone except "the landlord of New York," John Jacob Astor. The epitaph printed by the *New York Trade Reporter* perhaps came closest to what Stewart's legacy might have been: "What Newton was among scientists, Watt among inventors, such was A. T. Stewart among commercial men. He is doubtless destined to be a central figure in future histories of America, as being the first man who looms grandly up, Saul-like, from the level of the commercial age."

The move toward self-service became the hallmark of twentieth-century retailing, not only in department stores but in groceries as well. At this Piggly Wiggly in Memphis in 1918 — a predecessor of today's ubiquitous supermarket — customers helped themselves and paid as they left.

Montgomery Ward's "Wish Book"

S TEWART AND HIS IMITATORS brought a rich variety of goods to city dwellers
at unprecedented low prices. But before 1920 most Americans still lived in
rural settings, where they were largely denied this diversity of bargains. So an
opportunity to satisfy widespread demand was available to entrepreneurs in retailing and a few, indeed, met the challenge of bringing mass merchandising to
the countryside.

Aaron Montgomery Ward of Chicago built the first great mail order enterprise. Born in 1843 in Chatham, New Jersey, Ward moved with his family to
Michigan, where he went to work as an apprentice while still in public school
and then switched to barrel making at age fourteen. Five years later he began
his lifetime career in retailing when he secured a job at a local general store.
Adapting well, he was put in charge of the store at the age of twenty-one. At the
end of the Civil War, Ward switched to Chicago's Marshall Field's Department
Store, where he stayed for two years before moving to still another wholesaler.

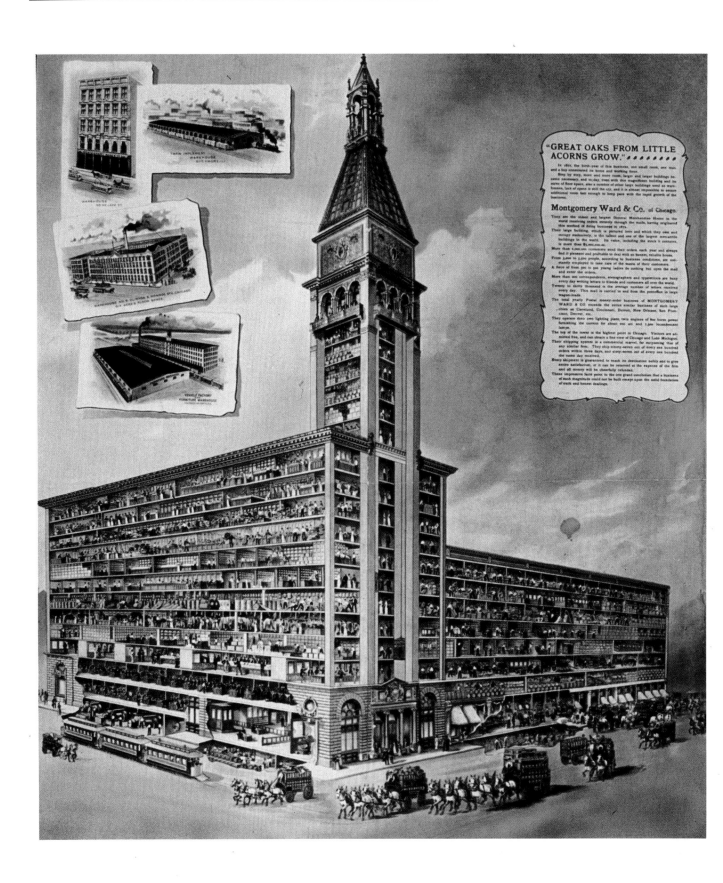

Ward's next post, as a traveling salesman, provided him with the experience and inspiration he needed to start his mail order enterprise. Traveling widely throughout the rural West and conversing with its residents, Ward recognized an important fact: people outside large cities wanted to buy, but they were unhappy with the poor selection and high prices that still characterized stores in rural, especially farm, areas.

Just as Ward was ready to start his mail order business in 1871, his savings went up in flames in the great Chicago fire. Undaunted, he recruited a partner, his brother-in-law George Thorne, and in 1872 the two men each contributed $1,600 to found the business. They issued their first "catalogue," a one-page list of items for sale at very low prices, from their operations headquarters in a Chicago livery loft.

In addition to low prices, Ward's emphasized its guarantee of customer satisfaction. This was critical, for without such a commitment customers would fear investing in goods from an unseen seller. The business did well the first year, but the turning point came in 1873 when the company was awarded a contract to be the supplier of the National Grange, a massive farmers' collective. Ward carefully cultivated this account, offering Grange members ten days' credit, and from 1873 to the 1880s publicized the fact that his company was "The Original Grange Supply House."

By 1884 the slim catalogue had grown to 240 pages and contained over 10,000 items. Sales topped $1 million for the first time four years later, and the company received still another spur in 1895, when the government (under the guidance of Post Master General John Wanamaker) instituted Rural Free Delivery. But this change favored other mail order houses as well, including Ward's arch rival, Sears, Roebuck, which had moved its aggressive mail order business to Chicago in 1893. As the majestic Ward Tower went up in Chicago at the turn of the century, harbingers of trouble were already apparent. Within a few years, Sears passed Montgomery Ward in catalogue sales. Still, in 1913 Ward was a giant, with annual sales of $40 million and 6,000 employees, bracing for a good fight.

In the 1920s, however, the competitive arena changed. Both Ward's and Sears began building chain stores to compensate for the fact that farm income drastically declined from $17 billion in 1920 to $11 billion in 1924. By 1927 Ward's had expanded its chain store network faster than Sears and was already operating 36 units. In 1931, when the company had twice as many chain locations as Sears, however, it became suddenly and chillingly clear that the expansion had come too quickly. Buying had fallen precipitously with the coming of the Depression, and some 450 of Ward's stores were already operating at a loss.

Ward himself had long since passed from the scene, but his company was able to realign its strategy under the new management of Sewell Avery of U.S. Gypsum Company and made a spectacular recovery by the end of the 1930s. The founder's primary contribution, the mail order business, somewhat overshadowed by the chain of retail outlets, continued to bring a rich variety of low-priced goods to relatively isolated American buyers, who used "Monkey" Ward's colorful catalogue as a source of endless entertainment and as a valuable link to the world of mass retailing.

The ever-changing retail scene forces continuous adaptation. Stewart moved from wholesaling and retailing into manufacturing, while Ward's and Sears went on from the mail order business to become huge chains. The Montgomery Ward company has recently discontinued its catalogue business; but rising entrepreneurs such as Lillian Vernon Katz of Mount Vernon, New York, who since 1951 has built a $100 million mail order business by offering upscale specialty items, have shown that the possibilities in the mail order business have hardly been exhausted.

William C. Procter: From Manufacturing to Marketing

MASS RETAILERS AROSE at the expense of America's middlemen. From about 1815 to 1860, these middlemen had played an indispensable role in the economy, gathering bulk products from a variety of producers, breaking them into smaller lots and branding them, and distributing them to scores of merchants, while providing both with much-needed capital in the process.

But by the late 1900s these intermediaries were squeezed from both directions: by mass merchandisers such as A. T. Stewart and Montgomery Ward, and also by an increasing number of large manufacturers who decided to distribute directly to retailers. This came less from competitive strategy than economic necessity. The fact was, some products simply could not be handled adequately by jobbers, wholesalers, and commission brokers. A growing number of large manufacturers recognized that they would either integrate forward into distribution or they would perish.

The drive for manufacturers to distribute the goods came mainly from technology. The techniques of large-batch production, developed in many late-nineteenth-century industries, doomed middlemen. Products poured out of factories like a river in desperate search of outlets. Machinery had to run ceaselessly to realize a proper return on investment; if the flow to consumers was interrupted, profits plummeted. The mechanization of industry not only made higher profits possible but also made imperative mass distribution and its handmaiden, advertising.

A striking example of significant alterations in retailing caused by mechanization and promotion was Procter & Gamble, the nation's preeminent marketer of mass consumption products. P&G is a company whose beginnings can be traced to the kind of vision that animated Gustavus Swift as he peered into Bubbly Creek, considering ways to use every part of the steer or pig so there would be no waste. Enormous amounts of fat were generated in the carving of carcasses, but none was discarded. Fats had several uses in the mid-nineteenth century. They were employed as lubricants, for example, and were an ingredient in cosmetics, dyes, and paints. But the two most important fat-based products were soap and candles. At a time when farm families still used fats from their animals to make products for themselves, urban dwellers were purchasing candles from dry goods stores and having the proprietor cut bars of soap from a slab he purchased from one of the many local soap manufacturers or its distributor.

Wherever there was a packing plant, candle and soap makers would be nearby, and cities where meat packing was big business had the largest of these. One such place was Cincinnati, the "Porkopolis" of the West, and it was there that William Procter, a British candle maker, and his wife's Irish-born brother-in-law, James Gamble, a soap manufacturer, formed their partnership in 1837. In addition to candles and soaps, they processed and sold lard and lard oil, also by-products of hog butchering. The business prospered, and on the eve of the

Procter & Gamble made a niche for itself in the soap market by capitalizing on Ivory's unique qualities, proclaimed in this 1898 ad.

An imaginative practitioner of modern advertising, P&G spends large sums to come up with new ideas to promote its products worldwide. This German ad proclaims Ivory "the favorite soap of the Maharaja."

Civil War P&G was the largest company of its kind in Cincinnati. Thanks to government contracts to supply the army with candles and soap, P&G broadened its scope, breaking out of the mold of regionalism to start entertaining national aspirations.

As with all manufacturers hoping to have more than local distribution, P&G came to rely heavily on wholesale merchants, who would take consignments of soap and candles and sell them to small retailers in their service areas. Such middlemen had been employed by Francis Cabot Lowell and other textile manufacturers of the early nineteenth century, and they flourished during the pre–Civil War period, when the railroad was bringing goods far from their place of manufacture.

These wholesalers generally were in the business of buying goods from manufacturers and then trying to resell them in the most profitable fashion. As a result, they were inclined to offer preferential deals to favored retailers, which meant that a product's price at one store could be markedly different from that charged at another in the same town. As urbanization increased and customers shopped at several stores, they came to realize this, complained, and sparked discontent at the factory. In addition, the wholesalers speculated on future price movements by hoarding or selling off their consignments, and often confronted producers with orders on a schedule dictated less by ultimate use of the product than by their own financial and other manipulations. Still, in the post–Civil War boom, there seemed little way of conducting business without them.

William Procter and James Gamble each had three sons, and several of them, most notably James N. Gamble and Harley and William A. Procter, entered the business. While the Procters tended to concentrate on candles and the Gambles on soap, there was a general sharing of responsibilities, and the company was not bifurcated along product lines. In 1878 soap accounted for less than a quarter of the company's income, the rest deriving from candles and lard. But it was also becoming more and more evident that candles would soon give way to kerosene lamps and later, of course, to gas and electric lights. That there would always be a market for candles seemed axiomatic, but the real future was in soap, for as America continued to industrialize and urbanize, demand for factory-manufactured products increased.

That year James N. Gamble came up with a new soap. At the time, luxury bars contained olive oil and other fine, expensive ingredients; he wanted to create a product similar in fineness but based upon less expensive oil. "We thought it well to make the soap similar to the castile soap & I came in contact with a young man who was interested with others in making a soap of the same kind of ingredients, namely vegetable oils." The result was a white soap, not unusual or different from many others being turned out by the three hundred or so manufacturers of the time. Harley Procter then decided to place a groove in the laundry-size bar, so it could be cut in half easily, and claimed it was the only laundry soap that could be used in the bathroom and nursery.

What was unusual was the soap's special quality: the ability to float. Supposedly it happened that one of the workers left a mixing machine running too long and puffed the soap mixture more than usual. The batch was permitted to cool and was cut and packaged and sent to the wholesaler. Soon after, customers wrote asking for more of the "soap that floats." In this way, it was said, P&G had accidentally come up with something that differentiated its product from the others.

While the story was false, the company proved deft at capitalizing on the soap's special quality. Seeking a name for the product, Harley Procter came up with "Ivory," inspired by the Forty-fifth Psalm ("All thy garments smell of myrrh, and aloes, and cassia, out of the ivory palaces whereby they have made thee glad"). Advertising initially stated that "The Ivory Soap will float," and after several changes this became the slogan "It Floats!" Going further, Procter had Ivory analyzed and was told it contained 0.11 percent uncombined alkali, 0.28 percent carbonates, and 0.17 percent mineral matter, for a total of 0.56 percent useless impurities, which left 99.44 percent active soap. The slogan now was to be "The Ivory . . . is 99 and 44/100 percent pure."

As we have seen, this was an age of bunkum and ballyhoo, and Harley Procter was playing in a tough league, where rival soap makers put forth all kinds of claims for their products. Procter was one of the best: on the back of the Ivory package was a notice that doctors condemned colored soaps as "liable to produce skin diseases." Ivory was made of vegetable fats, so P&G asked, "Are you certain that the plate you eat and the cup you drink from have not been washed with soap made of diseased cattle?" The company warned, "The country is flooded with highly chemicalled and very dangerous soaps, the result of the fierce competition among soap makers, and the average housekeeper can not determine which is the safest to use." But help was at hand. "Practice makes perfect. The manufacturers of Ivory Soap have been making soap continuously since 1837, and the result of their long practical experience and intelligent experiments is the remarkable Ivory Soap, which chemists of national reputation pronounce to be without a superior."

P&G was hardly the originator of modern advertising, but it was one of the more astute practitioners, and on a large scale: by 1905 the company was spending $400,000 annually on advertising, a considerable figure for the time.

Shortly after the turn of the century, P&G experimented with several vegetable oil compounds that appeared likely to replace or at least challenge lard as a cooking fat. Out of this came a product that was more uniform than lard and less likely to turn rancid, which could also substitute for the more expensive butter in cooking. It started out in 1911 as Krispo, but the name was soon changed to Crisco.

In 1907 William A. Procter stepped down as president and was succeeded by his son, William Cooper Procter, whose first important success was bringing Crisco to market. Best known for his enlightened labor policies, William Procter was also one of the first to break the hold of the wholesalers over brand product distribution.

So long as P&G products were sold to wholesalers, the company could not plan efficiently and effectively. Procter could never know exactly how much soap and shortening to produce, since so much depended upon orders from the middlemen. Nor was there any way to accurately gauge the effectiveness of promotion and advertisement: consumer demand might not be translated into orders since they had to be filtered through the wholesalers. Production was becoming more mechanized, and Procter had to keep his machines operating at a high level to be efficient. This meant the flow from factory to consumer had to be regularized, which in turn meant the demise of the middleman.

Experiments began in the New York area and parts of New England, as scores of P&G salesmen went directly to the small retailers to seek orders. It seemed a risky and perhaps recklessly expensive proposition. The wholesaler could take orders for and deliver a wide variety of items, while the P&G salesman might spend the better part of an hour arranging for the purchase of a half-

Today P&G markets a wide range of products, from paper towels to potato chips.

dozen boxes of soap and a carton or two of Crisco. Was this economical? Procter thought it could be. Competition was intense; wholesalers couldn't be expected to favor one brand over another, while the P&G representatives could do so and thereby boost sales. In addition, wholesalers often set prices in a way manufacturers considered unwise and counterproductive; this would change with direct distribution. Procter put it this way in 1919, as the company prepared to put the program into operation:

> If we supplied the retailer with what he needs on a week-to-week basis, the outflow from our plants would likewise be a steady week-to-week flow. If we are to avoid periodic layoffs, the solution seems to be to sell so that we will be filling retail shelves as they are emptied. In that way, our outflow will be as steady as the retailer's. And we can stabilize our employment year-round to match the retailer's year-round sales.

As was to have been expected, the wholesalers rose in indignation, their very existence threatened. Some wholesalers said the change would crush the company. "P&G — Passed and Gone" was one of their slogans, and they tried to steer retailers into taking more of the brands manufactured by other companies. P&G retaliated with massive advertising and promotional campaigns, spending on advertising much of the profit it had realized through cheap production methods. They succeeded, with the result that later in the decade direct selling was imitated by P&G's competitors.

Direct sales to retailers was probably an inevitable development. Advertising was expanding greatly in this period, as manufacturers strove to differentiate their products in the eyes of customers. Such large firms as American Tobacco, P&G, Carnation, Colgate-Palmolive-Peet, H. J. Heinz, Quaker Oats, and others were expending large sums to create consumer recognition and demand, and sooner or later they would insist upon taking distribution out of the hands of middlemen.

The Resors: Advertising Comes of Age

THE RISE OF MODERN ADVERTISING created new entrepreneurial opportunities for those ready to cultivate them. Manufacturing and marketing giants such as American Tobacco and P&G sometimes created large staffs of professionals to promote their products, but often they subcontracted this work to others. With this, a new breed of business was created: the advertising agency. At first these companies acted as auxiliaries to their powerful host. But as their own scope and influence grew and businesses at every level in the economy demanded their services, they came to comprise an industry strong and influential in its own right.

For many years Lydia Pinkham's company used the services of an advertising agent named Harlan Page Hubbard. In those days such agents acted as brokers between those who wanted to advertise and the owners of publications, charging each whatever the traffic would bear. Normally they represented the magazines and newspapers, or, rather, speculatively purchased space from them for resale at their own risk. When the Pinkhams learned that Hubbard's cut comprised as much as half of their huge advertising budget during the 1880s, they tried to get him to disclose and limit his commission; failing this, they

replaced him in 1890 with a new agent who agreed to hold his fee to no more than 10 percent.

Despite such difficulties, it was becoming increasingly clear to the Pinkhams and others that advertising paid. Between 1890 and 1900, when the Pinkhams spent an average of 44 percent of revenues on advertising, their total sales climbed an astounding 2,500 percent. But advertising agents such as Hubbard, who were becoming a necessary evil, were giving the business a bad name. Thus was the stereotypical ad man, the fast-talking hype artist of dubious scruples, born. To some extent the image lives today; as advertising historian Stephen Fox has noted, "At cocktail parties, people in the advertising business wince when asked what they do for a living."

Still, advertising is now far more professional than it was in Hubbard's day. To a large extent this is because of the work of a special breed of advertising entrepreneurs who, during the early twentieth century, helped transform the industry, one which, despite the large size of some agencies, proved to be unusually personal because key entrepreneurs set the tone and direction for large enterprises as well as the entire profession. Yet for all of their influence on modern life (the J. Walter Thompson agency today alone serves markets that include over 1 billion people), the pioneers of advertising — Albert Lasker, Claude Hopkins, Bruce Barton, Raymond Rubicam, Leo Burnett, David Ogilvy, and William Bernbach, to name a few — remain virtually unknown.

James Walter Thompson, the namesake of what was for decades the world's largest advertising agency, was born in Saratoga, New York, moved to New York City as a young man, and worked his way up through a small advertising agency founded in 1864 in Manhattan by William J. Carlton and Edmund A. Smith. In 1878 Thompson, then the firm's bookkeeper, bought out his employer for $1,300, then quickly instituted several important strategies, which would help redirect the course of advertising history.

For one, he recognized that women, who controlled the bulk of disposable household income, were a powerful force in the marketplace. He also geared his advertising efforts toward magazines, a highly effective yet largely unused advertising medium. In this way, Thompson catered well to both of his agency's clients: advertisers, who got more for their dollar by advertising through national magazine consortia, which Thompson engineered; and publishers, who increased their revenues from nationally prominent firms. By the end of the century, when he had already earned the title "father of magazine advertising in America," Thompson held a virtual monopoly on such advertising and was diversifying into other print media. In 1896 Thompson incorporated the firm as the J. Walter Thompson Company, since then referred to as "J. Walter" or simply "JWT."

By 1916 JWT had offices in several major cities and was the largest advertising agency in the United States. But Thompson himself was weary from his ongoing struggle against arch Philadelphia competitor N. W. Ayer and sensed that the business was at a peak. Others have claimed that Thompson, after nearly four decades of pioneering work, was losing touch with the business. In any event, Thompson sold the firm for $500,000 in 1916 to a syndicate headed by one of his most promising employees, Stanley Resor. In one sense, Thompson's critics were proved right, he had been losing touch; in fact, he had seriously miscalculated. The firm was far from declining: as powerful and influential as JWT had become, it was just on the verge of its heyday.

Cincinnati-born Stanley Resor attended public school in his hometown before entering Yale. While he was in college, his father, a successful stove manufacturer, suffered a serious financial setback, thus sending Stanley's chances of taking over the family business up in smoke. After graduating in 1901, Resor held a variety of jobs before being hired as a salesman by Procter & Collier (P&G's in-house ad agency) in 1904. Four years later, he was recruited by J. Walter Thompson in New York. Resor drove hard at JWT and soon distinguished himself for his emphasis on brand-name development as well as his advertising strategies that encouraged middle-class consumers to emulate the buying habits of the rich.

Soon after his purchase of JWT, Resor played out his strategies. He streamlined the agency, closing less productive branches, firing many employees, and,

A Skin you love to touch

can be yours when you understand the skin and its needs

So few people really understand the skin, that "a skin you love to touch" is rarely found.

Whatever the condition that is keeping your skin from being beautiful, it can be changed. Is your skin colorless, sallow, coarse textured or excessively oily? Are there little rough places in it that make it look scaly when you powder?

Whatever the trouble is, you can make your skin what you would love to have it. Like the rest of your body, your skin is continually being rebuilt. As *old* skin dies, *new* forms. Every day, in washing, you rub off the dead skin. This gives you your opportunity.

In the books that noted skin specialists have written you will find this advice: The best way to make this new skin so strong and healthy that it will truly be "a skin you love to touch" is by proper cleansing with a soap carefully prepared to suit the nature of the skin.

It was to meet the need for such a soap that John H. Woodbury, after thirty years' study and treatment of the skin, prepared the formula for his now famous Woodbury's Facial Soap.

Begin tonight to get its benefits

To make your skin "a skin you love to touch," begin this treatment tonight. Just before retiring, wash with Woodbury's in the following way: With warm water work up a heavy lather of Woodbury's in your hands. Then work this cleansing, antiseptic lather into your skin—always with an upward and outward motion. Rinse with warm water, then with cold. Then rub your face for several minutes with a *lump of ice.*

Use this treatment persistently, and in ten days or two weeks your skin should show a marked improvement. Use Woodbury's regularly thereafter, and before long your skin will take on that finer texture, that greater freshness and charm of "a skin you love to touch." A 25c cake of Woodbury's is sufficient for a month or six weeks of this treatment. Get a cake today and begin tonight to get its benefits.

Write for the beautiful picture above

Clarence Underwood's beautiful painting of "A Skin You Love to Touch" shown above has been reproduced in full colors by a new and beautiful process. It is twice the size shown here. No advertising matter appears on it. We want you to have this picture as a constant reminder that you, too, can have "a skin you love to touch." Mail the coupon below with ten cents in stamps or coin, and we will forward you the picture, together with a cake of Woodbury's Facial Soap large enough for a week's treatment. Mail the coupon today. ADDRESS THE ANDREW JERGENS CO., 202 Spring Grove Ave., Cincinnati, O.

Woodbury's Facial Soap

For sale by dealers everywhere throughout the United States and Canada.

Canadians: *The Woodbury products are now manufactured also in Canada, and sold by Canadian druggists from coast to coast. For picture and sample, address The Andrew Jergens Co., Ltd., 202 Sherbrooke St., Perth, Ontario.*

most important, dropping over 200 of the firm's 300 clients, retaining only the largest. The following year, 1917, Resor achieved another important consolidation: he married a co-worker named Helen Landsdown. Resor had met Landsdown when he was at Procter and Collier, then hired her as a copywriter at Thompson. During the next several decades, Stanley and Helen proved to be a remarkable creative and managerial team, guiding the company through a sustained period of growth and international expansion and building it into the world's leading advertising agency.

Stanley Resor also began to staff the agency with college graduates, then a rarity in the business. In this way, Resor, who explicitly hoped to create a "university of advertising," made important advances in the professionalization of the industry. By 1928 a quarter of the company's staff of 600 held degrees, four of them doctorates. But his interest was not simply abstract: Resor looked to scholars to better his understanding of human nature and thereby make his advertising efforts more effective. For a time, the novelist John P. Marquand worked at JWT, but he proved to be a frustrated and unsuccessful copywriter.

Psychologists, a still rarer breed in the 1920s, filled a special role at the firm. They contributed knowledge and credentials to Resor's persistent search for an understanding of the nature of basic human drives. At an early age, Resor had been influenced by the work of William Graham Sumner, among others, who postulated that human beings evolved slowly, driven by primitive urges like sex, fear, vanity, hunger. Sharing this basic view was psychologist John B. Watson, one of the founders of "behaviorism," who was brought on board by Resor.

Watson instituted several interesting practices at JWT, including what were probably the first "blind" taste tests in the industry. Conducted with various cigarettes, these tests determined that consumers were unable to distinguish their own brands, and this led to the conclusion that consumer preferences were irrational. Watson was eventually made a vice president and an account executive at the company but remained somewhat disgruntled by the fact that the firm's orientation generally remained "intuitive" rather than "scientific" as he would have liked.

If his interest in psychology and philosophy reflected his desire to "understand the customer" on the most personal level, Resor also sought to understand the customer in more objective ways, as reflected in demographic, geographical, sociological, and other quantifiable trends. As early as 1912, the agency conducted a mammoth market survey for Red Cross Shoes, for which it gathered statistics on thousands of retail establishments and about every town in the United States with more than 500 residents. These data were published as *Population and Its Distribution*; updated versions of the book were used by some 2,300 companies as well as the U.S. government in its compilation of the census. Resor also put a professor from the Harvard Business School, Paul Cherington, in charge of his research department in 1922. A disciple of Frederick Taylor's scientific management methods, Cherington conducted a number of "scientific" surveys of consumer habits. Thus, with research and professional psychology, Stanley Resor sought to understand the customer more thoroughly and systematically than probably ever before in the advertising industry.

While Helen Resor was also the product of an early life of hard work and creative drive, her skills and style contrasted sharply with those of her husband. Born in Grayson, Kentucky, the second youngest of nine children, Helen lost her father through divorce when she was four and faced a childhood that demanded thrift and responsibility. A serious, hard-working student, she graduated valedictorian of her high school class. At Procter & Collier, and later at J. Walter Thompson, Helen Resor demonstrated exceptional abilities to understand customers and craft effective advertising.

Many of her greatest strengths emerged from her perspective as a woman. This was especially timely, given the consumer products boom of the 1920s, when many new products were specifically designed for female consumption. "In advertising these products," she would later reflect, "I supplied the feminine point of view." Influential national women's magazines of the day, such as *Ladies' Home Journal* and the *Saturday Evening Post,* became her primary vehicles of expression.

Helen Resor's advertising approach powerfully combined the visual and sensual with the informative. Beautiful, often romantic, pictures accompanied a compact but informative text, touting the product and frequently offering a bargain or free sample. Perhaps the most famous of this breed was her ad for Woodbury's Facial Soap. Beneath an Alonzo Kimball painting of an embracing couple, which highlighted the phrase "A Skin You Love To Touch," were several key points telling women how they would benefit from the soap, capped off by a special offer. For this ad, Helen Resor has been credited with the first important use of "sex appeal" in advertising.

Her greatest contributions to the agency, however, were her superb copywriting and aesthetic abilities, which allowed her to compose striking, sumptuous, and effective advertisements. Helen practiced a more informal brand of psychology; one important "fact" about people, she believed, was that they were highly influenced by the convictions of others, especially those who were prominent, celebrated, or otherwise laudable. Because of this, she relied heavily on "testimonials," an advertising technique that remains a standard practice in the industry.

Testimonials had been used before Helen Resor by the likes of the patent medicine hawkers, but never on such a grand scale. Helen's first important testimonial appeared in 1917 for Pond's skin cream, and by 1926 she had signed up the queen of Spain, New York socialite and feminist Mrs. O. H. P. Belmont, the queen of Rumania, Mrs. Reginald Vanderbilt, and the duchess of Richelieu. Doctors were used to testify for Fleischmann's Yeast, and when American physicians balked, JWT found willing physicians in Europe. After the company secured the important Pan American Airways account in 1942, the Resors signed up the archbishop of Canterbury, Archbishop Samuel Stritch of Chicago (both distinguished men of the cloth were poor seconds to the original target, the pope!), philosopher John Dewey, and George Bernard Shaw.

An ingenious method for securing cheap testimony from stars was developed by JWT's Hollywood representative, Danny Danker. In exchange for a crate of Lux soap, unknown aspiring stars would promise Danker that they would endorse the product if they ever "made it big." Many did. For a free case of soap, such superstars as Clara Bow, Joan Crawford, and Janet Gaynor became Lux sponsors.

Helen Resor proved to be a pioneer among female executives. During her first years with the agency, she was transferred from Cincinnati to the New York headquarters, where she composed fine copy for important clients such as Yuban coffee, Cutex, and Lux detergent. In 1911, when Procter & Gamble broke with tradition and contracted outsiders to handle their Crisco account, Helen

Resor became the central force in the campaign and the first woman to attend P&G board meetings. According to Resor, "I was the first woman to be successful in writing and planning national, as opposed to retail, advertising."

As part of its path-making use of magazine advertising, JWT under the Resors became the first to replace pen-and-ink drawings with fine photography in printed advertising on a large scale. With other communications media, especially radio, which blossomed during the 1920s and 1930s, the Resors proved equally progressive. JWT sponsored not only ads but radio programs, producing them in its own Hollywood studios. In 1930 it had a dozen and a half clients who sponsored 23 hours of radio each week. The "Lux Radio Theater" and the "Kraft Music Hall" were two of the most successful Resor creations. Dozens of stars, including W. C. Fields, Edgar Bergen and Charlie McCarthy, Groucho Marx, Bing Crosby, Al Jolson, and Burns and Allen, got their start in this way.

Together the Resors were a dynamic, winning combination. Their managerial styles blended nicely, and both operated the agency in a freeform manner, without strict hierarchies, so that ideas and communication flowed through informal channels. Offices were decorated according to the taste of each individual, creating an eclectic atmosphere. Still, a few rules were steadfast at JWT. Nepotism was discouraged and, despite the example set by the owners, marriage (among employees and with members of client firms) meant dismissal for at least one of the partners. Finally, the couple, especially Stanley, maintained an unusually low profile for professionals of their stature. Stanley slipped inconspicuously in and out of work, rarely gave speeches, and shielded the details of his personal life from journalists and biographers.

The 1920s was an especially fertile creative period at J. Walter Thompson, setting the pattern for future growth, which took on an increasingly international orientation. A London branch was opened in 1923, but a turning point was reached in 1927 when General Motors, a JWT client, convinced the agency to open a branch in every country where the auto maker operated. During the next half-dozen years, JWT opened 23 European offices, as well as branches in Australia, South America, India, Africa, Southeast Asia, and New Zealand. The amount of advertising placed (the standard industry gauge) climbed from $3 million in 1916, the year Resor took over the agency, to $10.7 million in 1922, then rose precipitously to $23 million in 1927, $100 million in 1947, and three times that amount a decade later.

The Resors consistently positioned JWT to favor large advertisers, and while this was a critical early strategy during the 1920s, when advertising expenditures rose by 300 percent, it paid off handsomely during later decades. By the 1960s JWT's roster of clients was studded with the likes of Lever Brothers, RCA, Liggett & Myers Tobacco Company, the New York World's Fair, Kodak, Pan American World Airways, Standard Brands, 7-Up Company, Scott Paper Company, Quaker Oats Company, Kraft Foods, and Ford.

Henry Resor served as president of JWT until 1955 and chairman until 1961, the year before he died. During his final years, he seemed to be losing touch with current trends in the industry, just as Thompson had nearly a half century earlier.

For, despite its power, JWT and its sisters comprise an auxiliary industry, which functions symbiotically with the manufacturing and marketing giants in the economy, much as the tickbird thrives at the side of the rhinoceros. Both kinds of business are subject to the relentless vicissitudes of the marketplace, where the ability to adapt is never outmoded.

Associating a product with technology of the future has become a standard advertising strategy.

Sublime or ridiculous, the gimmick's the thing. Advertising is based on the truism that catching the public's attention is the first step toward selling a product.

Advertisers' willingness to capitalize on American icons (*left*) is parodied with biting humor in a travesty (*right*) that takes a dim view of the excesses of the marketing world.

By the 1960s less direct methods of selling — the use of self-deprecation and humor — were coming into vogue under the creative direction of entrepreneurs such as Mary Wells Lawrence, who were outsiders in the advertising establishment. In addition, television was becoming the dominant advertising medium, and JWT seemed far from the cutting edge of TV advertising. But Norman H. Strouse, the new president of JWT, proved responsive to these changes, and the agency continues to thrive today.

Since the 1950s, of course, no one in the marketing business can afford to ignore television's influence, springing as it does from its power to wed the nation together in one instantaneous electronic moment. More and more advertising dollars are being poured into the medium. One 30-second commercial spot during the Super Bowl now commands $550,000 and costs up to $1 million to produce, but it also reaches one-third of the entire U.S. population.

As CEOs such as Frank Perdue of Perdue Chicken, Lee Iacocca of Chrysler, and Victor Kiam of Remington mount the airwaves to pitch their companies' wares, as electronic networks and psychology are used to conduct and analyze market research, and as complicated computer matrices are developed to ease and speed the flow of detergents or cigarettes or video cassettes from factory to shelf, some observers speak of important new trends in marketing. Barnum might have laughed at this, as would, no doubt, a host of his marketing peers since the first stirrings of the craft.

VI

Instant America

DISTANCE AND TIME have always shaped the contours of American economic growth. Improvements in transportation weakened the effects of these barriers, speeding the movement of people, goods, and information. But the melding of technology and entrepreneurship led to the instantaneous conveyance of only one of these business components: information. And until Einstein's postulate that only energy, not matter, can travel at the speed of light is overthrown, humans and their artifacts will remain burdened by their very bulk and mass.

The impact of this information revolution on society, and on the way business has been conducted, has been profound. Computer banks, woven together by transcontinental communications networks, now process and transmit trillions of "bits" of information each second, while broadcast media blanket the globe with entertainment and news. Everyone in business has been forced to adapt to these changes, but only a few entrepreneurs actually shaped them, taking chances with the new technologies while trying to discern the emerging shape of the instantaneous world.

The business of "expressing" information began with the overland mail companies of the early nineteenth century, founded by men such as Alvin Adams, John Butterfield, William H. Russell, and Henry Wells, but the first instantaneous form of communication was the telegraph. This important industry, based on Samuel Morse's technological developments, became a viable, large-scale business in the hands of Hiram Sibley. The telephone had an even greater impact on American life, especially after it was forged into the giant AT&T network by Theodore Vail. Using airwaves instead of wires, radio and television then became the most powerful communications media yet devised, and David Sarnoff of RCA played a key role in their development. Meanwhile, the electronic components needed for modern communications technologies — from the radio to the computer — were first manufactured by companies such as Motorola, directed by Daniel Noble and Thomas Galvin. Today, pioneers such as Gerard O'Neill, founder of a satellite communications company called Geostar, continue to pursue new entrepreneurial opportunities.

It was only recently, however, that information began to move faster than goods and people. Apart from face-to-face meetings, handwritten letters were the primary means of communication between businessmen until well into the twentieth century. Lacking the means to send and receive messages, orders, payments, and other information rapidly, regularly, and with some degree of assurance that delivery would be made, merchants and bankers preferred close personal ties. The same was true for other individuals, for whom letter writing is now either a half-forgotten art or an onerous chore.

In the fifteenth century, the powerful Fugger banking family resolved the problem by settling relatives in Europe's money centers, knowing that relying on blood was more prudent than resting important decisions on the transmission of oral or written messages. The same reasoning motivated the partnership of Francis Cabot Lowell and his brother-in-law Patrick Tracy Jackson. The young J. P. Morgan's position in New York, depending as it did on his connection with his father's London firm, was hardly unusual in post–Civil War America.

The speed at which information could be transmitted depended on available technology. The horse-drawn carriages of the late Colonial period were little improvement over those of Elizabethan times. Indeed, messages were trans-

The romantic riders for Butterfield's Pony Express traveled day and night through dangerous territory to deliver the mail. In the mid-nineteenth century, the Pony Express and the telegraph served America's growing need for rapid delivery of information to all parts of the country.

mitted more swiftly through the Roman Empire a millennium and a half earlier, since the roads were better.

Attempts to develop improved methods of rapid communication are as old as civilization. Smoke signals, fire beacons, homing pigeons, and even "lung telegraphs," by which individuals blessed with powerful voices shouted, yodeled, or whistled, were used for communicating across relatively short distances. The Greeks employed a system of fire signals to report the victory in the Trojan War across 170 miles to Mycenae, and Pheidippides ran the 22 miles from Marathon to Athens to bring news of the great victory over the Persians in 490 B.C. In the thirteenth century, Ghengis Kahn utilized a relay of horses with stations 25 miles apart, which covered 300 miles in twenty-four hours. Ships used semaphores in ancient times to communicate with one another, and they are still employed today. Napoleon's engineers created a line of 224 line-of-sight stations to transmit messages by semaphores. In the United States, the first such system was built in 1800 by Jonathan Grout to run from Martha's Vineyard to Boston to send information regarding ship arrivals; seven "telegraph hills" between the island and the city still mark the route, just as San Francisco's Telegraph Hill is a reminder of that city's use of a semaphore system during the gold rush.

COPYRIGHT 1903.

U.S. Mail outposts like this one could be found even in remote areas in 1903. But while the government played a role in express mail delivery, it was private entrepreneurs who offered reliable, guaranteed service.

During Colonial times, intercontinental communications depended on available carriers; an exchange of letters between London and New York required four months. When Frederic Tudor sent orders to his agents in Calcutta, he realized the reply would not arrive for more than a year — if at all.

The Founding Fathers appreciated the need for improved communications, if only because many of them were merchants or farmers who sold their crops in distant markets. Both the Articles of Confederation and the Constitution gave the central government responsibility for providing a postal service. But deliveries would be erratic and slow while America remained essentially agrarian. Mail was carried between New York and Philadelphia only once a week in 1785, and five years later there were only 75 post offices in the entire United States.

This lack of frequent, regular postal service encouraged private individuals to enter the field, offering "express" service to those needing it. No one knows just when this began or who was involved; in all probability frequent travelers, noting they were often asked to deliver letters and parcels, made a small business of it toward the middle of the eighteenth century. By then, too, they made their presence known through notices like this one in the *Boston Sentinel* in 1789:

> The proprietors of the mail stages be leave to inform the public that they have employed two faithful trusty persons, who go in the Stages from this town to New York and back, and who will execute any commissions they shall please to intrust them with, on reasonable terms. Newspapers from either place, carefully delivered at 2s 3d per annum. Inquire at Stage House, near the Mall, January 31, 1789

Express service would be irregular and erratic in the agrarian era, giving the government its chance to dominate the market for mail and small articles. Most federal funds flowed to the coastal corridor between Baltimore and Boston, but the early-nineteenth-century economic boom and transportation mania sparked by the opening of the Erie Canal and the development of the early railroads caused interest to turn westward. As Chicago, St. Louis, and other western cities grew, bankers, merchants, and others there and in the East felt a pressing need for improved communications. By the mid-1830s, shippers realized that, in time, this would be provided by the railroad, but in 1836 the nation had only slightly more than 1,000 miles of track, and businessmen wanted action immediately. That year Congress authorized a postal express service to transport the mails from the East Coast to St. Louis, New Orleans, and Nashville. The carriers were to travel on horseback, "at the rate of eleven to twelve miles an hour, day and night," or about twice the rate of carriages.

By then, too, the express business had expanded to the point where companies were making regular deliveries of mail, parcels, and bills, usually faster and often at a lower price than the postal services. One of them, William F. Harnden, worked for a while as a railroad conductor and happened to be on one of the first trains to bring ice to Boston. Ailing and seeking less taxing employment, he took the suggestion of a friend who worked as agent for a steamship line, who thought he might deliver packages for customers who called at the offices, asking if anyone could carry them at the other end of the line. Soon Harnden drifted into the express business and apparently was the first person to call himself an "expressman," announcing in 1839 that he would "run a car through from Boston to New York and vice versa four times a week" to collect drafts and make deliveries. Soon other expressmen were going into the South and West, in competition with the post office, performing a vital business function.

Expressing the Mail

ONE OF THE FIRST EXPRESSMEN was Alvin Adams, who started out as a partner in an express company that made deliveries between Boston and Worcester, Massachusetts. Business was poor, and the proprietor was more than pleased to sell out to Adams in 1841 for $100. Sharper and more aggressive than most, Adams expanded operations to New York and then on to Albany. By 1850 the service had entered Philadelphia and Baltimore, growing through partnerships and acquisitions. Adams leapfrogged to the West Coast after the gold discoveries in 1848, initially carrying letters and parcels along the coast and then entering the gold-hauling business. Adams purchased Harnden & Company in 1854 and, renaming his company Adams Express, worked to fill in the area between New York and San Francisco. Within four years he was in St. Louis, Cincinnati, and Louisville, with New Orleans the next stop. In an industry noted for small units, Adams Express was a giant.

Dozens of individuals were engaged in the business. One of the more typical was John Butterfield. Born in Berne, New York, in 1801, Butterfield devoted his entire adult life to transportation. Indeed, his career recapitulates its history in the first two-thirds of the nineteenth century. As a youth, Butterfield worked as a stage driver out of Albany. After accumulating sufficient funds, he moved to Utica, purchased a horse and coach, and went into the livery business on his own. In time Butterfield would take interests in Great Lakes steamers, Erie Canal barges, and the construction of plank roads in the Utica area. He then entered the street-railroad business and, toward the end of his life, dabbled in the telegraph as well.

In 1849 Butterfield and another expressman, James D. Wasson, organized a service to transport goods and mail by rail from New York to Buffalo. Another Butterfield company soon operated between New York and Cleveland, while a third carried freight across the isthmus of Panama. These were hardly industry leaders but rather typical small operations; indeed, there wasn't much of an industry at the time, merely a heterogeneous collection of individuals scraping to make their livings by supplementing the Postal Service, offering rapid delivery to businessmen in a fashion not unlike that Fred Smith would provide at Federal Express more than a century later.

Henry Wells, a former teacher who specialized in curing speech defects, was attracted by the express business. Perhaps bored by teaching and wanting a more lucrative career, Wells went to work for Harnden, who at the time intended to concentrate on populated areas along the eastern seaboard. Perceiving opportunities in the West, Wells urged him to go there as well. When told of this by an associate, Harnden replied, "If Mr. Wells chooses to run an express to the Rocky Mountains, he may — I would not do it."

In 1842 Wells resigned from Harnden's employ to strike out on his own. He started on the run between New York City and Buffalo, considered the gateway to the West, charging 6 cents a letter, 19 cents less than the post office. Wells flourished despite government attempts to shut him down and competition from Adams, Butterfield, and others, who were drawn to the route by Wells's success. Additional companies followed, and Wells was recognized as a growing influence in the business.

As competition intensified, the operators considered uniting to form a community of interests. In 1850 Wells joined with Butterfield & Wasson and a third company, Livingston, Fargo & Company, to form the American Express Company, which served a large area in the Midwest. The company was a huge success but, like Harnden, it remained east of the Mississippi, much to Wells's chagrin. Like many other Americans, Wells had his eyes on California gold.

Getting mail to the trans-Mississippi West was a complex and difficult affair. In the 1840s the government had subcontracted mail service there to private interests, often expressmen, who devised ingenious ways to make deliveries. One popular method employed an oceanic route. Mail to the Pacific coast could be brought from the East by boat to Nicaragua or Panama, hauled overland to the Pacific by the Butterfield and other operations, and then placed aboard a California-bound vessel. If all went well, letters might make the passage from Boston to San Francisco in a month or so, but this was quite rare. Troubles at sea, the weather, Central American politics, and other chronic problems could be counted on to intervene.

The alternative was overland passage. Mail might be carried by train, coach, or steamship to Missouri, and then either due west through the Rockies to Salt Lake and on to San Francisco, or south through New Mexico and Arizona to Southern California and from there to San Francisco.

This served fairly well, so long as the local population was small and generally agrarian. Then came the gold finds, causing an onrush of miners and others to the area. California's population, 93,000 in 1850, swelled to 380,000 ten years later, by which time it was a state, and the business communities at Sacramento and San Francisco had an urgent need for better communication. Many established express companies entered the state, while new ones were formed to provide better service than that provided by the post office. Adams remained the leader there, in 1851 carrying most of approximately $60 million

American Express was among the first to deliver the mail to the Midwest at high speed. The telegraph that ran along these tracks in 1884 helped move things along by coordinating railroad schedules.

in California gold to New York. Wells wanted to challenge Adams for this business and in the process clashed with Butterfield and others on the American Express board. He lost and, together with another director, William G. Fargo, left to form another company, Wells Fargo, intending to concentrate on the California market.

During the early 1850s, Congress debated various plans to support a transcontinental railroad to run from the Mississippi to the Pacific, believing this would resolve all problems of connections with the West. Politics intervened, however, and as war between the North and South grew closer, each congressional contingent blocked the other's attempt to win a railroad originating in its section. Some other way had to be found to facilitate communications, if only on a stopgap basis.

In 1857 Postmaster General Aaron Brown, a former governor of Tennessee with pro-South proclivities, solicited bids for a mail service to California. Adams, American Express, and Wells Fargo were not interested; why carry mail when there was gold to be transported? By then, however, Butterfield had caught the California fever and was prepared to seek the contract. Well placed politically — he was a personal friend of President James Buchanan — he won the award. Knowing the territory, Butterfield would have preferred a northern operation, passing through more settled territories and states, where the Indians were better controlled. But Brown insisted that he go south and took a personal hand in drawing up the route, which was to run from St. Louis to Tipton, Missouri, by train, then by stage to San Francisco.

The Butterfield Overland Mail made its first stagecoach trip on September 16, 1858, carrying passengers and mail from Tipton to San Francisco in a half hour under twenty-four days — a day under the limit set by the contract. The 2,800-mile operation cost over $1 million to organize, with the government to pay Butterfield $600,000 a year for his services. Butterfield had one major rule, which he repeated ad nauseam: "Remember boys, nothing on God's earth must stop the United States mail!" Butterfield by and large delivered on promises, but dissatisfied northern businessmen agitated for a route more favorable to their interests. The catalyst was California senator William M. Gwin, who in 1854, at the age of forty-nine, traveled on horseback from San Francisco to the Missouri River. Gwin was an ardent supporter of a regular postal service to the West and, as a member of the Senate Committee on Post Office and Post Roads, was in a position to do something about it.

Joseph Holt of Kentucky, who favored the North, replaced Brown as postmaster general in 1859 and promptly arranged for such a line. The contract was won by the flamboyant William H. Russell, who was one of the many expressmen in the area. A familiar figure in the pre–Civil War West, Russell had been one of the founders of the city of Denver, made and lost fortunes in mining, and was an astute lobbyist for the region's interests in Washington. In 1855 he had organized a freight firm, Russell, Majors & Waddell, a union of his interests with those of two other freight haulers, Alexander Majors and William B. Waddell. The firm obtained a contract to carry army materials to all posts west of Leavenworth, Kansas. In 1857, a conflict erupted between the federal government and the Mormons at Salt Lake. Ordnance shipments increased, making Russell, Majors & Waddell the largest carrier west of the Mississippi. Business fell off after the fighting ended, so the mail contract seemed ideal.

Russell won the contract by agreeing to deliver mail from New York to San Francisco. The specified time was to be thirteen days for a letter sent by train from New York to St. Joseph, Missouri, and then by horseback to San Francisco, or nine days if telegraphed from New York to St. Joseph and then carried by couriers to the West Coast city. The charge was to be $3 for a half-ounce letter taken from San Francisco to Salt Lake City, and $5 a half ounce beyond that, to which telegraph charges were to be added. These were premium prices, but even they would not pay for costs; the remainder was to be made up by federal subsidies. It was considered an amazing feat, more impressive to the businessmen of 1860 than Fred Smith's pledge of overnight delivery by Federal Express would be to their counterparts a little more than a century later.

In 1859 Russell chartered the Leavenworth & Pike's Peak Express to operate a weekly freight service, which the following year was reorganized as the Central Overland California & Pike's Peak Express Company, a subsidiary of which would be the Pony Express Company, organized to carry out the contract. To establish the company, Russell had to purchase 500 fine horses, establish 190 stock stations for changing horses and riders, hire 200 station attendants to care for the horses and have them ready, saddled and bridled, for the switches, and take on 80 riders. According to one of Majors's sons, Russell spent approximately $100,000 to establish and equip the line, far less than Butterfield's freight service.

Everyone involved recognized that the Pony Express might draw all of the mail business from Butterfield, leaving him with the freight and passenger trade, which might be insufficient to provide profits. "They are playing a bold game for a fat contract to carry a tri-weekly mail to Placerville [California], and are not the set of persons to give up without a sharp contest," observed the *Alta California* on March 23, 1860, adding that Russell beat Butterfield to the draw. "If their Horse Express enterprise is successful, the contract is sure; if the Southern route is proved the quickest, they lose it. But Butterfield understands all this, and will do all in his power to prevent success in the first case and defeat in the last."

On April 3, 1860, a rider carrying a bulging mail pouch galloped from San Francisco to Sacramento, threw it to another rider on a fresh horse, who took it to Placerville, and so on to Salt Lake City and from there to St. Joseph and the Hannibal & St. Joseph train depot, the Pony Express Special, and the telegraph office. Seventy-five riders and horses were used that first trial, and the trip took ten and a half days. Although Russell never achieved the advertised delivery time, the service was quite popular.

There was much romance in the Pony Express, and even now the name evokes images of derring-do. Riders were tough, innovative, resourceful, and brave, having to outrace Indians and on occasion dodge arrows, on their 75- to 100-mile runs. Buffalo Bill Cody was one rider, and Wild Bill Hickok ran a station. The oath of fidelity they were obliged to take indicates the nature of the business:

> I, _____, do hereby swear, before the Great and Living God, that during my engagement, and while I am an employee of Russell, Majors & Waddell, I will, under no circumstances, use profane language; that I will drink no intoxicating liquors, that I will not quarrel or fight with any other employee of the firm, and that in every respect I will conduct myself honestly, be faithful to my duties, and so direct all my acts as to win the confidence of my employers. So help me God.

A round trip was made twice a week, for which each rider's salary was $50 to $150 per month. Should the next rider be disabled, the previous one was expected to jump on the fresh horse and do double duty. One actually rode continuously for 329 miles in twenty-one hours and forty minutes. In his frontier novel *Roughing It*, Mark Twain described the crowd that often came out to witness the spectacle of a rider's arrival:

> Here he comes! Every neck is stretched further, and every eye strained wider. Away across the endless dead level of the prairie a black speck appears against the sky and it is plain that it moves. Well, I should think so. In a second or two it becomes a horse and rider, rising and falling, rising and falling — sweeping toward us, nearer and nearer, and the flutter of hoofs come faintly to the ear — another instant, a whoop and a hurrah from our upper deck, a wave of the rider's hand, but no reply, a man and a horse burst past our excited faces, and go winging away like a belated fragment of a storm!

The Pony Express ran into trouble in the form of the Washoe Indian war, which erupted two months after the service began, and this cost the company $75,000. The Indians captured the mailbag once — the only time in Pony Express history that letters were lost. Russell hoped for steeply increased governmental support, but Congress failed to come up with the amount needed to subsidize such an operation. By the end of 1860, Russell had $1 million in losses and no hope for anything better. Now Butterfield Overland, which had itself been taken over by Wells Fargo, took charge of the Pony Express and so may be said to have won the contest.

It wasn't much of a victory. The service continued on for a few months, but the losses mounted. In October 1861 it made the final ride, exhausted by lack of funds and the emergence of a more powerful and cheaper competitor: the telegraph, whose line from New York to San Francisco was completed that year. "The pony was fast," wrote a historian of the venture, "but he could not compete with lightning."

Samuel F. B. Morse developed the technology for the first instantaneous form of communication, the telegraph, in the 1830s. This portrait is by Matthew Brady, the first great American photographer.

Samuel F. B. Morse and Hiram Sibley: Men of Lightning

THE LIGHTNING had been provided by Samuel F. B. Morse, an artist whose career was heading nowhere in the mid-1830s, when a congressional committee rejected his application to paint a fresco in the rotunda of the new Capitol building. In addition to his artistic work, Morse had made a foray into inventing: with his brother he had patented a piston pump for fire engines. He also had attended several series of lectures on electricity. His artistic career seemingly at a dead end, he turned once more to invention.

Morse's interest in the telegraph was piqued while traveling home from Europe by ship in 1832. On board he met Charles Jackson, a Bostonian, who dabbled in electromagnetism and was pleased to find so congenial a companion. Watching a demonstration, Morse remarked, "If the presence of electricity can be made visible in any part of the circuit, I see no reason why intelligence may not be transmitted instantaneously by electricity." For the rest of his life, Jackson would complain bitterly that Morse took his ideas for the telegraph from these conversations.

The system Morse had in mind was actually quite simple. Electricity provided from "intensity batteries," invented in 1836 by Joseph Henry, would be sent over a wire. A key would interrupt the flow; by holding it down for longer or shorter periods, the operator could tap out a stream of dots and dashes, to be recorded on a printer or interpreted orally. Working with an assistant, Alfred Vail, and a colleague, Leonard Gale, Morse developed a practical working model of the telegraph in 1836. The following year he filed a caveat for it at the U.S. Patent Office, in which he said the apparatus for a display of his invention was not yet completed, and he "prays protection of his right till he shall have matured the machinery." Morse perfected his sending and receiving code in 1838, organized a corporation and made Gale and Vail his partners, and then traveled to Washington to seek federal support for a demonstration line.

Telegraphy interested Congressman Francis Smith of Maine, who became an ardent supporter of the plan. As chairman of the House Committee on Commerce, Smith undertook to get $30,000 for the construction of an experimental link between Washington and Baltimore and persuaded the inventor to part with half of the shares he had promised Gale and Vail. As it turned out, Smith was of little help; the bill providing the funding wasn't passed under his chairmanship, and he failed to be reelected. But Morse got his appropriation in 1843 and went to work.

There was an immediate problem. As the episode with Smith indicated, Morse had no talent for business and no idea of how to construct the line. He foolishly opted to lay the wires underground, inside a pipe along the Baltimore & Ohio right-of-way, correctly realizing this would eliminate problems caused by vandalism and climate but unaware of costs and technical problems. Morse hired a young man named Ezra Cornell, who had invented a trench digger, and they began work — only to learn that laying eight miles of wire took half the

appropriation. Moreover, the wires failed due to faulty insulation, and Morse had trouble locating the break. With only $7,000 left, he switched to the now-familiar telegraph poles, and by May 1 was within fifteen miles of Baltimore, where the Whig Party had just nominated Henry Clay for the presidency. The news was rushed to the temporary terminal and sent by wire to Washington, arriving there an hour and a half before it came by rail. Encouraged, as even skeptics were being won over, Morse and Cornell proceeded toward Baltimore, and on May 24, 1844, before a group of dignitaries gathered in the Supreme Court chambers, Morse dispatched a message to Vail in Baltimore: "What hath God wrought?"

That the telegraph was an exciting new technology with enormous potential was obvious. Now Morse started to accept messages. A Baltimore merchant wired the Bank of Washington to discover whether a check drawn by a depositor was good; news that the Democrats had nominated James K. Polk was sent over the telegraph; a Washington family had heard rumors of the death of a relative living in Baltimore and by using the telegraph learned it was not true.

In retrospect it could be seen that Morse's invention would be used by businessmen, financiers, journalists, and private citizens, and would be of vital importance for railroads. Given access to the telegraph, merchants could place orders at distant factories and learn of market and political changes from newspapers using the same technology; the need for independent agents such as those employed by commercial interests for millennia would swiftly come to an end. Financiers could gather capital from all parts of the country. Regional stock exchanges would close down, as brokers and investors could have instant links to the central market in New York. Railroad dispatchers could reroute trains and make schedule changes when necessary, in the process lowering the accident rate. Best of all, it need not be an expensive proposition. Capital costs varied depending upon terrain and maintenance problems but in the 1850s and 1860s would turn out to average around $150 a mile.

Yet acceptance of telegraphy was initially slow, perhaps because it was so revolutionary an idea, its use so disruptive of familiar ways of conducting business. Even after the Washington to Baltimore link was completed, it was more a curiosity than anything else, and for a while Vail promoted chess games between the cities simply to advertise its possibilities. In time these difficulties would be overcome, as all involved became more familiar with the technology. Yet time alone wouldn't resolve another problem. Lacking in 1845 was any clear idea of an industry structure.

With little notion of how the invention could be marketed, Morse hoped the government would purchase rights to it. Over Smith's objections, he offered to sell them to Postmaster General Charles Wickliffe, who demonstrated interest, for $100,000. By that time, however, Congress was considering war with Mexico and the possibility of annexing Texas, and so nothing was decided.

President Polk took office in March 1845, and Postmaster General Cave Johnson, who had opposed federal support while a Tennessee congressman, rejected the plan and even established a charge of 1 cent on every 4 characters so as to recover the original subsidy. But Johnson did want the government to regulate the service. "The use of an instrument so powerful for good or evil cannot with safety to the people be left in the hands of private individuals uncontrolled by law." So there would be private ownership but public regulation.

This decision had long-range significance. European countries would place the telegraph under government control, usually through the post office, and the precedent would later be applied to telephones, electricity generation and distribution, and even broadcasting. Had Morse and Wickliffe been successful, all of these industries might have been operated by the government. As it was, Morse cast about for licensees and had no trouble finding them.

Morse started out by hiring Amos Kendall as his agent in locating potential buyers. Formerly Andrew Jackson's postmaster general, the wily Kendall had been a businessman and newspaper publisher and quickly realized just how valuable the telegraph could become. In addition, he had many contacts and had no difficulty locating interested parties, though few were willing to make significant financial commitments. By the spring of 1845, however, Kendall managed to attract a group of still skeptical backers, who subscribed $15,000 and formed the Magnetic Telegraph Company, which was to construct a line from Washington to New York.

New telegraph companies were formed as Morse sold licenses with a free hand, hoping to make money out of telegraphy this way. The New York & Boston Magnetic, the Boston & Portland, the New York, Albany & Buffalo, the Lake Erie, the Erie & Michigan, the Atlantic & Ohio, the Pittsburgh, Cincinnati & Louisville, and the Washington & New Orleans were all operating or constructing lines by early 1847, their names indicating location and service areas. Companies were elbowing one another aside in the East and Midwest, and new entries with transcontinental ambitions came into being in what appeared to be the same kind of expansion the railroads were witnessing.

Now systems based on rival technologies made their appearances. Royal H. House, a Vermont resident who later relocated to Rochester, New York, was awarded a patent on his telegraph and printer device in 1846, and two years later Alexander Bain, a Scotch scientist, received his patent. Others would follow, complicating matters since the technologies were incompatible. In the mid-1850s, Morse-based companies operated a large majority of the nation's wires, but several key markets were wedded to other systems. Finally, there were internecine struggles, as Morse, Francis Smith, Charles Jackson, and others quarreled over rights, with suits and countersuits flying. The stakes were large, since by then the telegraph's utility was becoming manifest. In 1847 *The Republican*, a St. Louis newspaper, rhapsodized on its impact:

> The Magnetic Telegraph has become one of the *essential means of commercial transactions*. Commerce, wherever lines exist, is carried on by means of it, and it is impossible, in the nature of things, that St. Louis merchants and businessmen can compete with those of other cities, if they are without it. Steam is a means of commerce — the Magnetic Telegraph is now another, and a man may as well attempt to carry on a successful trade by means of the old flatboat and keel, against a steamboat, as to transact business by the use of the mails against the telegraph.

By then Boston and New York were exchanging more than 100 communications per day, and lines were strung between almost all the major eastern commercial centers. "Every day affords instances of the advantages which our business men derive from the use of the telegraph," wrote the *Commercial Review of the South and West.* "Operations are made in *one day* with its aid, by repeated communications, which could not be done in from two to four weeks by mail — enabling them to make purchases and sales which otherwise would be of no benefit to them, in consequence of the length of time consumed in negotiation."

It would not be going too far to say that at that time the telegraph surpassed the railroad in usefulness and importance. Certainly businessmen thought this was so. In addition, there was a romance about telegraphy not dissimilar to that attending the railroad. As noted, Carnegie and Edison were telegraphers, and as will be seen so were other nineteenth-century tycoons. "At its very birth it [the telegraph] became the handmaiden of commerce." So said the *National Telegraph Review and Operator's Companion*, an admittedly not unbiased publication that made its appearance in 1853. At the end of the previous year, there were more than 23,000 miles of wire covering the eastern United States, bringing some 500 cities and villages in contact with one another.

By then, too, there was much talk of creating a national entity. It made little sense for a message going from one city to another to pass through more than one company or to have to be translated for the incompatible systems. Moreover, the telegraph rivalries hampered business, making service erratic and unreliable. Telegraph operators might "steal" a message sent by another company through their territory. Rates were uneven and price wars frequent; there was no method for establishing who had priority to use a line. The companies Kendall controlled were committed to the principle of equal access to all parties, but others took thinly disguised bribes from customers wanting priorities over their business rivals. Finding some way out of this chaos resulting from the failure of government to take charge was one of the budding industry's prime concerns.

As the person who transmitted hot news of financial deals, the man with his finger on the telegraph key had his finger on the pulse of American business.

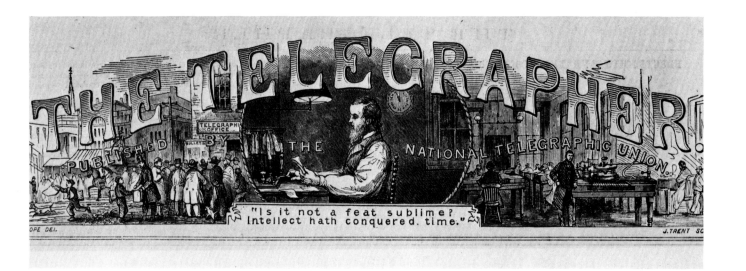

A start toward resolving the problem was brought about by Hiram Sibley, who today perhaps is the least-known major businessman of the nineteenth century. Born in North Adams, Massachusetts, in 1807, Sibley was educated in the local schools and then drifted from job to job; at one time or another he was a shoemaker, wool carder, and machine shop operator.

In 1838 Sibley moved to Rochester, New York, where he entered the banking and real estate businesses, and five years later was elected sheriff of Monroe County. By then a local celebrity with a reputation for dabbling in many enterprises, he was introduced to Samuel Selden, who held the House telegraph patent rights and became intrigued with his apparatus. In 1849 Selden proposed they build a telegraph line in the area, even though it already was served by the Morse-based New York, Albany & Buffalo Telegraph Company. Sibley agreed and, together with several associates, organized the New York State Printing Telegraph Company, which made little headway against the New York, Albany & Buffalo.

Not surprisingly, Sibley rejected Selden's suggestion that they form a second company to expand into the west, having learned a lesson about the industry from the experience. Referring to the jumble of companies and systems in operation, Sibley asked, "Why should we erect just one more line to add to the hopeless confusion of the West?" Rather, he said, any new company should have more grandiose ambitions, namely to acquire all of the telegraph companies west of Buffalo and unite them into a single system. Selden approved the idea, and Sibley purchased an interest in the House patents, intending to use the technology as the basis of the ambitiously named New York & Mississippi Valley Printing Telegraph Company, which was chartered in 1851. Capitalized at $360,000, of which $83,000 was called initially, it was one of the largest ventures in the industry to that time. With this, Sibley started to build and seek out other companies willing to be part of a larger entity.

Sibley had little success those first years, though once again he was becoming more astute regarding the industry. Funds exhausted, he recapitalized his company in 1854 under the same name and set out on an ambitious construction and acquisition campaign. Most of the early takeovers were carried out through alliances that required almost no cash expenditure. For example, Sibley

By the turn of the century, scarcely a town in the nation lacked a telegraph office. Like this one in New Haven in 1905, the offices were owned by private companies but regulated by the government.

THE LAYING OF THE CABLE—JOHN AND JONATHAN JOINING HANDS.

When Hiram Sibley's Western Union Telegraph Company moved into Latin America, it widened the use of the transatlantic cable to the entire Western Hemisphere and gave the American company control of a vast international communications network.

arranged for the construction of a line to Detroit and Chicago by three railroads, which in return would receive stock in the telegraph company and free use of the service for railroad business.

By then, Sibley realized the House system was far inferior to the Morse. Moreover, his way west appeared to be blocked by Ezra Cornell who, together with associates Jeptha H. Wade and John J. Speed, owned many of the Morse rights and had intentions of becoming a regional and then national force by expanding his Erie & Michigan Telegraph to other parts of the nation. At this time Sibley made his shrewdest move. He approached Speed and Wade and negotiated for the purchase of the Morse rights for the Midwest for $50,000. This was done without Cornell's knowledge and to his dismay. Now Cornell's ambitions seemed thwarted. He railed against his associates. "Speed sold all the Morse patents, my interest as well as his, thus giving the House folks our own tools with which to defeat us in our operations for extending our lines, and fortifying and protecting our business," he exclaimed. "This is the foulest piece of treachery toward me that I have ever known and the reason assigned is appropriate; it is the reason for which Judas betrayed his Lord, and for which Arnold betrayed his country." Although they were later reconciled, Cornell never completely forgave Sibley for what he deemed a betrayal.

With this one bold move, Sibley began the switch to the superior Morse system, won entry into a promising territory, and, in taking Wade into his organization, obtained the services of one of the most knowledgeable managers of the time, who would be his protégé and successor. Together they negotiated the takeovers of additional companies, culminating in 1855 with wresting the Erie & Michigan from Cornell after a bitter struggle, thus making the New York & Mississippi Valley the dominant force in the Midwest. The lines merged, and Cornell won a minor concession. The Erie & Michigan would place two men on the board of the new company, which was to be known as the Western Union Telegraph Company.

There were still scores of small local operations, but by then telegraphy was dominated by large enterprises, which, like the Western Union, were growing through acquisitions and building programs. The most important of these was the American Telegraph Company, organized in 1854 by retired merchant Cyrus Field, who had the audacious plan of throwing a telegraph line to the West Coast and simultaneously running a cable on the floor of the Atlantic Ocean to the British Isles. He proposed to accomplish the former by leasing existing lines — Magnetic Telegraph, the Washington & New Orleans, the New York, Albany & Buffalo were some — on generous terms, after which he would erect lines from their western limits to the California coast. Field also won control over a new printer developed by David Hughes, a music teacher from Kentucky who dabbled with electrical devices, which he claimed was superior to that employed by the Morse interests. American Telegraph clearly represented a threat to the older forces in the industry — men like Amos Kendall, who still controlled Magnetic — and the newer ones such as Sibley.

In order to meet this challenge and end what he considered ruinous competition, and to develop an alliance with American against Western Union, Kendall called a conference in late June 1857 for the purpose of "devising a plan for harmonizing all interests and protecting existing lines." The situation had become highly complicated, made more so by Field's insistence that no community of interests would be possible unless all agreed to use — and pay for — the Hughes printer, and the fact that he was employing Morse to help with planning the Atlantic cable. Enough plots and counterplots abounded to satisfy the most avid reader of detective murder mysteries. Most of those assembled were engaged in secret negotiations, and each player had a different view of what was happening. For example, Sibley had encouraged Kendall to call the conference, not knowing of his intentions to work out a deal with American, all the while discussing with Field his own plan for an alliance with that company to share the industry between them.

It should have come as no surprise that nothing came of the meeting, after which Kendall went to Washington and many of the others scattered. But soon after, Sibley assembled some of the younger telegraph leaders interested in ridding the field of Kendall and his generation and arriving at terms with American. Six companies were involved: in addition to American and Western Union, there were New Orleans & Ohio, Illinois & Mississippi, Atlantic & Ohio, and New York, Albany & Buffalo. Under Sibley's leadership, they came together in what was to be known as the "Treaty of the Six Nations." As Field had insisted, the members would pay for the patent rights to the Hughes printer as a precondition to dividing the American telegraph market into six slices, with Western Union obtaining Ohio, Indiana, most of Michigan, and smaller parts of New York, Pennsylvania, and Virginia. Known as the North American Telegraph Association, it was a model for and precursor of the many industrial pools of the post–Civil War period.

Any hope that the association might bring some harmony to telegraphy was short-lived. Field wanted the others to support his Atlantic cable, while Sibley tried to persuade them that priority should be given the transcontinental line. He was unable to convince his own board of the viability of such an undertaking, as directors cited the difficulty of locating trees for telegraph poles in desert areas and the presence of hostile Indians. There was rivalry from the Pony Express as well. Undaunted, Sibley opted to go it alone through a privately owned entity and lobbied in Washington for governmental aid.

In 1860 Congress passed and President James Buchanan signed the Pacific Telegraph Act, which authorized the secretary of the treasury to seek bids on such a project. The subsidy was so small — assistance in construction plus $40,000 a year for ten years — that there were only three bidders, and two of these dropped out, leaving Sibley with the contract.

Sibley began by dispatching Wade to California to unite the small local companies into the California State Telegraph Company. This in turn organized the Overland Telegraph Company, which was to handle construction eastward from Carson City, Nevada (where it joined with existing California state lines), to Salt Lake City. Meanwhile, Sibley created the Pacific Telegraph Company to build westward from Omaha, Nebraska, to Salt Lake City. Stock was sold in both companies, loans arranged, and Sibley invested almost everything he had in the undertaking.

The actual work took a year to complete, the last link placed by October 1861, and cost less than $500,000. Since the government provided $460,000, the companies' out-of-pocket expenses were approximately $40,000. Soon after, both were merged into the Western Union, which paid for them by issuing $12 million in stock, much of which went to Sibley. As noted, the telegraph put the Pony Express out of business and made Sibley the leader in his industry, the head of the only telegraph company that could claim to be transcontinental in scope.

Sibley was unwilling to let it go at that. By then the rivalry with Cyrus Field and American had intensified. Field's attempt to lay an Atlantic cable had failed in 1857 and 1858, and, though he continued to work on the project, there was general dismay at headquarters. Perhaps hoping to best Field at his own game, Sibley decided to attempt to lay a cable across the Bering Strait to Russia, and then run a line through Siberia to Moscow and St. Petersburg and on to connect with European lines. Feeders might be sent into Japan and China as well; though this was an afterthought, it nonetheless indicates the scope of Sib-

The expansive telegraph network, dominated by Western Union, transformed the look of every Main Street in America and was a boon to businesses nationwide.

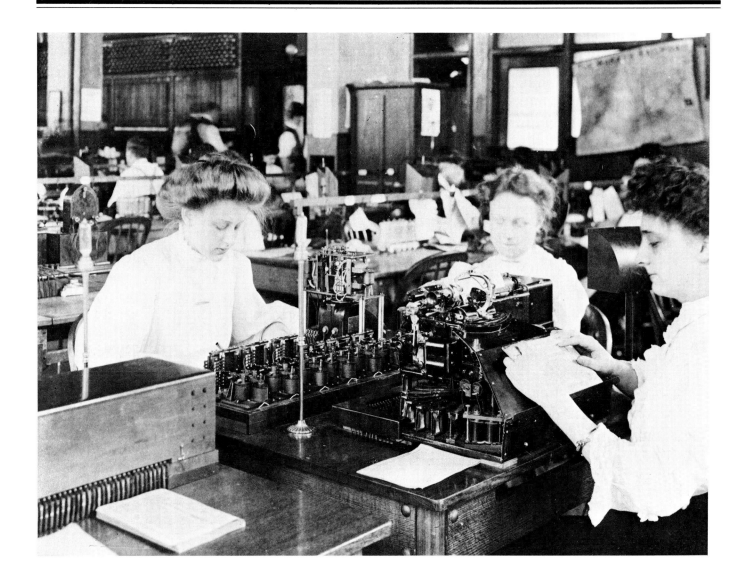

ley's ambitions. Thus a link would be created between the United States, Europe, and Asia by going west and not east.

Sibley visited Russia, won approval, and an announcement to that effect was made in March 1864. By then rumor had it that Western Union would also invade Latin America, opening the rest of the hemisphere to the telegraph. The thought of a vast network enabling an individual in Argentina to contact one in London, and all of this under the control of an American, was awesome to say the least. Sibley started to string wire up the Pacific coast and into Alaska, but work was slowed and then halted when Field's Atlantic cable went into commercial operation in 1866. American was triumphant, and Western Union lost $3 million on the venture.

The company had some consolation in its dominance of the market. By then, Western Union had only two important rivals: the recently formed United States Telegraph and American. In February Western Union absorbed the former, and that spring it merged with American Telegraph, the understanding being it would be the surviving company. For all practical purposes, Western Union was the sole significant factor in the industry.

Many women were trained to use telegraph instruments and to relay messages, and they made up a large part of the work force of offices such as this one in Washington, D.C., in 1908.

Sibley was there to witness this triumph, but ailments had obliged him to relinquish the presidency to Jeptha Wade the previous year, and it was Wade, in some respects his most important acquisition, who arranged the United States and American takeovers. Gradually Sibley appeared less often at headquarters, but his health recovered sufficiently for him to enter new endeavors: land speculation and development, railroads, banking, and even the seed and nursery business. Sibley had started out as a serendipitous businessman, and he ended the same way.

Theodore N. Vail: Architect of American Telephone & Telegraph

THE TELEGRAPH was the first instantaneous communications medium in America. It permitted the far-flung coordination of complicated railroad networks and revolutionized the intercity transmission of commercial information. But it was used primarily by business. Widespread instantaneous communication for consumers was achieved by a different technology, the telephone.

In the telegraph business, Hiram Sibley made the technological developments of Samuel Morse commercially viable. In the same way, entrepreneur-inventors in the telephone industry such as Alexander Graham Bell were followed by system builders, and of this group, none was more important in building and shaping America's telephone network than Theodore Vail.

By the mid-1870s scarcely a town or village in the nation lacked a telegraph office. Once they became accustomed to it, businessmen involved in a regional or national market found it difficult to conduct operations without the telegraph. Together with the railroad, the technology had altered the commercial scene sharply and forever.

But it did not alter the everyday lives of most people. In Europe the telegraph was used by individuals for personal correspondence, but Americans still preferred the familiar letter. Since messages had to be sent from a telegraph office, privacy was lost, and there was a measure of inconvenience as well. Some farsighted students of the telegraph dreamed of instruments in homes, with links to others elsewhere, and indeed private telegraph systems of this type did exist. But in such cases, the people involved had to learn the code, and since creating links between more than two points posed problems, little further consideration was given the matter.

Several inventors worked on what one of them called "a voice telegraph." Antonio Mucci, an Italian, may have demonstrated such a device in Havana in 1849 or 1850. A German inventor, Philipp Reis, wrote of his successful experiments in 1857, and three years later an American, Daniel Drawbaugh, transmitted sound over a "variable resistance device." While none of these men is usually credited with originating the new technology, their experiments indicate that the concept was in the air.

On February 14, 1876, Alexander Graham Bell of Boston, a teacher of the deaf with a lifelong fascination with sound, filed an application for his telephone patent. On the same day, Elisha Gray filed a caveat at the U.S. Patent Office, claiming to have developed "a new art of transmitting vocal sounds telegraphically." And if they had not done so, doubtless someone else would have soon after. The concept was too obvious, the technology too available, and the need too present for the telephone not to have appeared in the last quarter of the nineteenth century.

Bell wasn't much interested in business, but in Gardiner G. Hubbard he had an adviser who could offer assistance. A wealthy lawyer with interests in gas, water, and trolley utilities, and a member of the United States Railway Commission, Hubbard was familiar with the telegraph and saw how Bell's invention might become a superior method of transmitting information. In his fantasies he considered going into competition with Western Union, but a conflict with that $40 million giant really was unthinkable, so he planned instead to offer to negotiate some kind of financial settlement with the telegraph interests.

With the financial support of another Boston businessman, leather merchant Thomas Sanders, and Bell's laboratory partner Thomas Watson, Hubbard had organized the Bell Patent Association to carry out further research and development. He wrestled with the question of whether telephones should be sold or rented. Although the Patent Association had limited funds, he favored rentals, having had a good experience with this as attorney for a machinery company that followed the practice. Funds would be raised by royalties on patented instruments, which could be leased to licensees who earned a commission.

Bell seemed already to have a clear vision of the form the technology would take. He rejected the idea that telephones should follow the telegraph's model and establish "telephone offices" to which individuals would go to place calls. If the telephone could be made sufficiently simple, devices could be placed in homes. The lines might be gathered at local offices, and these interconnected through main cables to other locals. In this way, any two individuals in the nation might converse whenever and with whomever they wished, and not leave their homes or offices.

Even before making plans for marketing the telephone, Hubbard had approached Western Union and, with Bell's approval, offered to sell it all the patents for $100,000. He was refused. Whether Western Union was so shortsighted as to have little regard for the telephone is unknown. More likely, management believed that no serious threat could be expected from the likes of Bell and Hubbard. So the two men decided to go ahead on their own. Within a year Hubbard replaced the Patent Association with the Bell Telephone Company and created a second entity, the New England Telephone Company, which was to concentrate on locating franchises in that part of the country, while the Bell Company concentrated on New York and elsewhere.

Initial success prompted Western Union to take action by organizing the American Speaking Telegraph Company, which obtained the Gray patents and others owned by another inventor, Amos E. Dolbear. Hubbard promptly sued Western Union, charging patent infringements, but this show of raw power awed the Bell interests. "How on earth can we make our position better by fighting with nothing to fight with?" asked Sanders. Accustomed to bare-knuckle tactics, Western Union was a hard competitor, and Sanders claimed his customers and suppliers had been frightened off by the giant firm. "My business has suffered, that is, my notes have been thrust onto the market at a high rate from the feeling that I am largely interested in a shaky concern."

Hubbard decided to change this image. He began by uniting Bell and New

Alexander Graham Bell, here about to conduct an aerial experiment, was less interested in business than inventing. He left the marketing of his telephone technology to Theodore Vail, who built the mammoth AT&T Company.

England Telephone to form National Bell Telephone. Hubbard had never managed a firm, and so he cast about for someone with the competence to throw back Western Union and capitalize on the technology and other resources available. A few years earlier, in his capacity as railway commissioner, he had met Theodore N. Vail, then general superintendent for the U.S. Railway Service. Thirty-three years old in 1878, Vail was characteristically seeking a new challenge. Hubbard hired him as general manager of the Bell Telephone Company in May and stepped down as president of National Bell the following March, being replaced by William Murray Forbes, a scion of one of Boston's most respected families.

Growing up on an Ohio farm, Vail at different times had considered entering the ministry, medicine, and law; he was no more settled as a young man than he would be later. Starting out as a clerk in a store that had a telegraph, he was fired from that job, but not before learning to use the instrument. At nineteen he moved to New York, where he obtained a position as an operator at Western Union, and reveled in big-city life. His fondness for nightlife and billiards soon lost him that job, too, and he moved back with his parents to Iowa to try his hand at farming. In 1868 he took a post as telegrapher for the Union Pacific Railroad in Pinebluff, Wyoming, but soon left because he didn't want to take his bride-to-be to the frontier. A mail clerkship in Omaha, Nebraska, was more to his liking, and before long Vail was chief clerk at the Union Pacific, leaving there in 1873 to go to Washington to work for the U.S. Railway Service, where he succeeded to the general superintendency three years later. By 1878 Vail was considered the nation's top expert on mail delivery. But he was growing restless under the constraints of government bureaucracy and wrote to a friend, "I shall keep an eye open for something there is more to."

By then, Vail had become interested in telephones and even had one installed in his home while purchasing Bell shares. This was typical of the man; Vail was always a gambler and was entranced by romantic notions about the company. Bell Telephone needed a general manager, and Vail wanted a change of scene. He accepted the offer from Bell Telephone with alacrity, even though it meant a cut in salary.

When Vail arrived at Bell in the summer of 1878, he found the company in disarray. He immediately recognized the paramount importance of two actions: establishing Bell as *the* telephone company, which meant coming to terms with rivals, and creating a structure for achieving a national patent monopoly. Vail went to Menlo Park to meet with Edison, considered Western Union's greatest asset in the telephone contest, and returned with assurances that Edison accepted Bell as inventor of the telephone but was developing improved models for American Speaking Telephone. Compromise was called for and, after some negotiations, a settlement was reached. Western Union would sell its 56,000 telephones in 26 cities to Bell and grant it control over the competing telephone patents until 1894, in return for 20 percent of Bell's licensing fees. In addition, Western Union would pay 20 percent of the costs of defending the Bell patents, while the telephone company pledged not to enter the telegraph business. Thus Bell had one of the greatest strategic coups in American business history. Given its superior resources, Western Union might have crushed Bell. At the time, however, it was staving off a raid by financier and railroad magnate Jay Gould and wanted to be free to concentrate on that; so the giant firm withdrew from the field, leaving it to the much smaller entity.

Working out of New York, Vail corresponded with company president William Forbes in Boston and fashioned a sound and workable strategy for expansion. He licensed five producers to make auxiliary equipment for the telephone as demand grew, driven by the company's broadening base of operating franchises. In 1880 National Bell was rechartered as the much larger American Bell Telephone Company. It was empowered to issue eventually permanent licenses to local groups, permitting them to use its patented instruments and Bell equipment, on the understanding that they would invest funds to develop their service areas, sign over from 35 to 50 percent of their common shares to Bell, and pay fees of $20 per telephone per year. Forbes reflected that "by pursuing this plan the company will gradually acquire a large permanent interest in the telephone business throughout the country, so that [it] will not be dependent upon royalties when the patents shall have expired." Like Vail, he expected that in time many of the operating companies would become subsidiaries of American Bell. At the same time, Forbes and Vail began to consider ways of connecting

FIGHT THE FLAMES BY TELEPHONE

Where the telegraph had been used primarily by businesses, the telephone became a household utility, offering privacy, convenience, and a resource in emergencies.

cities with long-distance lines, which greatly increased the technological complexity of the business.

In order to provide equipment for its expanding and increasingly complex technologies, American Bell would need a larger and more sophisticated manufacturing arm. One was acquired in 1882 through a cross-licensing arrangement with Western Electric, organized in 1869 by Western Union to supply it with telegraph gear. Now that Western Union was out of the telephone business, it was persuaded to dispose of its own interest in this unit. Soon after, American Bell purchased a controlling interest in Western Electric and expanded its holdings over the years.

The strategy, then, was integration forward into operations and backward into production. It worked. By 1885 American Bell franchises had 155,000 telephones in operation. The company's assets had reached $60 million, and revenues that year came to $10 million. Payments from franchises, only $11,000 in 1881, rose to $597,000. Over time, the company's size and technological complexity would make it difficult, if not impossible, for potential competitors to emerge on a comparable scale.

This success bred a struggle at headquarters. Vail would have preferred to plow all the profits back into operations, knowing such resources would be

Unlike the telegraph, which sent messages from separate offices, the telephone originally used a system of "switching" through lines gathered at a local office. Operators here work the switchboard in Hamburg, New York, in about 1910.

[249]

needed when the original patents ran out; but, anxious to reward investors, Forbes insisted on a liberal dividend policy. The president and his general manager clearly entertained differing views of the company. Forbes saw it as a money machine, grinding out profits in the form of payments from the operating companies, while Vail wanted to concentrate on connecting the independent systems with one another to fashion a national telephone service, such as Alexander Graham Bell had originally intended.

In 1884 the Southern New England Telephone Company completed a line between Boston and New York, but surprisingly little traffic developed on the route. This failure was one of the key reasons prompting the creation of American Telephone & Telegraph, originally an American Bell subsidiary, formed in 1885 to enter the long-distance market. This was also a way to ending the conflict that was brewing between the Boston group and Vail. Under the arrangement, Vail resigned as general manager to become president of AT&T and was replaced by John Hudson, a Boston Brahmin, attorney, and classics scholar. Such were the legatees of Francis Cabot Lowell and Frederic Tudor.

Vail set up shop in New York, proclaiming his object was nothing less than

> to connect one or more points in each and every city, town, or place in the State of New York, with one or more points in each and every other city, town, or place in said state, and in each and every other of the United States, and in Canada and Mexico; and each and every of said cities, towns, and places is to be connected with each and every other city, town, or place in said States and countries, and also by cable and other appropriate means with the rest of the known world.

Such vaulting ambition would require large-scale financing. AT&T's first line was completed in 1886 between New York and Philadelphia, but Forbes generally did not share Vail's ambition to enlarge long-distance service on a grand scale. Vail's only course was to remain on good terms with the board and hope that when Forbes stepped down he would be selected to lead American Bell. Forbes did resign in 1887, but the board chose Howard Stockton, another Bostonian, as his replacement.

Vail, who by now was suffering from frustration and exhaustion, went to his farm in Vermont. Although wealthy enough to retire, he soon began to cast about for other opportunities. He invested in a variety of schemes, including farming interests in the Argentine, where he spent winters and helped build the Buenos Aires subway. Vail retained his shares in American Bell, which, in 1899, was merged into AT&T, and profited from the generous dividends. Meanwhile, AT&T's basic patents had expired in 1894, and unless the company held a commanding lead in all areas, it might anticipate a challenge from rival interests.

Such indeed was the case. In 1894 there were only 7 local telephone companies outside of the American Bell orbit; 87 independents were organized that year alone, and eight years later the total number had risen to more than 4,000, united in the National Association of Independent Telephone Exchanges, considered the first step toward the creation of a rival corporation to AT&T. By then these companies had more than a million telephones in service, against AT&T's 1.3 million, and they were growing more rapidly. In 1899 a New York combine headed by tycoons P. A. B. Widener and William C. Whitney organized the Telephone, Telegraph & Cable Company, capitalized at $30 million, with avowed intentions of providing long-distance service. Soon after, it was joined by another group, backed by none other than John D. Rockefeller. The two united, and their Erie Telegraph & Telephone Company, which owned more than 100,000 telephones in the Midwest, appeared a formidable competitor.

The telephone had enormous consequences for American business. At the New York Stock Exchange in 1929, this "telephone clerk" calling a member on the floor could relay stock transactions in a matter of minutes.

But not for long. Erie went bankrupt and was acquired by AT&T. That left four major forces in communications at the turn of the century: Western Union; Postal Telegraph, a holding company second only to Western Union in size; AT&T; and the independent telephone companies. Morgan intended to unite AT&T and Postal Telegraph to have a company to crush the independents and then absorb Western Union.

T. Jefferson Coolidge, a Boston banker and Morgan ally, entered the picture at this point. Together with other Morgan interests, he purchased control of Telephone, Telegraph & Cable. These were transferred to AT&T in return for stock in that company. Other purchases followed, as the Morgan group slowly took control of AT&T, and a merger with Postal Telegraph now seemed inevitable. It didn't take place, due largely to the opposition of Postal's president, Clarence Mackay, who had the temerity to challenge Morgan by making his own bid for AT&T. This failed, however, and Morgan took over completely in 1907 and offered Vail the presidency.

Vail had returned to AT&T's board in 1901 and might have become president then had he been willing to work with the Boston group and accept its terms. But he remained opposed to the company's conservative, short-range financial policies which forced it to go frequently to the marketplace to raise funds. He also noted that the independents were luring customers away from AT&T with their aggressive willingness to offer better service at lower prices. "The worst of the opposition has come from the lack of facilities afforded by our companies," he said, "that is, either no service, or poor service."

Vail said that no less than $200 million over a five-year period would be needed to change the situation for the better. Morgan would provide this through borrowings, while permitting the Boston group to retain the dividend. All the while, however, he was coming to recognize Vail's abilities and was won over to his point of view. Vail knew that once Morgan took over, he might have the presidency but wasn't sure he wanted it. Sixty-two years old in 1907, grown heavy and sluggish, and still interested in the Argentinian ventures, Vail was initially reluctant to accept the assignment. But he could hardly refuse; he had waited for a chance at independent leadership, and Morgan offered him carte blanche. Vail's return was hailed by the press, which called him one of the industry's pioneers and the person capable of bringing unitary order to the industry. This seemed reflected in his first report to the stockholders:

> The strength of the Bell System lies in its universality. It affords facilities to the public beyond those possible on other lines. It carries with it also the obligation to occupy and develop the whole field. . . . Two exchange systems in the same community, each serving the same members, cannot be conceived of as a permanency, nor can the service in either be furnished at any material reduction because of competition, if return on investment and proper maintenance be taken into account. Duplication of plant is a waste to the investor. Duplication of charges is a waste to the user.

On the operational level, Vail stressed long distance; this was expected. Not so was his vigorous attempt to carry out the Morgan mandate. In 1909 AT&T purchased a 30 percent interest in Western Union and then embarked on a program to take over the independents as well. Morgan discouraged other investment bankers from financing rivals, and buyouts were made whenever possible. But the most common device was to offer lower rates and superior service. It worked. When Vail took over in 1907, AT&T affiliates had 3 million telephones in service and the independents a like number; by 1912 AT&T had over 5 million telephones and the independents 3.6 million.

Vail's success led to talk of antitrust prosecution and possible government ownership, as was the case in Europe, which would reverse the policy set down by Postmaster General Cave Johnson in 1845. Anticipating this, Vail spoke often of the need for a "regulated monopoly," a modern version of the Johnson approach. This didn't impress outgoing president William Howard Taft, who in 1912 indicated that Attorney General George Wickersham would initiate action aimed at breaking up AT&T, and such a suit was filed that year in Oregon. Learning of his intention, Vail dispatched one of his vice presidents, N. C. Kingsbury, to meet with Wickersham to see if some kind of compromise might be reached.

"The Kingsbury Commitment," as it was known, was achieved with little fanfare and much satisfaction on both sides. AT&T would divest itself of the Western Union shares and abandon attempts to absorb that company. Vail would end plans to take over some midwestern telephone companies, but there was no requirement to cease takeovers altogether, and AT&T's ownership of Western Electric was not affected. Vail had reason to be satisfied. AT&T would retain its dominant position; the natural monopoly doctrine was accepted, and the company would remain intact for almost seven more decades.

While working as a wireless operator for the Marconi company, young David Sarnoff gained experience that eventually catapulted him into management positions and ultimately to the leadership of RCA.

David Sarnoff: The Entrepreneur As Dreamer

WHILE THE TELEGRAPH was a revolutionary device, and the telephone destined to become a household utility, both had shortcomings, the most important being the need for wires. Although not as expensive as railroad tracks, the lines did have to be maintained, and this was costly. They might easily be downed in a storm, and throwing them across rivers presented great difficulties. The first Washington to New York link, for example, ended on the New Jersey shore and had breaks for the Susquehanna and other rivers. It would be years before submarine cables were perfected that were capable of bringing the lines to Manhattan. When Cyrus Field dreamed of an Atlantic cable and Hiram Sibley of a link to Siberia they, too, had to overcome tremendous technical difficulties.

This was why Guglielmo Marconi's invention of the wireless in 1895 was so important. Its significance was immediately grasped by naval officers, who saw in it a vast improvement over the semaphore at a time when Europe was preparing for war. Telegraph and telephone interests were also enthusiastic about the wireless, and Marconi had no trouble obtaining financing for his company, the Wireless Telegraph and Signal Company organized in London in 1897. Two years later, Wireless Telegraph established a subsidiary, known as American Marconi Wireless, to develop the market in the United States.

As expected, the wireless played a critical part in World War I. When the United States became a combatant in 1917, American Marconi's assets were seized, and the company was run by the navy. After the war, naval officers, aided by Assistant Secretary of the Navy Franklin D. Roosevelt, labored to retain control of American Marconi, arguing that it was contrary to the national interest for so significant an entity to be controlled by foreigners. British Marconi protested, to no avail. The only question that remained was just who should own the property, private interests or the government. Some congressmen favored federal control, while others thought the American telephone and telegraph companies might take over and run it as a consortium.

The latter had their way, perhaps because it had become the dominant tradition. A new company would be formed with a threefold mission: to wrest control from Great Britain of wireless communication worldwide; to hold radio-related patents on behalf of the owners; and to act as merchandiser for equipment produced by the parent companies. At the time, few imagined wireless would have any other role.

But the technology was in place for other uses. In 1905 an American, Lee De Forest, had invented the audion tube, which enabled wireless operators to transmit words as well as signals. De Forest organized a company soon after to develop what he believed would be a wireless telephone, a device to revolutionize that means of communication and put him into competition with AT&T. Another inventor, Reginald Fessenden, was working in the field and, on New Year's Eve, 1906, sent a message out over the air, which was picked up by United Fruit ships. Before the war, De Forest, Fessenden, and many other technicians in America and Europe were experimenting with "wireless telephony," as it was then known, but they were uncertain as to its uses, and their efforts were barely noticed by those concerned with wireless telegraphy.

The consortium led by Owen D. Young that obtained control of American Marconi was comprised of United Fruit and equipment manufacturers General Electric and Westinghouse, which each took a share. Western Union was not included, but AT&T came into the group soon after. At the time, it was understood that GE, Westinghouse, and United Fruit, soon to be known as the "Radio Group," would concentrate on wireless telegraphy, while AT&T would develop wireless telephony. Arrangements were completed by 1919, when American Marconi became Radio Corporation of America, with Young, a General Electric vice president, its first chairman.

David Sarnoff was commercial manager for American Marconi, which meant he was the de facto chief operating officer. Twenty-eight years old at the time, he had been born in Russia and immigrated with his parents to the United States in 1900. His father died in 1906, and David left school to look for work. Happenstance took him to American Marconi, where he was hired as an office boy. In his spare time, Sarnoff learned to operate the telegraph ticker, and in 1908 he was hired by American Marconi as a marine operator. It has long been believed that Sarnoff catapulted to fame in 1912 when, as operator at the Marconi office in New York, he relayed news of the sinking of the S.S. *Titanic*,

Here Warren G. Harding delivers one of the first presidential radio addresses, in 1921. The development of broadcasting permitted the transmission of words and music to anyone who tuned in.

but recent scholarship disclaims this myth. Still, Sarnoff was elevated to the post of assistant chief engineer but soon switched to management, telling a friend, "An engineer or scientific experimenter is at the place where the money is going out. The place to make money is where the money is coming in. I am going to quit trying to be an engineer, therefore, and am going to solicit the sale of contracts and service that will bring money into the company."

Edward Nally, Marconi's president, took the same position at RCA, while Young, its chairman, divided his time between that company and General Electric. Sarnoff remained at his post and, while aware of the importance of the wireless, became intrigued with some experiments then going on at Westinghouse. Frank Conrad, one of the company's leading scientists, was sending music over the air, and he discovered it was being picked up by amateurs who owned crude receivers. This stimulated the sale of Westinghouse equipment and caught the interests of management.

The wireless companies were concentrating on "narrowcasting," the transmission of signals from one person to another, in much the same way that the telegraph and telephone were used. Conrad had stumbled on to "broadcasting," the transmission of music and information to whomever wanted to tune in. The market for narrowcasting was large but would be dwarfed by the one for broadcasting. Yet at the time these experiments, like those of Fessenden and others before the war, were scarcely noticed.

Sarnoff had thought of broadcasting even earlier, having written a memo on the subject to Nally in 1916. "I have in mind a plan of development which would make radio a 'household utility' in the same sense as the piano or phonograph. The idea is to bring music into the house by wireless." He went on to describe the device, "a box which can be placed on a table in the parlor or living room, the switch set accordingly, and the transmitted music received." The offerings need not be limited to music, thought Sarnoff, and he went on to sketch what amounted to a wireless classroom. "Events of national importance can be simultaneously announced and received. Baseball scores can be transmitted by air. . . . Farmers and others living a distance from urban areas could be greatly benefited. By the purchase of a 'Radio Music Box' they could enjoy concerts, lectures, recitals, etc. which might be going on in the nearest city within their radius."

Nally, an old telegraph man, wasn't interested, but Sarnoff continued to press for broadcasting at American Marconi and later at RCA. He received little encouragement. In 1921 Sarnoff was named general manager and, the following year, vice president. The new president was General James Harbord, who knew little about radio but had military credentials and connections in Washington, both factors considered important to a wireless company. As it happened, Harbord and Sarnoff worked well together; the general recognized the younger man's talents and respected his knowledge. In all but title, Sarnoff was RCA's chief operating officer.

By then the demand for radio receivers was increasing exponentially. In his early memos, Sarnoff had predicted total sales of 1 million units by 1922 at $75 each. In actuality, radio sales were $60 million in 1922, $130 million in 1923, and $358 million in 1924. Sarnoff met this demand by increasing RCA's sales organization from 14 people in 1921 to a nationwide network of 200 offices in 1922. In the process, RCA's revenues rose from $11 million in 1922 to $22.5 million in 1923, and to $50 million in 1924.

A major new industry was being born, one as exciting as and in some ways more revolutionary than automobiles. During the early 1920s, perceptive observers could envisage a time when major broadcasting networks would entertain and inform a nation glued to their radios. Even then there was talk of television within the industry and of some connection with motion pictures. But none realized how these media would affect not only the economy but leisure-time activities and the very way people would interpret the world around them. The telegraph had been an improvement over the mails, the automobile a clear advance over the horse and buggy. But radio, and then television, would affect the way the vast majority of the world perceived almost every facet of their lives. Not since the invention of movable type by Johann Gutenberg some four

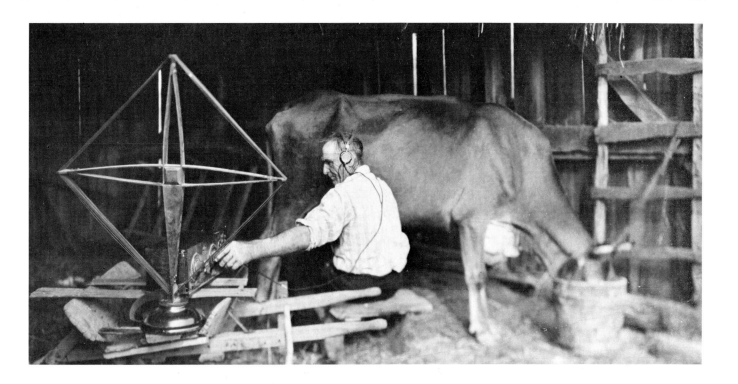

Radio was the first technology to create an electronic web in the airwaves, allowing it to be received in every American home — even in every barn.

hundred years earlier had there been such an alteration in mankind's view of itself and the world. Moreover, radio and television would be the precursors of the ongoing electronic revolution.

At the center of all this visible and forthcoming change was Radio Corporation of America, led by the visionary David Sarnoff, who was pondering television when others were still intrigued by the fact that Marconi's inventions made possible a superior form of the telegraph and perhaps the telephone.

The new company and industry grew rapidly and faced many problems. One was the role of broadcasting. Initially, most in the industry believed it was an adjunct to receiver sales and that manufacturers would have to develop programming in order to win customers for their sets. To them the radio business was centered around hardware and not the more ephemeral show business aspects.

It wasn't long before all involved realized that large profits might be made through broadcasting. By the end of 1922, there were 576 stations in operation; the previous year there had been 28. Both RCA and AT&T started to organize their networks, and this brought AT&T into conflict with the Radio Group, now comprised of RCA, GE, and Westinghouse. So long as RCA was concerned with wireless, there had been few problems. Now that it was becoming the central force in radio, the alliance broke down. Fearing antitrust action, both sides acted cautiously, and in 1926 AT&T sold its network to RCA, which promptly announced the formation of the National Broadcasting Company. Later that year Congress passed and President Calvin Coolidge signed legislation creating the Federal Radio Commission, which was to regulate broadcasting in the future·and which, in 1934, was transformed into the Federal Communications Commission.

During the late 1920s, Sarnoff's attention was riveted on exploring new areas of opportunity and obtaining independence from GE and Westinghouse. When Warner Brothers released the first full-length sound motion picture, *The*

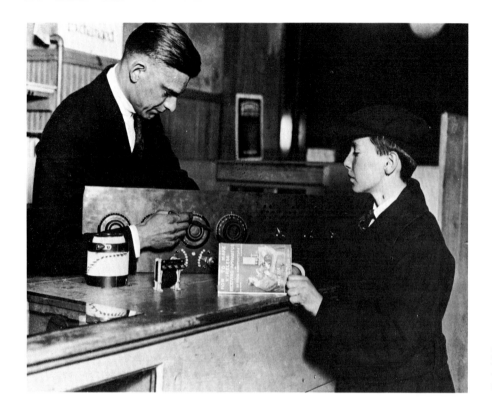

At radio shops like this one in Brooklyn in 1922, boys caught up in the radio craze that swept the nation bought parts to build their own sets.

Jazz Singer, in 1927, Sarnoff decided this would be a promising area. Warner used an AT&T system, and this would bring RCA into another conflict with its former parent. Sarnoff obtained patents for a rival technology from GE and formed a union with Joseph Kennedy's budding film operation. He then took over several groups of theaters in 1928, forming Radio-Keith-Orpheum, better known as RKO, in which RCA had an initial 20 percent stake. Naturally, the theaters purchased RCA sound equipment, and RKO utilized the technology in production. RCA remained in second place behind AT&T in this area, but the move did demonstrate that Sarnoff was willing to expand.

For years Sarnoff had tried to effect some kind of alliance with a phonograph manufacturer. "Technically the Radiola and the phonograph are both trying to do the same kind of job, to reproduce as faithfully as possible speech or music," he wrote in 1922. In tandem with GE and Westinghouse, RCA purchased the Victor Talking Machine Company, one of the industry's leaders, and renamed it RCA Victor. The move was another example of expansion into a related area, but to Sarnoff it was more than that. The takeover included Victor's major production facility in Camden, New Jersey, which had obtained permission from GE and Westinghouse to manufacture radios and radio-phonograph combinations on its own. Independence would have been inconceivable without such a capability, and so the takeover was also seen as a prelude to a break with GE and Westinghouse.

By 1930, when the government instituted an antitrust suit against the so-called Radio Trust, RCA had added two large music publishers, Leo Feist and Carl Fisher, and had started a talent agency. It now was an integrated entertainment company — with a wireless operation on the side. Sarnoff talked of artists appearing on NBC programs to be heard on RCA radios, making motion pictures at RKO studios to be exhibited at RKO theaters equipped with RCA sound systems, recording music published by Feist or Fisher for Victor and played on Victrolas, and being represented by an RCA agent. In addition, RCA had an interest in the new Rockefeller Center, where its corporate headquarters were relocated.

Two years later, in order to avoid a messy court battle, GE and Westinghouse agreed to divest themselves of their RCA holdings, leaving the company independent and Sarnoff the master in his own house. It was hardly a propitious time. The year 1932 was the bottom of the Great Depression, and, while NBC was doing well, radio sales fell off and RKO performed poorly, soon going into receivership. NBC sustained RCA through the Depression and continued to do so even after manufacturing recovered later in the decade. During World War II, RCA became a major supplier of radio and other gear to the armed forces and one of the largest research and development performers, in the process obtaining valuable experience with emerging electronics technology. Sarnoff, who had a Signal Corps Reserve commission, served tours of duty and was in charge of telecommunications for General Dwight Eisenhower on D-Day. Discharged with the rank of brigadier general, Sarnoff took great pride in his service record and for the rest of his life delighted in being addressed as General Sarnoff. Now Harbord retired, and Sarnoff became RCA's chairman in name as well as fact.

With the end of the war, Sarnoff turned to the next important new technology on the electronics scene: television. Experiments in this area went back to the mid-nineteenth century, but most credit Vladimir Zworykin, a Russian émigré who arrived in the United States in 1919, with having been its prime inventor. While working at Westinghouse in 1923, Zworykin perfected a rudimentary television camera he called the iconoscope. This was followed by a receiver called a kinescope, and the entire system was demonstrated in late 1929. Others were also conducting television experiments, among them GE and AT&T.

Naturally, Sarnoff became involved. In 1923 he wrote a memo predicting a bright future for television, "which is the technical name for seeing instead of hearing by radio." Sarnoff mused about how viewers might see and hear events from all parts of the globe while they were taking place and about a linkage with films. "I also believe that transmission and reception of motion pictures by radio will be worked out within the next decade. This would result in current events or interesting dramatic presentations being literally broadcast by radio through the use of appropriate transmitters and, therefore, received in individual homes or auditoriums, where the original scene will be re-enacted on a screen with much the appearance of present-day motion pictures."

By 1929 Sarnoff was in regular contact with Zworykin, and the following year he arranged for the scientist to be transferred to RCA. During the 1930s, Sarnoff poured millions into television, which was demonstrated at the 1939–40 New York World's Fair, while experiments continued. Were it not for the war, commercial television might have been introduced soon after.

By then a number of motion picture companies had become involved with the technology, and for a while its future was uncertain. Was television to become motion pictures in the home (not unlike today's cable television) or radio with pictures? The motion picture companies moved slowly, while Sarnoff plunged ahead. It might have been otherwise had the connection with RKO been intact. As it was, Sarnoff's work and that of other radio manufacturers and broadcasters dictated that the radio and network connection would prevail.

Sarnoff's role in early television was his finest hour, enabling him to demonstrate his mastery as an innovator and corporate strategist. Despite resistance from the radio industry, including executives in his own company, he sidestepped pitfalls and did not allow the new technology to be restrained and distorted by the old. Within RCA he hired new leadership, bypassing existing dealer organizations to establish RCA Service to ensure that television's particular needs for skilled maintenance would be met.

The development of television was in many ways a repeat of the radio experience, only this time all involved had a model to follow. NBC geared up to produce programs, while several RCA factories turned out receivers. While not an instant success, due to irregular programming, the high cost of sets, and their early unreliability, it was evident from the first that television would make major contributions to RCA and NBC. In 1946 RCA manufactured 10,000 television sets; by 1954 it was turning them out at the rate of 1 million a year.

As with radio, RCA had many rivals in television, the foremost in the area of broadcasting being William Paley's Columbia Broadcasting System. Both RCA and CBS had been working on color television, which all believed was destined to replace monochrome. The two technologies differed radically. While the CBS version was generally deemed superior, it was not compatible with existing receivers, which is to say the monochrome sets would not be able to receive programs sent out under the CBS system. RCA's system was compatible but had many flaws.

Sarnoff, who over the years had developed keen political instincts, proceeded on several fronts. While his scientists and technicians labored feverishly to perfect the RCA system, he employed stalling tactics at the FCC, knowing that each monochrome set purchased would count as a vote against CBS. Would the FCC dare render obsolete every set in the nation? Perhaps so, when there were only a few of them, as was the case in the mid-1940s. But the situation would change as television became ubiquitous.

In 1947 only 14,000 homes had television sets. By 1949, when the FCC came down in favor of CBS, the number had increased to 940,000. Now Sarnoff was assisted by the outbreak of the Korean War, during which activities were suspended. During the next three years, RCA redesigned its system, and in 1953, when over 20 million America homes had monochrome sets, the FCC approved its version. It was a resounding victory — if not the greatest of Sarnoff's career, at least the most satisfying.

Sixty-two years old in 1953, Sarnoff was hailed as one of the nation's premier businessmen. That he was farsighted and imaginative was obvious, as were his penetrating intellect and gifts for strategic planning. In fact, Sarnoff was one of the most dazzling corporate leaders of his time, but within the industry and among students of the business scene, there was a growing realization that he was a poor manager in professional terms.

Sarnoff never concentrated on honing the managerial skills needed to operate so large and complex a corporation as RCA had become. He had not devoted sufficient time and energy to creating a staff to carry his ideas forward. Perhaps it would have been otherwise had he been interested in management, but such was not the case. The collection of speeches and articles he collected in a volume entitled *Looking Ahead* makes this lack of interest clear. The book is full of perceptive statements about technology, society, and, of course, radio and television. But, significantly, only one of the papers contains the word "management" in the title, and that is "The Management of Environmental

Following RCA's lead, rival companies exploited radio's potential as an entertainment medium. Here Rosalind Russell (*right*) and Lurene Tuttle enact a scene on the popular CBS "Suspense" show in 1949.

On April 30, 1939, Sarnoff dedicated RCA's pavilion at the New York World's Fair — before a television camera. It was the first TV coverage of a news event. Combined, radio and television have had a profound effect on the way people perceive the world around them.

TV was the realization of Sarnoff's media dreams. By 1949 nearly a million American homes had TV sets, and network shows featuring such stars as Bob Hope were a phenomenal success.

Forces." Unlike J. Edgar Thomson, Alfred Sloan, Frederick Weyerhaeuser, and many other businessmen discussed and analyzed here, Sarnoff was deficient in creating a structure to contain and carry forth his program.

Sarnoff held RCA together by force of personality, intellect, and direct intervention. As a result, the corporation became a hotbed of intrigue, with various cabals organized to protect vested interests and woo the leader. Sarnoff was famous for his rough treatment of both line and staff managers. On one occasion, Sarnoff encountered former president Harry Truman in an elevator. Sarnoff had injured a leg and was wearing a cast. "Well, General," cracked Truman in characteristic salty fashion, "I guess now for a while you'll have to kick people in the ass with the other leg, won't you?"

Sarnoff delighted in seeking new challenges, but this meant he devoted insufficient attention to nurturing maturing businesses, which hurt RCA. The company pioneered in radio receivers but lost the lead to others; by the 1930s Philco was the top producer. At first NBC was the dominant network, but the much smaller CBS soon led in some areas. Likewise, RCA was television's pioneer, but Zenith became a larger manufacturer of monochrome sets, and in time RCA was an also-ran in color as well. There was the failure of RKO, and even while besting CBS in color television, Sarnoff lost out in phonograph records, where the CBS technology at 33 1/3 revolutions per minute was a clear winner over RCA's 45 rpms. Yet to come was a disastrous attempt to carve out a niche in data processing that almost wrecked the company and a misbegotten foray into conglomerization from which RCA is only now recovering. In 1966 David Sarnoff placed his son, Bob, in charge of the company, a dubious move at best, and then continually second-guessed him.

Finally, Sarnoff licensed technology with a free hand, necessary in the 1920s and 1930s to fend off antitrust actions but foolhardy after the war. Beginning in 1957, RCA sold technology to Japanese consumer-electronics firms on a wholesale basis; in some years license fees provided the major portion of the corporation's earnings. It wouldn't be going too far to suggest that, absent RCA's assistance, the Japanese would have had far more trouble entering the American market than they did. Perhaps recognizing this, the Japanese gave Sarnoff the highest honor they ever conferred upon a foreign businessman, the Order of the Rising Sun, third class.

David Sarnoff's career indicates how a forceful and energetic businessman can mold an industry — indeed, more than one, in his case. At the same time, the problems RCA underwent in his last years and under his successors demonstrate the importance of fashioning an organization and staffing it skillfully to make possible future growth and development.

Today's news broadcasts combine TV's two greatest attributes: entertainment and transmission of information.

Daniel Noble displays the device that inspired the Motorola Company name — the car radio.

Paul Galvin, Daniel Noble,
and the Transformation of Motorola

In 1929 David Sarnoff and Alfred Sloan of General Motors organized a joint venture, General Motors Radio Corporation, whose mission was to dominate the market for car radios. This company never amounted to much, although even the car radio market was really created during the Great Depression. The reason was that GMRC was bested by a much smaller rival, capable of taking the measure in this area of the likes of David Sarnoff and Alfred Sloan.

The company was Galvin Manufacturing, organized by Paul V. Galvin in 1928 and in 1947 given a name more in line with its first important product: Motorola.

Born in the small town of Harvard, Illinois, in 1895, Galvin spent two years at the University of Illinois at Urbana. He enrolled in an officer's training program shortly before the United States entered World War I, served in France, and after his discharge took a job at the Chicago-based D&G Storage Battery Company. In 1921 he joined with Edward Stewart to form the Stewart Battery Company, and they located their manufacturing facility in Marshfield, Wisconsin. In the same industry as D&G, Stewart and Galvin's enterprise turned out roughly 150 units a day, all of which sold in the Midwest. It was a highly competitive business, and neither Stewart or Galvin had much experience. Stewart Battery, located in rural Wisconsin, was far from critical markets and transportation networks, and its finances proved wobbly. Nor did the depression of 1921–22, hitting at a time when radios were just starting to sell, help matters. The company failed in 1923, obliging Galvin to look for work elsewhere. From 1923 to 1926, he held a sales post at Brach Candy Company, which in time would become a major force in its field but was then a small operation in Chicago. When Brach decided to retire in 1926, Galvin took the opportunity to go off on his own and, together with Stewart, reentered the battery business.

They decided to specialize in radio batteries, in those years quite different from what they are today. The first household tube receivers were clumsy affairs, powered by direct-current storage batteries, but everyone involved from David Sarnoff on down realized that it was only a matter of time before some method would be found to utilize alternating current. Until then there would be a gap in the market, which was what Galvin hoped to fill. He came up with a device known as the "A-Eliminator," which transformed AC into DC and worked in conjunction with a battery. The owner of an eliminator would plug it into the electric outlet and then plug his radio into the eliminator. The radio would draw power from the eliminator, and the AC current would keep the battery charged.

Still, the technology was changing rapidly, and the market for the product was underdeveloped. The company folded once more, but this time Galvin mustered his last dollars to buy the company's resources in the liquidation sale and started a new enterprise on his own. Now he would focus on the production of eliminators rather than batteries. Galvin believed that this might offer a solution to the problems that had plagued the earlier businesses because the short-term market for eliminators was strong.

Aware, however, of the transitory nature of these devices, Galvin sought other products to keep his new company alive. In 1929 he started producing car radio receivers for private-label sales. By then the technology was fairly straightforward and RCA was licensing it quite liberally. The move proved successful, but Galvin continued to seek a product that would be unique and hold higher profit potential. One came from the idea of placing radios in cars. This was not completely novel; there were radio-equipped cars at the time, placed on a custom basis. Galvin told how he first learned of them:

> I was in New York working out a compromise with one of my suppliers on merchandise I no longer needed when he mentioned there were a couple of fellows over on Long Island making custom installation of radios in cars. Just a backyard, garage-operated operation. They would take the dashboard off the car and build a breadbasket chassis and stick it back of the panel. They drilled holes so that the tuning knobs poked out the front of the dashboard. They put a little aerial under the running board or up into the header in the top of the car, and a little four inch cone speaker under the dash. He told me that all of this, with added provision for the bulky "B" batteries, made the unit the devil to put in and the fellows charge up to $240 for an installation.

From Galvin's perspective, the problems were straightforward. These installations, requiring a minimum of eight hours, could be eased if the car manufacturers made provisions for radios. In addition, the radios were balky, played sporadically and poorly, and the separate battery made little sense at a time when most automobile manufacturers were switching from the hand crank to battery-powered starters.

Galvin returned to his company, considering how the process might be altered. A method came from the fertile mind of William Lear, one of the nation's most perspicacious inventors, who would later develop the Lear Jet. At the time, Lear operated his own firm, Radio Coil & Wire, but also did designing work for Galvin. Together with an associate, Elmer Wavering, he had invented

The car radio, which originally employed vacuum tubes, was one of the first devices to take advantage of power transistors.

a broadcast receiver that would play in a moving automobile. Galvin obtained manufacturing rights and demonstrated it at an auto show in 1929. The price was $110 to $130 installed, depending on accessories.

At a time when the battery-powered radio was leaving the home, then, it was reappearing in a different form in the nation's automobiles. The car radio immediately boosted sales and helped alter the industry. Two years later, company engineer Ray Yoder invented a vibrator-type power supply to replace the B batteries, which moved Galvin Manufacturing to the front of the industry and led to the demise of GMRC.

Ever an original thinker, Galvin wondered whether it would be possible to develop a mobile version of AT&T's long-discussed wireless telephone. Some police departments recognized the need for one as early as 1930, when radios were placed in their cars so they could receive emergency messages, which would interrupt commercial broadcasts. Clearly this could not last because their signals were still carried over AM bands, where they interrupted regular broadcasts and could be monitored by criminals. Police departments were demanding their own continuously operating frequencies. Motorola engineers started working on the technology in 1931. "There was a need and I could see it was a market that nobody owned," Galvin recalled.

In the mid-1930s, Edwin Armstrong experimented with frequency modulation, a static-free method of broadcasting far superior to what then existed, amplitude modulation, save for one problem: AM signals followed the earth's curve, while FM went out in straight lines, making reception limited to the horizon. While this was a drawback for broadcasting, it mattered little for police radio. Daniel Noble, a professor at the University of Connecticut, created an FM mobile communications system for the state police and, in 1940, wrote of his work in an academic journal. Galvin read the article and perceived in Noble a person who was not only thinking but actually working along the same lines as he.

The two men met, and Noble agreed to take a year's sabbatical and spend it with Motorola. He was one of several imaginative technicians in the growing research arm. In this period, for example, Don Mitchell, a Galvin Manufacturing engineer, invented a two-way portable radio communications device called the "Handie-Talkie," which with some modifications by Noble — conversion from AM to FM and reduction of size and weight — later became familiarly known during World War II as the "Walkie-Talkie." Both mobile and portable radio communications products became staples of Motorola's business, and Noble remained on to direct research. In time, the company would expand into other areas as well, most prominently television-set production.

Noble, who was more a scientist than a businessman, took the company into a new area: electronics. He had become intrigued with developments in solid-state physics, envisioning the use of new components for Motorola's communications products. He persuaded Galvin to establish a research facility in Arizona and moved there to work on defense contracts.

Demand for Motorola's consumer and communications products meant the company had to purchase ever-increasing supplies of vacuum tubes from other companies, RCA in particular. Not wanting to be overly dependent on this competitor, Motorola's leaders considered acquiring a company that made such equipment. Convinced solid-state devices would soon render tubes obsolete, Noble persuaded Galvin that this was akin to buying a dead horse. Galvin gave Noble a budget and carte blanche to develop such components.

The Walkie-Talkie, developed by Motorola, was vital equipment during World War II. The portable two-way communication device used "frequency modulation," or FM, to transmit messages.

After securing licensing rights from Bell Laboratories in 1952, Noble and his staff spent the next several years laboriously trying to develop the first germanium power transistors, a task made almost insurmountable by the lack of high-quality materials, nonexistent manufacturing technology, and spotty research knowledge. Noble was fighting the calendar, for after a few years with no product in hand, pressure from headquarters was increasing to resurrect the plan to acquire a tube-manufacturing facility. But he developed his first germanium transistors in the mid-1950s, and soon after Motorola used them in car radios.

The transistorized car radio was a great improvement over tube-powered models. For one thing, the transistors did away with the highly unreliable radio "vibrator" used to alternate and amplify voltage to drive the vacuum tubes, which had been the single largest source of problems and unreliability in all car radios since their invention. Equally important, as far as Motorola was concerned, the company's entry into the electronics field assured a steady supply of advanced components and placed the company squarely in a lead position in an exciting new area of technology.

Noble's arguments regarding vacuum tubes proved correct. By remaining wedded to vacuum tubes for too long, RCA and other manufacturers lagged behind and were unable to make the switch in time to assume leadership. No vacuum-tube manufacturer became an important and leading semiconductor producer as Motorola was to become.

In achieving that position of leadership in the fledgling industry, one of Noble's greatest problems involved production. Lead wires in early transistors were applied by hand with tweezers, for example, and such refinements as "clean rooms" were far in the future. Having mastered transistors, he turned to semiconductors, which, in the late 1950s, were a new and crude product, as was their manufacture; since demand was still small, they were turned out in laboratories, not factories. Materials chronically became contaminated, which not only made the product unreliable but forced up prices and costs. Until this

To beat out competitors in the field, Motorola mass-produced solid-state electronics components such as this tiny computer chip and sold them at low cost, eventually divesting itself of its consumer goods divisions.

changed, semiconductors would never be much more than a laboratory curiosity, custom-made for individual needs, and there would be few of these.

So promising was the technology, however, that a market developed almost spontaneously. An auto maker was interested in using six semiconductor components, known as diode rectifiers, in its alternator, but the market price of these, about $2.50 apiece, exceeded the cost of all the other materials for the alternator. Noble was notified that it would place a substantial order if Motorola would undertake to supply the parts at a price of 75 cents each and decrease the cost the second year to 50 cents and then to 25 cents.

It was a major gamble, for, by accepting the order, Motorola would be guaranteeing a price schedule that might prove highly unprofitable, in addition to creating a new form of production line that might not be workable. But there was no alternative if semiconductors were ever to become anything more than experimental devices. Noble agreed to accept the offer and, after receiving approval from top management, enlarged and reorganized his staff. As expected, there were losses the first year, but Motorola broke even the second year and actually made sufficient profits the third year to more than balance the early deficits. In the process, Motorola emerged as one of the nation's top three semiconductor manufacturers, developing new products and capturing new markets.

This experience in mass production also taught the fledgling operation another valuable lesson. While other semiconductor manufacturers would often lead the way in innovating, Motorola could always be counted on as a "fast follower," able to out-manufacture its rivals once the technology reached the point where economies of scale were realizable, in the process dramatically lowering costs and gaining market share. Motorola's low-cost production, pioneered by Noble, permitted the company to create the largest array of semiconductor products of any American producer.

Motorola has followed this basic strategy in the development of semiconductors ever since. Although the company fell behind in the production of integrated circuits (several components on a single chip) in the 1960s, it raced ahead in the development of microprocessors (just behind Intel) with the creation of the 6800 in 1974 and the 68000 in 1979 (from 5,000 to 200,000 components on a single chip). These two generations of devices serviced traditional customers such as the automotive industry but found new applications in places where Motorola components had not been widely used — such as the computer industry — with the 68000 becoming the base for the new super computers of the 1980s.

Thus Motorola started out as a manufacturer of batteries and then car radios, went on to become the dominant force in two-way communication products, and entered the components field in a classic fashion by integrating backward. The experience with semiconductors had altered the company's position. In time, the tail would wag the dog: the company that started out as a radio and then television manufacturer and went into components to integrate backward sold off many of its consumer-goods divisions to concentrate on electronic components. At one time, Motorola's Quasar line of television sets was deemed the class of the field. Then it was sold to Matsushita, in a dramatic example of how the Japanese were taking over American consumer electronics — but with a difference: Matsushita and other Japanese companies purchased Motorola components, for these could compete with any in the world for reliability and cost.

Gerard O'Neill and Geostar

E NTREPRENEURSHIP THRIVES in America, where more new enterprises were started in 1985 than in any other year. These ranged from companies offering lawn-mowing services, to the merchandising of premium ice cream, to novel methods of producing steel, to exotic restaurants. But the generation and transmission of information is at the cutting edge of American business today. It is where much of the glamor and excitement are to be found.

As we have seen, change is the one constant in American business history; the imperatives that motivated Frederic Tudor and De Witt Clinton are to be found in the dozens of high technology enclaves scattered throughout the country from Massachusetts's Route 128 to California's Silicon Valley. Today the world's largest industry is petroleum; it now appears fairly certain that, in the early twenty-first century at the very latest, it will be displaced by information generation and transmission.

The reason is obvious: the need to transport products, which motivated Americans to lay down turnpikes, dig canals, and create railroads, is not growing nearly as fast as that of generating and transmitting knowledge. We have seen how Fred Smith created Federal Express to move small packages and mail more swiftly and reliably than could the Postal Service; today Smith's most exciting new service is Zapmail, by which letters and other documents are sent electronically, by bouncing signals off space satellites, with most deliveries made within two hours of transmission. The program began in the summer of 1984; approximately 5,000 machines were in place a year later, with plans to double the number within another year. "The revolution in telecommunications will have enormous implications in the way Federal Express does business and we need to be aggressive in this area," said Smith. Zapmail may soon be Federal Express's major product, displacing parcels and the "old-fashioned" letters.

Others are mining the same rich lode. One of these is Gerard O'Neill, a Princeton physics professor, who talks about the possibility of every person on the planet being able to contact anyone else, no matter where, in a microsecond. Indeed, the sender need not even know where the person to be contacted happens to be at the time. O'Neill says this will be done through "a synthesis of communications satellites and high-speed computer technology." This is not a science fiction fantasy: much of the technology already exists, and O'Neill is one of dozens of small entrepreneurs at work in the field, along with many of the nation's largest electronics and telecommunications companies.

O'Neill is planning what he calls the "Geostar Satellite System," which has three components: ground-based computers, four satellites hovering in stationary orbit 22,300 miles above the continental United States, and a network of consumer two-way communications devices of various sorts, such as pocket-size, battery-operated "transceivers," with liquid-crystal displays and small keyboards, and onboard transceivers for airplanes, trucks, ships, and other likely places.

Physics professor Gerard O'Neill of Princeton University, Geostar's founder, chairman, and CEO, is one of several entrepreneurs developing satellite systems that could make instantaneous communication possible for everyone on the planet.

If O'Neill's plans are ever realized, an individual wishing to send a message would "place a call" through the transceiver. The transceiver would send it to a satellite, which would transfer it to the computers, which, in turn, would locate the person by means of a continual coded signal sent out by his or her own transceiver. It would be possible to pinpoint a transceiver to within a few yards.

Signals could be sent for various purposes. For example, SOS signals from mugging victims could summon police in a way early users of Motorola two-way radios could hardly have imagined. Lost or injured skiers or hikers could be easily located; kidnappers would be dissuaded from their activities. Home, business, and automobile burglar alarms could similarly alert police and fire personnel, giving them license numbers, addresses, and other pertinent information. Individuals with special medical conditions could be monitored and distress signals sent in emergencies. Airlines could replace their present radar air-traffic control systems with Geostar, which would be more accurate and offer uninterrupted coverage. Truckers, taxi companies, and other fleet operators could greatly enhance their dispatching capabilities. Just as their ancestors were amazed by the wireless, which so dramatically altered shipping, so maritime interests would benefit greatly by a system whereby all carriers could communicate with one another when the need arose. The possibilities are staggering.

O'Neill claims the transceivers might initially be priced at about $450, with annual charges running $30 to $40. The cost of a message would be based on the number of characters but would average about the price of a local telephone call. The best estimate made so far indicates that Geostar will require a

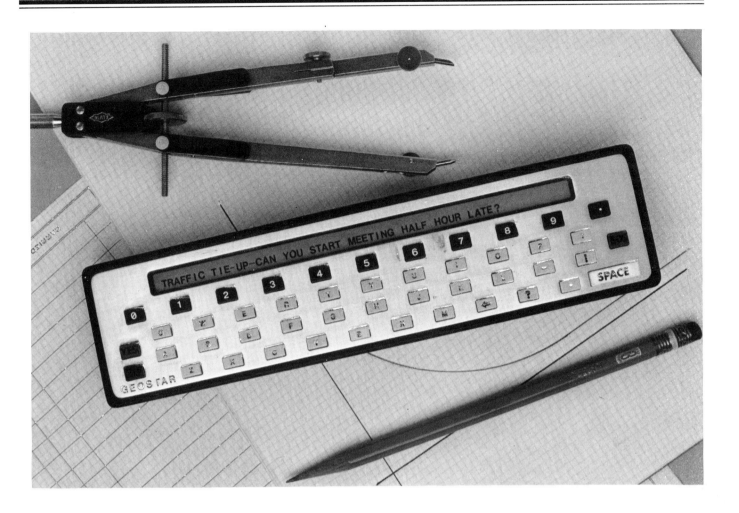

Using a transceiver no bigger than a pocket calculator, businesses could relay important messages within a microsecond.

capital investment of less than 1 percent of what is spent on the Federal Aviation Administration *alone* over a ten-year period.

The Geostar System was granted its first patent in 1982, and the corporation was organized the following year; within a few months, $1.5 million in stock was offered and subscribed to almost immediately. According to one estimate, Geostar will require another $198 million before it can begin operations in 1987. Following the path first blazed by Morse, Cave Johnson, and the telegraph, all of this will come from private sources.

Few people have even heard of Geostar, but perhaps in a few years its technology will be commonplace, altering the lives of Americans as radically as the telegraph, telephone, and radio once did. Since the required technology already exists, the missing ingredient for success will be effective entrepreneurship. This has proved critical throughout American business history, and will continue to be so as long as individuals like Gerard O'Neill open new industries at an accelerating pace.

Entrepreneurship remains an elusive commodity, as this gallery of distinct and notable practitioners makes clear. At each turn, history has insured that every entrepreneur face a unique set of challenges. Yet it is because of this striking diversity of circumstances that common elements of entrepreneurship can be seen.

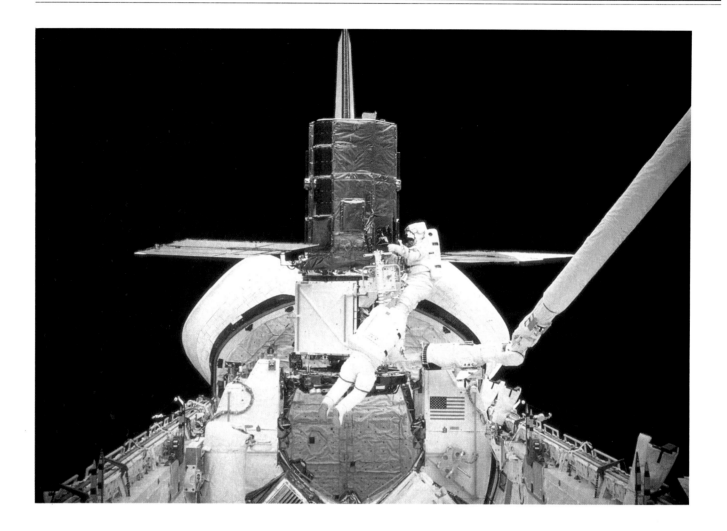

The willingness to take risks is, of course, one common denominator. Still, entrepreneurs from Samuel Slater to Fred Smith remind us that those who are deeply embedded in an industry and can control and minimize risk are more likely to prevail than their daredevil counterparts.

Imagination is another recurrent quality that seems necessary if the entrepreneur is to succeed by combining in a new way factors that are also available to competitors. Some analysts now believe that entrepreneurship, like many other skills, can be taught, but this belies the truth in Leonardo da Vinci's inspired dictum that there are those who see, there are those who see when they are shown, and there are those who don't see.

Nor is imagination enough, for the entrepreneur must be an achiever as well as a visionary, and many display a dogged determination to succeed at the entrepreneurial game that sometimes borders on fanaticism.

Seen in this way, the entrepreneur emerges as one who imagines opportunities to be realized by combining actual or potential factors in a new way and who takes risks and drives hard to realize this vision. Still, such a neat definition must never deny the messiness of history, where the adventure of American entrepreneurship has thrived.

O'Neill's vision is not far from becoming a reality. The technology is already in place, with commercial satellites like this one being launched on NASA flights.

Selected Bibliography

General Works

Chandler, Alfred D., Jr. *The Visible Hand: The Managerial Revolution in American Business.* Cambridge, Mass., 1977.
———, and Richard S. Tedlow. *The Coming of Managerial Capitalism: A Casebook on the History of American Economic Institutions.* Homewood, Ill., 1985.
Livesay, Harold C. *American Made: Men Who Shaped the American Economy.* Boston, 1979.
Pusateri, C. Joseph. *A History of American Business.* Arlington Heights, Ill., 1984.

I   The Entrepreneurs

Ash, Mary Kay. *Mary Kay.* New York, 1981.
———. *Mary Kay on People Management.* New York, 1984.
Conot, Robert. *A Streak of Luck.* New York, 1979.
Cruse, Harold. *The Crisis of the Negro Intellectual.* New York, 1967.
Erwin, Will. *The House that Shadows Built.* New York, 1928.
Josephson, Matthew. *Edison: A Biography.* New York, 1959.
Lovelock, Christopher H. *Federal Express,* 3-case series, Harvard Business School, 1976–78.
Passer, Harold. *The Electrical Manufacturers, 1875–1900.* New York, 1972.
Puryear, Alvin. *Black Enterprise, Inc.* Garden City, N.Y., 1983.
Schumpeter, Joseph. "The Creative Response in Economic History." *Journal of Economic History* 7 (November 1947):149–59.
Sigafoos, Robert A. *Absolutely Positively Overnight!* Memphis, 1983.

II   The Land and Its People

Anderson, Oscar E., Jr. *Refrigeration in America: A History of a New Technology and Its Impact.* Princeton, N.J., 1953.
Boorstin, Daniel. *The Americans: The Democratic Experience.* New York, 1973.
———. *The Americans: The National Experience.* New York, 1965.
Carroll, Charles F. *The Timber Economy of Puritan New England.* Providence, 1973.
Chandler, Alfred D., Jr. *The Visible Hand: The Managerial Revolution in American Business.* Cambridge, Mass., 1977.
Clemen, Rudolf A. *The American Livestock and Meat Industry.* New York, 1923.
Cummings, Richard O. *The American Ice Harvests: A Historical Study in Technology, 1800–1918.* Berkeley, Calif., 1949.
Dublin, Thomas. *Farm to Factory: Women's Letters, 1830–1860.* New York, 1981.
Fries, Robert F. *Empire in Pine: The Story of Lumbering in Wisconsin, 1830–1900.* Madison, Wis., 1951.
Goodspeed, Thomas W. "Gustavus Franklin Swift, 1839–1903." Reprinted from *The University Record.* Chicago, 1921.
Hauberg, John H. *Weyerhaeuser & Denkmann: Ninety-Five Years of Manufacturing and Distributing Lumber.* Rock Island, Ill., 1957.
Hidy, Ralph W., and Muriel E. Hidy. *Pioneering in Big Business, 1882–1911: History of the Standard Oil Company [New Jersey].* New York, 1955.
Hidy, Ralph W., Frank Ernest Hill, and Allan Nevins. *Timber and Men: The Weyerhaeuser Story.* New York, 1963.
Kujovich, Mary Yeager. "The Refrigerator Car and the Growth of the American Dressed Beef Industry." *Business History Review* 44 (1970): 460–82.
Nevins, Allan. *John D. Rockefeller.* 2 vols. New York, 1941.
Neyhart, Louise A. *Giant of the Yards.* Boston, 1952.
Sobel, Robert. *The Entrepreneurs: Explorations Within the American Business Tradition.* New York, 1974.
Swift, Louis B. *The Yankee of the Yards: The Biography of Gustavus Franklin Swift.* Chicago, 1927.
Williamson, Harold F., and Arnold F. Daum. *The American Petroleum Industry: The Age of Illumination, 1859–1899.* Evanston, Ill., 1959.

III   Expanding America

Allen, Frederick Lewis. *The Great Pierpont Morgan.* New York, 1949.
Allen, Oliver E. *The Airline Builders.* Alexandria, Va., 1981.
Bender, Marylin, and Selig Altschul. *The Chosen Instrument: Pan Am, Juan Trippe; The Rise and Fall of an American Entrepreneur.* New York, 1982.
Bobbe, Dorothie. *De Witt Clinton.* New York, 1933.
Carosso, Vincent P. *Investment Banking in America.* Cambridge, Mass., 1970.
Chandler, Alfred D., Jr. *Giant Enterprise: Ford, General Motors and the Automobile Industry.* New York, 1964.
———. *Strategy and Structure: Chapters in the American Industrial Enterprise.* Cambridge, Mass., 1962.
Daley, Robert. *An American Saga: Juan Trippe and His Pan Am Empire.* New York, 1980.
Goodrich, Carter, ed. *Canals and American Economic Development.* New York, 1961.
Hughes, Jonathan. *The Vital Few.* Boston, 1965.
Livesay, Harold C. *American Made: Men Who Shaped the American Economy.* Boston, 1979.
Satterlee, Herbert L. *J. Pierpont Morgan.* New York, 1939.
Shaw, Ronald E. *Erie Water West: A History of the Erie Canal, 1792–1854.* Lexington, Ky., 1966.
Sloan, Alfred P., Jr. *Adventures of a White Collar Man.* New York, 1941.
———. *My Years with General Motors.* New York, 1962.
Solberg, Carl. *Conquest of the Skies: A History of Commercial Aviation in America.* Boston, 1979.
Taylor, George Rogers. *The Transportation Revolution, 1815–1860.* Armonk, N.Y., 1951.
Ward, James A. *J. Edgar Thomson: Master of the Pennsylvania.* Westport, Conn., 1980.

IV   Made in America

Asimov, Isaac. *Robots: Machines in Man's Image.* New York, 1985.
Chandler, Alfred D., Jr. *Giant Enterprise: Ford, General Motors, and the Automobile Industry.* New York, 1964.
Edwards, Junius. *The Immortal Woodshed.* New York, 1955.
Edwards, William B. *The Story of Colt's Revolver: The Biography of Col. Samuel Colt.* Harrisburg, Pa., 1953.
Engelberger, Joseph F. *Robotics in Practice: Management and Applications of Industrial Robots.* New York, 1980.
Hounshell, David A. *From the American System to Mass Production, 1800–1932.* Baltimore, 1984.
Leland, Mrs. Wilfred C., and Minnie Dubbs Millbrook. *Master of Precision.* Detroit, 1966.
Lewis, David L. *The Public Image of Henry Ford.* Detroit, 1976.

Logsdon, Tom. *The Robot Revolution.* New York, 1984.

Minsky, Marvin, ed. *Robotics.* New York, 1985.

Nevins, Allan, and Frank Ernest Hill. *Ford: The Times, the Man, and the Company.* New York, 1954.

———. *Ford: Expansion and Challenge, 1915–1932.* New York, 1957.

———. *Ford: Decline and Rebirth, 1933–1962.* New York, 1962.

Rae, John B., *The American Automobile Industry.* Boston, 1984.

Rivard, Paul E. "Samuel Slater, Father of American Manufactures." Slater Mill Historic Site, 1974.

Sobel, Robert. *The Entrepreneurs: Explorations Within the American Business Tradition.* New York, 1974.

Sward, Keith. *The Legend of Henry Ford.* New York, 1948.

Tucker, Barbara M. *Samuel Slater and the Origins of the American Textile Industry, 1790–1860.* Ithaca, N.Y., 1984.

V   Giving 'Em What They Want

Barnum, Phineas T. *Struggles and Triumphs; or, The Life of P. T. Barnum.* Edited by George B. Bryan. New York, 1927.

Carson, G. *The Old Country Store.* New York, 1954.

Fox, Stephen J. *The Mirror Makers: A History of American Advertising and Its Creators.* New York, 1984.

Harris, Neil. *Humbug: The Art of P. T. Barnum.* Boston, 1973.

Hower, Ralph M. *History of Macy's of New York, 1858–1919.* Cambridge, Mass., 1943.

———. "Urban Retailing 100 Years Ago." *Bulletin of the Business Historical Society* 12 (December 1938): 91–101.

Lief, Alfred. *"It Floats": The Story of Procter & Gamble.* New York, 1958.

Mayer, Martin. *Madison Avenue, U.S.A.* New York, 1958.

Pope, Daniel. *The Making of Modern Advertising.* New York, 1955.

Resseguie, Harry E. "A. T. Stewart's Marble Palace — The Cradle of the Department Store." *New York State Historical Society Quarterly* 48 (April 1964): 131–62.

———. "Alexander Turney Stewart and the Development of the Department Store." *Business History Review* 39 (Autumn 1965): 301–22.

———. "The Decline and Fall of the Commercial Empire of A. T. Stewart." *Business History Review* 36 (Fall 1962): 255–86.

Schisgall, Oscar. *Eyes on Tomorrow.* New York, 1981.

Smith, Mary Ann. "John Snook and the Design for A. T. Stewart's Store." *New York State Historical Society Quarterly* 58 (January 1974): 18–33.

Stage, Sarah. *Female Complaints: Lydia Pinkham and the Business of Women's Medicine.* New York, 1979.

Wallace, Irving. *The Fabulous Showman: The Life and Time of P. T. Barnum.* New York, 1959.

Young, James Harvey. *The Toadstool Millionaires.* Princeton, N.J., 1961.

VI   Instant America

Barnouw, Erik. *A History of Broadcasting in the United States.* Vol. I. New York, 1966.

Braun, Ernest, and Stuart Macdonald. *Revolution in Miniature: The History and Impact of Semiconductor Electronics.* 2d ed. New York, 1982.

Brooks, John. *Telephone: The First Hundred Years.* New York, 1976.

Dreher, Carl. *David Sarnoff: An American Success.* New York, 1977.

Garnet, Robert W. *The Telephone Enterprise: The Evolution of the Bell System's Horizontal Structure, 1876–1909.* Baltimore, 1985.

Graham, Margaret B. W. *RCA and the Videodisc Innovation: The Business of Research.* Forthcoming from Cambridge University Press.

Hafen, Le Roy R. *The Overland Mail, 1849–1869: Promoter of Settlement, Precursor of Railroads.* Cleveland, 1926.

Paine, Albert B. *Theodore N. Vail: A Biography.* New York, 1921.

Petrakis, Harry M. *The Founder's Touch: The Life of Paul Galvin of Motorola.* New York, 1965.

Reid, James D. *The Telegraph in America.* New York, 1897.

Rich, Wesley E. *The History of the United States Post Office to the Year 1829.* Cambridge, Mass., 1924.

Scheele, Carl H. *A Short History of the Mail Service.* Washington, D.C., 1970.

Smith, George David. *The Anatomy of a Business Strategy: Bell, Western Electric, and the Origins of the American Telephone Industry.* Baltimore, 1985.

Sobel, Robert. *The Manipulators: America in the Media Age.* Garden City, N.Y., 1976.

Thompson, Robert L. *Wiring a Continent.* Princeton, N.J., 1947.

Index

Picture Credits

Frontispiece: Library of Congress. **I. The Entrepreneurs** *Library of Congress:* 1, 6, 8, 9, 13, 14, 20, 23, 28, 42. *Western History Collections, University of Oklahoma Library:* 2. *Warshaw Collection, Smithsonian Institution:* 4 (left and right), 5, 26. *Henry Ford Museum, Dearborn, Michigan:* 10. *Gillette Company:* 16, 17, 19. *Historical Collection, Security Pacific National Bank, Los Angeles:* 21. *Culver Pictures, Inc.:* 24. *Parker Brothers:* 29, 30 (© 1935, 1985). *Johnson Publishing:* 32, 34, 35. *New York Public Library:* 33. *Mary Kay Cosmetics, Inc., Dallas, Texas:* 38 (photo by Ted Munger), 40 (top and bottom). *Federal Express Corporation:* 45, 47 (All rights reserved). **II. The Land and Its People** *National Archives, Washington, D.C.:* 49. *Library of Congress:* 50, 52, 53, 54, 55, 56, 58, 59, 60, 66, 69, 70, 72, 73 (top and bottom), 74, 75 (top), 76, 82, 83, 86, 87, 90. *Weyerhaeuser Company Archives:* 64. *Warshaw Collection, Smithsonian Institution:* 75 (bottom). *Perdue Farms, Inc.:* 77, 78 (left and right), 79. *Culver Pictures, Inc.:* 84. *Massachusetts Historical Society:* 89. *Rhode Island Historical Society:* 93 (top). *State Historical Society of Wisconsin:* 93 (bottom). **III. Expanding America** *Library of Congress:* 95, 96, 98, 101, 103, 104, 107, 108 (top and bottom), 110, 111, 113, 115, 116, 121, 122, 123, 124, 125, 133, 135. *Schenectady County Historical Society:* 99. *Pennsylvania State Archives:* 105. *United Technologies Corporation Archives:* 119. *Warshaw Collection, Smithsonian Institution:* 120, 130, 131. *MIT Museum:* 127. *Pan American World Airways:* 134, 137 (top and bottom), 138. *Massport:* 139. **IV. Made in America** *Manchester (New Hampshire) Historical Society:* 141. *Library of Congress:* 142, 143, 144, 146, 147, 149, 154, 156, 157, 158, 159, 160, 161, 162, 168, 173, 174, 175, 179. *Warshaw Collection, Smithsonian Institution:* 151, 153, 171 (left and right). *Martin W. Sandler Collection:* 165, 176, 177. *Burton Historical Collection, Detroit Public Library:* 167. *Unimation, Inc., A Westinghouse Company, Danbury, Conn.:* 181, 182 (top). *Stock Boston:* 182 (bottom; photo by Peter Menzel), 183 (photo by Stacy Pick). **V. Giving 'Em What They Want** *Library of Congress:* 187, 188, 190, 191, 197, 203, 209, 213 (top), 216 (bottom), 222 (top). *Warshaw Collection, Smithsonian Institution:* 193, 194, 200, 202, 213 (bottom), 222 (bottom), 223 (left and right). *Schlesinger Library, Radcliffe College:* 195. *Culver Pictures, Inc.:* 198, 201, 216 (top). *Gaby Monet:* 199. *New-York Historical Society:* 204. *New Haven Colony Historical Society:* 205. *Martin W. Sandler Collection:* 206. *Chicago Historical Society:* 210. *Procter & Gamble Company:* 214. *Andrew Jergens Company from the J. Walter Thompson Company Archives:* 218. **VI. Instant America** *Library of Congress:* 225, 227, 228, 231, 235, 236, 239, 240 (bottom), 243, 244, 247, 249, 251, 255, 257, 258, 261 (top), 262. *Martin W. Sandler Collection:* 240 (top). *Warshaw Collection, Smithsonian Institution:* 248. *RCA:* 253, 261 (bottom). *H. Armstrong Roberts, Inc.:* 263. *Motorola, Inc.:* 264, 265, 267, 268. *Geostar Corporation, Princeton, N.J.:* 270, 271. *NASA:* 272.